Curriculum Development in Vocational and Technical Education

Curriculum Development in Vocational and Technical Education

Planning, Content, and Implementation

Curtis R. Finch
John R. Crunkilton

Virginia Polytechnic Institute and State University

Allyn and Bacon, Inc.
Boston   London   Sydney

To our parents,
wives, and children

Copyright© 1979 by ALLYN
AND BACON, Inc.,
470 Atlantic Avenue, Boston,
Massachusetts 02210.

Production Editor: Russell Mead
Mfg. Buyer: Peter Bennett
Series Editor: Robert Roen

Second printing . . . September, 1979
Library of Congress Cataloging in Publication Data

Finch, Curtis R., 1939-
   Curriculum development in vocational and technical
education.

Includes bibliographies and index.
  1. Vocational education—Curricula. 2. Technical
   education—Curricula. 3. Curriculum planning. I. Crunkilton, John R., 1942- joint author. II. Title.
LC1043.F56   375'.37011'3   78-8090

ISBN 0-205-06148-6

Contents

List of Figures

List of Tables

Preface

This book is meant to fill an obvious void in the professional vocational and technical education literature. For some time there has been a need for a book that presents sound, usable principles for curriculum development in vocational and technical education. We have accepted the challenge to meet this need and the result of our effort can be seen herein. Persons who will find this content directly applicable to their professional areas include vocational and technical teachers, curriculum coordinators, principals, directors, and state education agency staff, as well as training specialists in the private sector. Much of the material has relevance to anyone who is involved in curriculum development work.

The content focuses on vocational and technical education curriculum development from a general perspective. Basic curriculum principles and strategies are presented that apply to a number of vocational service areas. These, in turn, are supplemented by practical examples that deal with curriculum development in specific areas. Concerns associated with secondary and postsecondary curriculum development are discussed as appropriate to ensure that both of these important areas are adequately covered.

The three main sections in this book are preceded by an introductory chapter that gives an overview of curriculum development in vocational and technical education and describes how Sections I, II, and III may be utilized to best advantage. Although coverage of vocational and technical education curriculum development is designed to be comprehensive, the three sections serve to describe activities that constitute distinct portions of the development process.

Section I deals with the essentials of curriculum planning. Chapter 2 serves as a foundation for this planning in that it emphasizes the importance of systematic decision making in curriculum planning. The next two chapters describe how information may be collected and assessed as part of this decision-making process. Chapter 3 enumerates the ways that school-related data may be gathered, while Chapter 4 deals with community-related data in a similar manner.

Section II represents the next logical step in curriculum development, since it deals with establishing curriculum content. Once a decision has been made to proceed with the development of a curriculum or program, content must then be formalized. Chapter 5 describes the various strategies a curriculum developer may use when content is being established. The process of actually deciding what content to include is presented in Chapter 6. This is followed by Chapter 7, where the formulation of specific curriculum goals and objectives is detailed.

The actual business of implementing the curriculum is described in Section III. Chapter 8 deals directly with the identification and selection of relevant curriculum materials. If high quality materials cannot be located, Chapter 9 may be used as a guide for developing them. Chapter 10 explains how individualized, competency-based instructional packages may be developed. The final chapter deals with an area often neglected by curriculum developers: systematic evaluation of the vocational and technical education curriculum.

Collectively, these chapters provide the professional vocational and technical educator with a detailed set of guidelines for use in the systematic development of high quality vocational and technical education curricula. The content serves as a resource and reference to be utilized whenever any vocational and technical curriculum is being planned, content is being established, and curriculum implementation is taking place.

Curtis R. Finch

John R. Crunkilton

Curriculum Development in Vocational and Technical Education

Curriculum Development: An Overview

Introduction

Ever since the term "curriculum" was added to educators' vocabularies, it has seemed to convey many things to many people. To some, curriculum has denoted a specific course, while to others it has encompassed the entire educational environment. While perceptions of this term may vary, the fact must be recognized that the curriculum extends beyond a simple definition. Curriculum constitutes a key element in the educational process that is extremely broad in scope and touches virtually everyone who is involved with teaching and learning.

This volume focuses directly on curriculum within the context of vocational and technical education. In no other area has greater emphasis been placed upon the development of curricula that are relevant in terms of student and community needs and substantive outcomes. The vocational and technical curriculum focuses not only on educational process but also on the tangible results of that process. This is only one of many reasons why the vocational and technical curriculum is distinctive in relation to other curricular areas and why vocational education curriculum planners must have a sound understanding of the curriculum development process.

Historical perspectives

Several factors have appeared to affect differences that currently exist between the vocational and technical curriculum and curricula in other areas. Perhaps the foremost of these is historical influence. History has an important message to convey about antecedents of the contemporary vocational and technical curriculum and provides a most meaningful perspective to the curriculum developer. Curriculum as we know it today has evolved over the years from a narrow set of disjointed offerings to a comprehensive array of relevant student learning experiences.

Early foundations of curriculum

Education for work had its beginnings almost four thousand years ago. This earliest type of vocational education took the form of apprenticeship. Organized apprenticeship programs were recorded as having been started for scribes in Egypt as early as 2000 B.C. At about that time, schools were established that provided two stages of training:

> The first or primary stage consisted of learning to read and write ancient literature. The second was an apprenticeship stage during which the learner was placed as an apprentice scribe under an experienced scribe, usually a government worker (Roberts, 1971).

Thus, the earliest form of education for work was organized in such a way that basic knowledges could be developed in a classroom setting and applied skills could be developed "on the job."

Even as organized apprenticeship programs began to flourish, this same basic arrangement persisted. Apprenticeship programs initiated in ancient Palestine, Greece, and other countries followed a similar pattern with youngsters learning a craft or trade through close association with an artisan. Although apprenticeship programs expanded rapidly as various skilled areas became more specialized and differentiated, reliance continued to be placed on training in the actual work setting—which, in most cases, consisted of conscious imitation. The apprenticeship form of instruction thus remained virtually unchanged until the nineteenth century.

Alternatives to apprenticeship

By the sixteenth century, alternatives to apprenticeship were being strongly considered. The educational schemes of philosophers such as Comenius and Locke proposed inclusion of manual arts. Samuel Hartlib set forth a proposal to establish a college of agriculture in England. These and other events in the Realism Movement resulted in trade subjects and practical arts being introduced into formal education. The Age of Reason, likewise, became a catalyst for shifting away from the traditional apprenticeship system. Rousseau's concern about the value of manual arts in education served as a model for other educators such as Pestalozzi, Herbart, and Froebel. As Bennett (1926) indicates, Rousseau's "recognition of the fact that manual arts may be a means of mental training marked the beginning of a new era of education."

With the advent of the Industrial Revolution in the early 1800s, apprenticeship began a steady decline. The great demand for cheap, unskilled labor obviously could not be met through apprenticeship programs, and many newly established industrial firms did not desire persons with such extensive training as was provided through the traditional learner-artisan relationship. However, as the Industrial Revolution progressed, owners and managers soon began to realize that skilled workers would be a definite asset to the organization. This increased demand almost seemed to correspond with the rapid decline of formal apprenticeship programs in many skilled areas.

Toward systematic curriculum development

Perhaps one of the earliest forms of systematic curriculum building in vocational education may be attributed to Victor Della Vos, director of the Imperial Technical School of Moscow. At the Philadelphia Centennial Exposition of 1876, Della Vos demonstrated a new approach to teaching the mechanical arts that "became a catalyst for vocational education in the United States" (Lannie, 1971). Rather than learning through conscious imitation, the Russian system utilized shops where formal instruction in the mechanical arts could be provided. This system attempted to teach mechanical arts fundamentals

> (a) in the least possible time; (b) in such a way as to make possible the giving of adequate instruction to a large number of students at one time; (c) by a method that would give to the study of practical shopwork the character of a sound, systematical acquirement of knowledge; and (d) so as to enable the teacher to determine the progress of each student at any time (Bennett, 1937).

Using these basic principles, Della Vos set up separate shops in the areas of carpentry, joinery, blacksmithing, and metal turning where students completed graded exercises that were organized logically and according to difficulty (Lannie, 1971). The Russian system, which was noted by many Americans, had a most substantial impact on Calvin Woodward and John Runkle. Woodward initiated a manual training school at Washington University in Saint Louis that closely paralleled the system developed by Della Vos. Runkle, who served as president of Massachusetts Institute of Technology, favored the Russian system to the extent that practical shop instruction was initiated for engineering students, and a secondary school of mechanical arts was established on the M.I.T. campus. These pioneer efforts served as important precursors of the contemporary vocational and technical curriculum.

The successes of Runkle and Woodward generated great interest in this form of instruction, and soon manual training began to spring up in a number of schools around the United States. Shopwork was even introduced into the elementary schools and, by the late 1800s, it was a formal part of many grammar schools across the nation. However, this progress did not take place without criticism. Many felt that manual training did not serve as the best substitute for apprenticeship. Manual training and other forms of practical arts such as domestic science represented course work "of a vocational nature but these courses were incidental or supplementary to the primary function of the school" (Roberts, 1971). In response to this deficiency, schools began to organize so that students could be prepared to enter work in a variety of occupational areas. During the late 1800s and early 1900s, technical institutes, trade schools, commercial and business schools, and agricultural high schools began to flourish. Many of the offerings provided in these schools were similar in scope to those found in today's comprehensive high schools and community colleges. However, the standards associated with these programs were quite lax or even nonexistent. Quality was at best a local matter and, more often than not, did not extend beyond concern of the instructor. The result was a considerable amount of inconsistency in quality among programs across the nation.

By 1900, a rather strong public sentiment for vocational education had developed. As the Industrial Revolution continued to expand, a need for skilled workers increased. This need was expressed by both businessmen and labor leaders. Rural America began to seriously question the relevance of traditional education and sought to have agriculture play a more important role in the school program. These feelings were more formally presented to the federal government by way of national organizations. Groups such as the National Society for the Promotion of Industrial Education and the Association of Agricultural Colleges and Experiment Stations led the way in terms of securing federal aid for vocational education. The culmination of their efforts was passage of the Smith-Hughes Act in 1917.

The Smith-Hughes Act and subsequent federal legislation have had profound effects on the public vocational and technical curriculum. Not only has legislation provided funds for high quality education, but state and local education agencies were required to meet certain standards if they wanted to qualify for these funds. Even though legislation has stipulated that vocational education be under public supervision and control, the standards associated with federal funding have had great impact on curriculum development in vocational education. Types of offerings, targeted groups of students, scheduling, facilities, equipment, and numerous other factors have been incorporated into federal legislation supporting vocational education. These factors have, in turn, affected curriculum planning, development, and implementation, since they have required the local developer to be responsive to national level concerns.

The point should be made that the Smith-Hughes Act and more recent legislation have supported the concept of providing students with a broad experiential base in preparation for employment. This contrasts greatly with many of the early vocational offerings, which were more or less separate entities or consisted of single courses. A major impact of federal legislation on vocational and technical curricula, then, has been in the area of quality control. The various vocational education acts have assisted greatly in establishment of minimum standards for programs.

Contemporary perceptions of education

The present-day curriculum may be perceived as being a basic part of the more expansive area known as education. Education itself is often viewed as an amorphous term that defies description and explanation. In actuality, education is a concept that each curriculum developer needs to define and refine before the curriculum development process is carried out.

Education and its elements

In contemporary society, education may be viewed as being comprised of two basic elements: formal education and informal education. *Formal education* is that which occurs in a more structured educational setting. Representative of this element would be school and school-related activities such as taking a course, participating in a school athletic event, employment as part of a formal cooperative vocational education program, or involvement in a student club or organization. *Informal education* consists of that education which typically takes place away from the school environment and is not a part of the planned educative process. Part-time volunteer work in a hospital, babysitting, taking a summer vacation in Europe, and waiting on tables might be considered as informal education activities. Central to this element is the fact that a person chooses to engage in a nonschool activity, and this participation results in some form of education. Also central to this element is that education extends far beyond the four walls of the school and encompasses more than what is under a teacher's direction. Career awareness, exploration, and preparation may take place through one's own personal initiative or by way of a parent's encouragement. Education in its formal and informal spheres encompasses a great portion of one's life. From early childhood through adulthood, opportunities exist for participation in formal and informal education and the extent of a person's participation often corresponds with his or her capabilities to perform at certain levels in later life.

Goals of education

Superimposed on the formal and informal education elements are two types of education that reflect the broad goals associated with it. These two types of education may be referred to as *education for life* and *education for earning a living*. As may be noted in Figure 1-1, the two are not mutually exclusive. Dealing

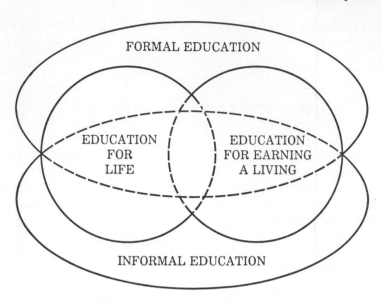

FIGURE 1-1.   **Education in our society**

with these two broad goals as separate entities is sometimes quite difficult, if not impossible. Thus each must be considered in light of the other. Basic preparation for life as part of one's high school education may serve as a foundation for postsecondary education in preparation for earning a living. Likewise, education for earning a living taken early in one's life might serve to let an individual know that a certain occupation should or should not be pursued. However, a continued interest in the field, together with education in that area, might nurture a strong avocational involvement.

One should remember that each of these types of education can be facilitated in formal and informal ways. For example, a youngster who takes a part-time job as a service station attendant to earn some extra money might find that some of this experience makes a direct contribution to a formal school-based auto mechanics program. On the other hand, this same experience could make him or her a better citizen by serving as a realistic example of how our free enterprise system operates. Whether experience might be preparation for life or earning a living, education may be provided through formal or informal means. While informal education may not be as deliberate and systematically structured as formal education, it nonetheless serves as an important contributor to the outcomes of education.

Toward a definition of curriculum

How, then, may we define curriculum? Referring to Figure 1-1, it can be noted that formal education, which includes education for life and education for earn-

ing a living, represents a vast array of learning activities and experiences. These learning activities and experiences are not merely specific class sessions or courses but extend to the entire educational spectrum of a particular school or schools. Within this context, curriculum may be perceived as being rather global in nature and representing a broad range of educational activities and experiences. Thus, curriculum may be defined as *the sum of the learning activities and experiences that a student has under the auspices or direction of the school.* Acceptance of this generic definition commits the curriculum developer to accept two additional supporting concepts. First, a central focus of the curriculum is the student. In fact, one may interpret this to mean each student has his or her own curriculum. Realistically, this interpretation is a sound concept, since students often select courses, experiences, and noncredit activities that align with their unique personal needs and aspirations. This might be pointed out by asking, "How often can it be found that two students have had exactly the same set of educational experiences?"

A second supporting concept has to do with the breadth of learning experiences and activities associated with the curriculum. Formal courses are not the only items considered to be a part of the curriculum. Clubs, sports, and other cocurricular activities are significant contributors to the development of a total individual and to curriculum effectiveness. Learning and personal growth do not take place strictly within the confines of a classroom or laboratory. Students develop through a variety of learning activities and experiences that may not necessarily be counted as constructive credit for graduation. Student vocational organizations, social clubs, and athletics are but a few of the many experiences that extend beyond the prescribed set of course offerings of a school. These experiences have the power to make contributions to student growth in ways that cannot be accomplished in classroom and laboratory settings.

Accepting the foregoing implies that we must consider the curriculum as encompassing general (academic) education as well as vocational and technical education. Realistically, whether at the secondary or postsecondary level, the curriculum includes work and experiences associated with preparation for life and for earning a living. This more global definition of curriculum enables us to consider not only what is offered in vocational and technical education, but how these learning activities and experiences should relate to the student's more general studies.

Curriculum and instruction

In order to better clarify the definition of curriculum it is important to examine how it may be distinguished from the concept of instruction. While curriculum constitutes a broad range of student experiences in the school setting, instruction focuses on the delivery of these experiences. More specifically, instruction may be perceived as *the planned interaction between teachers and students that [hopefully] results in desirable learning.* Sometimes, serious questions may be raised as to what exactly constitutes curriculum and what constitutes instruction. Some educators feel that any curriculum includes instruction, while others contend that sound instruction includes a sound curriculum.

A brief description of curriculum development and instructional development should aid in clarifying these apparent differences of opinion. Curriculum development focuses primarily on content and areas related to it. It represents a higher level of generalization than instructional development and always precedes it (Kindred et al., 1976). Instructional development, on the other hand, consists of planning done in direct support of student learning. Taken into account are the principles of human learning and the conditions under which it occurs (Kindred et al., 1976). Naturally, when curriculum development is taking place, the instruction that is to be built upon this framework must be kept in mind. Likewise, principles of learning are not avoided when a curriculum is being developed; they are merely considered from a higher level of generalization. Anyone who is developing instruction must be constantly aware of the content to be included in that instruction. In the case of instruction, content that has already been derived as part of the curriculum development process is further explicated and specific strategies are designed to aid the student in learning this content. Figure 1-2 provides a visual description of possible shared and unique areas associated with instructional development and curriculum development. While each area focuses on a number of rather unique concerns, many aspects of development could be classed as either curriculum or instruction. The shared aspects of curriculum and instructional development sometimes become unique to one area or the other based upon the person or persons involved in the development process as well as who will eventually benefit from this development. If one teacher were writing objectives for his or her course, this activity might be classed as instructional development. However, if a group of teachers were writing objectives for use in their courses and, perhaps, other teachers' courses, the activity might be considered as curriculum development. The distinguishing differences between these two areas become the scope of the development process and extent of generalizability. If the developmental process involves a number of professionals and the product of this effort will be usable by a number of teachers, the process is more correctly termed curriculum development. Instructional development is best viewed as usually involving one professional (typically a teacher) in the process of preparing for his or her own classes. Although the distinctions between curriculum development and instructional development are not as clear as many would like them to be, they serve to better identify each process.

Characteristics of the vocational and technical curriculum

Even though vocational and technical education is included within the overall framework of education, the vocational and technical curriculum has certain characteristics that distinguish it from the rest of the educational milieu. These

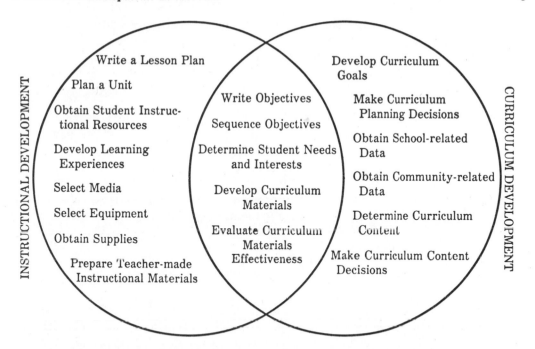

INSTRUCTIONAL DEVELOPMENT

CURRICULUM DEVELOPMENT

Write a Lesson Plan

Plan a Unit

Obtain Student Instructional Resources

Develop Learning Experiences

Select Media

Select Equipment

Obtain Supplies

Prepare Teacher-made Instructional Materials

Write Objectives

Sequence Objectives

Determine Student Needs and Interests

Develop Curriculum Materials

Evaluate Curriculum Materials Effectiveness

Develop Curriculum Goals

Make Curriculum Planning Decisions

Obtain School-related Data

Obtain Community-related Data

Determine Curriculum Content

Make Curriculum Content Decisions

FIGURE 1-2. Possible shared and unique aspects of instructional development and curriculum development

characteristics represent a curricular focus that may be best associated with curriculum building, maintenance, and immediate and long-term outcomes. While each of these characteristics is, to a greater or lesser degree, associated with other curricula (e.g., general or academic), their impact on the vocational and technical curriculum development process is important to note. Collectively, they represent the potential parameters of any curriculum that has as its controlling purpose the preparation of persons for useful, gainful employment. These basic characteristics of the vocational and technical curriculum include orientation, justification, focus, in-school success standards, out-of-school success standards, school-community relationships, federal involvement, responsiveness, logistics, and expense.

Orientation

Traditionally, the vocational and technical curriculum has been product- or graduate-oriented. While a major concern of vocational education has been to provide a means for each student to achieve curricular outcomes, the ultimate outcome is more far-reaching than the educational process. The ultimate success of a vocational and technical curriculum is not measured merely through student educational achievement but through the results of that achievement—results that take the form of performance in the work world. Thus, the vocational and technical curriculum is oriented toward process (experiences and activities within the school setting) and product (effects of these experiences and activities on former students).

Justification

Unlike its academic counterpart, the vocational and technical curriculum is based upon identified occupational needs of a particular locale. These needs are not merely general feelings; they are clarified to the point that no question exists about demand for workers in the selected occupation or occupational area. Thus, curriculum justification extends beyond the school setting and into the community. Just as the curriculum is oriented toward the student, support for that curriculum is derived from employment opportunities that exist for the graduate.

Focus

Curricular focus in vocational and technical education is not limited to the development of knowledge about a particular area. The vocational and technical curriculum deals directly with helping the student to develop a broad range of knowledges, skills, attitudes, and values, each of which ultimately contributes in some manner to the graduate's employability. The vocational and technical education learning environment makes provision for student development of knowledges, manipulative skills, attitudes, and values as well as the integration of these areas and their application to simulated and realistic work settings.

In-school success standards

While it is important for each student to be knowledgeable about many aspects of the occupation he or she will enter, the true assessment of student success in school must be with "hands on" or applied performance. For example, knowledge of the metric system is important to the extent that it contributes to student success in applied situations such as cutting metric threads on a lathe, administering medication, or repairing a part on a foreign car. In-school success standards are closely aligned with performance expected in the occupation, with criteria used by teachers often being standards of the occupation. The student may be required to perform a certain task or function in a given time using prescribed procedures, with each of these standards having its parallel in the work world.

Out-of-school success standards

The determination of success is not limited to what transpires in a school setting. A vocational and technical curriculum must also be judged in terms of its former students' success. Just as a college preparatory or community college transfer curriculum is judged on the basis of graduates' success in a four-year college or university, former vocational and technical students should demonstrate their success in the world of work. Thus, there is a major concern for the product or graduate of the curriculum, particularly with respect to employment-related success. Although success standards vary from school to school and from state to state, they quite often take the form of employer satisfaction with graduates' skills, graduates obtaining jobs in their fields of preparation, job satisfaction of graduates, graduates obtaining jobs related to their fields of preparation, and advancement experienced by graduates (Starr, 1975). There are certainly other standards that could be added to this list; however, the above items are out-of-school success standards that vocational education leaders rank as being very important curricular outcomes.

School-community relationships

While it is certainly recognized that any educational endeavor should relate in some way to the community, vocational education is charged with the responsibility of maintaining strong ties with a variety of agriculture, business, and industry-related areas. In fact, strong school-community partnerships exist in many locales. Since there are a number of potential "customers" in the community who are interested in products (graduates), the curriculum must be responsive to community needs. Employers in the community are, likewise, obligated to indicate what their needs are and to assist the school in meeting these needs. This assistance might consist of employers serving on curriculum advisory committees, donating equipment and materials to the schools, or providing work stations in the community for students enrolled in cooperative vocational education. Whatever relationship exists between the vocational curriculum and the community, it should be recognized that strong school-community partnerships may often be equated with curriculum quality and success.

Federal involvement

Federal involvement with public vocational education has existed for many years. Ever since the passage of the Smith-Hughes Act in 1917, schools that were qualified and desired reimbursement for the operation of vocational curricula have had to meet certain federal requirements. While these standards are basically developed and monitored at the state level, each state must have its plan of action approved at the federal level before funding is allocated. This, of course, means that if federal reimbursement is desired for an offering, state and federal requirements must be adhered to. The extent to which federal involvement affects the curriculum may constitute a distinct asset or a limitation. Requirements such as clock hours of vocational instruction and types of equipment used in the shop or laboratory might foster a higher level of quality. On the other hand, there may be certain requirements that place undue restrictions on curriculum flexibility, and thus hinder innovation or meeting the needs of certain student groups.

Responsiveness

Another basic characteristic of the vocational and technical curriculum is its responsiveness to technological changes in our society. Two hundred years ago, programs that prepared people for work were quite stable. Typically, the skills and knowledges developed in an apprentice program would be useful for the rest of one's productive life. Today, however, the situation is quite different. The Industrial Revolution and, more recently, the integration of technological concepts into our everyday life, have had a profound impact on vocational and technical education curricula. The contemporary vocational curriculum is responsive to a constantly changing world of work. New developments in the field are incorporated into the curriculum so that graduates can compete for jobs and, once they have jobs, achieve their greatest potential.

Logistics

Bringing together the proper facilities, equipment, supplies, and instructional resources represents a major concern to all persons involved in the implementation of vocational curricula. While logistics associated with maintaining any curriculum are often complex and time-consuming, the sheer magnitude of most vocational curricula makes this factor quite critical to success or failure. Some logistics concerns may be associated with any curriculum. Physics and chemistry equipment and materials must be available for experiments. Recording devices must be in proper working order when language laboratories are being used. Textbooks must be on hand when mathematics and history classes begin. However, all of the above types of items and many more might be needed in vocational laboratories across the country. The highly specialized equipment needed to operate quality programs usually requires regular maintenance and must be replaced as it becomes obsolete. Materials used in the curriculum must be purchased, stored, inventoried, replaced, and sometimes sold. The coordination of cooperative vocational programs that includes working closely with businesses and industries in the community to establish and maintain relevant work stations for students presents a unique set of logistical problems. The logistics associated with operating a vocational and technical curriculum are indeed complex; and these complexities need to be taken into account when the curriculum is being established and after it becomes operational.

Expense

Although the cost of maintaining a vocational curriculum is not inordinately high, dollars associated with operating certain vocational curricula are sometimes considerably more than for their academic counterparts. While this expense may depend upon the particular area of instructional emphasis, there are some items in the vocational curriculum that seem to show up quite regularly. These include basic operating costs such as heating, electricity, and water; purchase, maintenance, and replacement of equipment; purchase of consumable materials; and travel to work locations that are away from the school. Some of these costs are necessary to operate any school; however, the vocational and technical curriculum may often require greater basic operating expenditures because of facilities with a large square footage or equipment such as typewriters, welders, ovens, or computers that require large amounts of energy for their operation. Equipment must be updated periodically if the teacher expects to provide students with realistic instruction, and this updating process can be most expensive for a school to carry out. Ever increasing costs associated with the purchase of high quality equipment make this area one of tremendous concern to vocational educators. Finally, the purchase of consumable materials requires a sustained budgetary commitment to the curriculum. Dollars need to be available to buy consumables as they are used by students throughout the school year. These items are not limited to pencils and paper. They might include such diverse items as oil, flour, steel, wood, or fertilizer.

A rationale for curriculum development in vocational and technical education

The uniqueness associated with the vocational and technical curriculum raises a critical question. What is the basic direction that curriculum development in vocational and technical education should take? History tells us that, traditionally, curricula have been developed in a somewhat haphazard manner with little consideration given to the impact of the development process. Another point is that a vocational and technical curriculum soon becomes outdated when steps are not taken to keep it from remaining static. Finally, it must be recognized that the vocational and technical curriculum thrives on relevance. The extent to which a curriculum assists students to enter and succeed in the work world spells out success.

As a curriculum is being developed, the vocational educator is obligated to deal with these concerns in such a way that quality is built into the finished product or graduate. Any curriculum that is not developed systematically, or that becomes static or irrelevant, will soon have an adverse effect on all who come in contact with it. In order to avoid this difficulty, curriculum developers must give consideration to the basic character of the curriculum and build in those factors that contribute to its quality. While some of these factors might apply equally well to any sort of curriculum development, they are especially relevant to vocational and technical education. As the development process is going on, outcomes of this process must be made clear. It is hoped that these outcomes will be a vocational and technical curriculum that is data-based, dynamic, explicit in its outcomes, fully articulated, realistic, student-oriented, evaluation-conscious, and futures-oriented. Each of the above is important to the success of the contemporary vocational and technical curriculum; and, as will be seen, each is congruent with the character of vocational and technical education and the chapters to follow.

Data-based

The contemporary vocational and technical curriculum cannot function properly unless it is data-based. Decisions about whether or not to offer a curriculum need to be founded upon appropriate school- and community-related data. Curriculum content decisions are made after a variety of data such as student characteristics and the nature of the occupation being prepared for have been assembled and examined. The quality of curriculum materials is determined after data have been gathered from teachers and students who use them. In fact, the use of data as a basis for curriculum decisions cannot be overemphasized. The reason for this is that developers of traditional curricula have often neglected to place emphasis on relationships that should exist between data and curriculum decisions.

Dynamic

It might be said that the static curriculum is a dying curriculum. Just as vocational and technical education is in a dynamic state, its curricula must, likewise, be dynamic. Administrators, curriculum developers, and teachers must constantly examine the curriculum in terms of what it is doing and how well it meets student needs. Provision must be made for curricular revisions, particularly those modifications which are tangible improvements and not just change for the sake of change. This does not mean that once each year or so the curriculum is checked over by a panel of "experts." Provision must be made to redirect, modify, or even eliminate an existing curriculum any time it can be fully justified. The responsiveness of a curriculum to changes in the work world has much bearing on the ultimate quality of that curriculum and the contribution to student growth.

Explicit outcomes

Not only must the contemporary vocational and technical curriculum be responsive to the world of work, but it must also be able to communicate this responsiveness to both teachers and students. Broadly stated goals are an important part of any curriculum. However, these goals are only valid to the extent that they may be communicated in a more explicit manner. While it is recognized that we cannot state all curricular outcomes in specific measurable terms, many of these outcomes may be written in such a manner that broad curricular goals are made more quantifiable. To the extent that outcomes are explicit, we will be able to tell whether students achieve these outcomes and how outcomes relate to the occupation. This is perhaps the most commanding reason for ensuring that curriculum outcomes are clear and precise.

Fully-articulated

Although courses and other educational activities contribute to the quality of a curriculum, the way that they are arranged in relation to each other makes the difference between something that is merely satisfactory and something that is superior. Curriculum articulation may involve the resolution of content conflicts across different areas or development of a logical instructional flow from first year to second year. Articulation might extend to determining the ways cocurricular activities such as student vocational organizations lend support to the rest of the curriculum or deciding which mathematics concepts should be taught as a prerequisite to a particular technical course.

Curriculum articulation also takes place throughout levels of schooling. Reduction or elimination of instructional duplication at the secondary and postsecondary levels might be a major concern of the curriculum developer as well as those who are funding the offerings. Articulation across levels also enables both the secondary and the postsecondary instructor to teach what is best for his or her particular group of students and to do this in a more efficient manner.

Realistic

The vocational and technical curriculum cannot operate in a vacuum. If students are to be properly prepared for employment, curricular focus must be one of relevance. Content is not developed merely on the basis of what a person should know but also includes what a person should be able to do. Vocational curriculum content is typically based upon the actual worker's role with relevant tasks, knowledges, skills, attitudes, and values serving as a foundation for that which is to be taught. Consequently, great emphasis must be placed upon practicality. Since the bulk of a worker's time is spent in applied areas, many student experiences must, likewise, be of a practical nature. Hands-on experiences in a laboratory or cooperative education setting provide the student with a relevant means of transferring knowledges, skills, and attitudes to the world of work.

Student-oriented

Most curricula are, to some extent, student-oriented and curricula in vocational and technical education are certainly no exception. Currently there is a great deal of concern about how the curriculum can best meet students' needs. Various approaches such as team teaching, differential staffing, and individualized instruction have been used by teachers to help meet these needs. But, regardless of the approach a teacher uses, a basic question has to be answered. To what extent will the approach actually assist students in preparing for employment?

Another aspect of student orientation deals with the teaching-learning process. Not only must the curriculum meet group needs, but there is an obligation to meet the individual student's needs. In order for these needs to be met in an expeditious manner, arrangements could, for example, be made to provide instruction at various ability levels, to develop individual training plans, or to make available alternate paths for the achievement of course objectives. Whatever the means used to assist students, a basic concern should be with the individual and how he or she may be helped in the best possible ways.

Evaluation-conscious

Evaluation is perceived by many to be an activity that comes periodically in conjunction with accreditation procedures. Realistically, administrators and teachers cannot wait this long to find out how successful they have been. Curriculum evaluation has to be an ongoing activity—one that is planned and conducted in a systematic manner. Anyone who is involved with the vocational and technical curriculum should be aware that evaluation is a continuous effort. As the curriculum is being designed, plans must be made to assess its effects on students. Then, after the curriculum has been implemented and data have been gathered, school personnel may actually see what strengths and weaknesses exist. While most educators recognize that evaluation is not a simple activity, it is one that should be carried out concurrently with any curriculum effort.

Futures-oriented

Alvin Toffler's more recent book, *Learning for Tomorrow* (1974), has much to say about what the future may hold for education. Educators, particularly vocational and technical educators, are very much concerned about the future. What technological changes might affect the need for graduates? What types of school laboratories will be needed twenty years from now? What sorts of continuing education will be needed by students who are in school right now? These and other questions are often raised by vocational educators who think in futuristic terms. Persons responsible for the contemporary vocational and technical curriculum need to ensure that ongoing curricula are considered in relation to what will or may occur in the future. As decisions are being made about curriculum content and structure, thought should be given to the alternate futures that might relate to these decisions. Any curriculum that hopes to be relevant tomorrow must be responsive to tomorrow's as well as today's needs. The extent to which a curriculum is successful twenty, thirty, or even forty years from now will be largely dependent upon the futures-oriented perspective associated with it.

Utilizing Sections I, II, and III

This chapter sets the stage for the sections and chapters that follow. It serves as an overview of curriculum development in vocational and technical education by providing a brief historical framework as well as discussing contemporary perceptions of the curriculum and how it may be viewed within the context of vocational and technical education. The chapter points out that curriculum development involves few absolutes. It is one thing to build a chair or table to meet certain specifications and quite another to build a curriculum that may involve and affect numerous teachers, students, and employers.

The sections that follow relate to a common theme: decision making. The authors believe that, in order to develop and implement a sound curriculum, one must recognize the value of making realistic, systematic decisions. Decision making will be emphasized in each of the three sections, since it relates to many aspects of the curriculum development process.

Figure 1-3 provides a summary of the curriculum development process. Each of the blocks represents a section in the book that a reader might refer to if interested in one particular aspect of curriculum development. Section I deals specifically with planning the curriculum. This section would be relevant to persons who are developing a new curriculum or updating an existing one. The establishment of alternate decisions regarding the curriculum serves as a base for this section. Details about gathering school- and community-related data are provided so that the curriculum developer may obtain meaningful information to aid in the decision-making process.

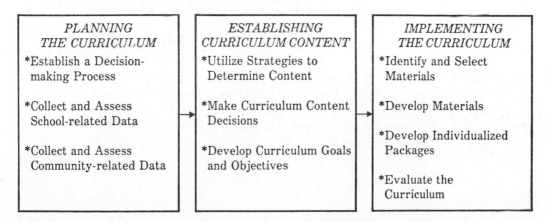

PLANNING THE CURRICULUM	ESTABLISHING CURRICULUM CONTENT	IMPLEMENTING THE CURRICULUM
*Establish a Decision-making Process	*Utilize Strategies to Determine Content	*Identify and Select Materials
*Collect and Assess School-related Data	*Make Curriculum Content Decisions	*Develop Materials
*Collect and Assess Community-related Data	*Develop Curriculum Goals and Objectives	*Develop Individualized Packages
		*Evaluate the Curriculum

FIGURE 1-3. **Curriculum development in vocational and technical education**

Section II focuses on the establishment of curriculum content. It is at this point that one has decided to actually develop the curriculum. This section would be of particular value to individuals who are ready to decide about content to be included in the curriculum. It contains details about the ways curriculum content may be determined and the procedures used to develop curriculum goals and objectives.

Section III is concerned with various aspects of implementing the curriculum. Persons who have gone through the planning and content establishment stages would find this section most meaningful. It first deals with the identification and selection of materials, since this is often the most inexpensive route to take. The development of curriculum materials is also detailed, including a practical description of how to develop individualized competency-based packages. A final aspect of Section III is curriculum evaluation. While the development process is certainly important, the quality of this development is determined through evaluation in realistic settings.

REFERENCES

Bennett, Charles A. *History of Manual and Industrial Education up to 1870*. Peoria, Ill.: Charles A. Bennett Company, 1926.

———. *History of Manual and Industrial Education, 1870 to 1917*. Peoria, Ill.: Charles A. Bennett Company, 1937.

Kindred, Leslie W.; Wolotkiewicz, Rita J.; Mickelson, John M.; Coplein, Leonard E., and Dyson, Ernest. *The Middle School Curriculum, A Practitioner's Handbook*. Boston: Allyn and Bacon, Inc., 1976.

Lannie, Vincent P. "The Development of Vocational Education in America, A Historical Overview," in Carl Schaefer and Jacob Kaufman, eds., *Vocational Education: Social and Behavioral Perspectives*. Lexington, Mass.: D. C. Heath, 1971.

Roberts, Roy W. *Vocational and Practical Arts Education*. New York: Harper and Row, 1971.

Starr, Harold. *Vocational Education Program Evaluation Inventory Study*. Columbus, Ohio: Center for Vocational Education, Ohio State University, 1975.

Toffler, Alvin, ed. *Learning for Tomorrow, The Role of the Future in Education*. New York: Random House, 1974.

Planning
the
Curriculum

Curriculum, as defined in the introductory chapter, encompasses the sum of the learning activities and experiences that a student has under the direction of the school. This implies that schools must assume the responsibility to develop, plan, and implement a curriculum which meets the needs of both students and society. Thus, the vocational and technical education curriculum development process must reflect the best thinking of educators and be carried out in a systematic and orderly fashion.

Section I concerns itself with beginning stages in the development of a curriculum or the revision of an existing curriculum. Topics in this section have application to vocational and technical education curriculum planning at any educational level. The three chapters in this section aid the curriculum developer in making decisions regarding whether or not a particular curriculum should be implemented.

Before any curriculum may be offered, a decision must be made to implement the curriculum and there are many factors to be considered before that decision can be made. Chapter 2 treats the decision-making process in education and serves to introduce the curriculum developer to this process. Emphasis has been placed upon sound decision making and how curriculum developers may work with others to achieve this end. The formulation of sound decision-making strategies as well as the development of standards for decision making and the identification of data needed for decision making provides curriculum developers with a basis for sound curriculum planning.

The latter two chapters of this section speak to the data that are needed if one is to make sound decisions in the curriculum development process. Chapter 3 deals entirely with data related to the school. Data associated with the current status of vocational offerings, dropout rates, students' interests, parent input, follow-up of former students, future enrollments, and facilities are examples of information vital to sound curriculum decisions. Data related to the community are discussed in Chapter 4. These include sources of employment, labor supply and demand, and the identification of various resources.

It is recommended that all three chapters be read and application of planning information be made to the curriculum developer's local situation before decisions are made about vocational curriculum development. Meaningful vocational and technical education curricula will materialize only if the curriculum developer follows a systematic decision-making process based upon accurate information about the school and the community.

Making Decisions in Planning the Curriculum

Introduction

The entire curriculum development process is interlaced with decision-making situations. Questions such as, "Should we take this approach or that approach?", "Should we offer Program A or Program B?", and "Which objectives reflect the goals of our program?" are typical of practical problems faced by the curriculum developer. At first glance, these problems appear to be relatively simple ones to solve. However, after reflecting on the decision-making process associated with finding their solutions, it may be readily seen that few curriculum development problems can be properly attacked unless people are willing to make major time and resource commitments to this end.

Curriculum development is an extremely complex and intricate process involving many decision situations. Decisions must be made about policy statements, priority determination, education program and course selections, standards, and many other aspects of the total curriculum. Although decisions are made at different levels in an educational system, decision making influences the total curriculum regardless of the level at which a decision is made.

This chapter deals directly with decision making as an integral part of curriculum planning. Special emphasis is placed upon the decision-making process, the value of systematic decision making, the effect of philosophy and sociopsychological factors on decision making, the establishment of standards for making decisions, and the types of data needed to make sound curriculum decisions.

Decision making in education

Any discussion about decision making cannot take place unless several basic factors are presented. First, consideration must be given to the distinction and relationship between policy making and decision making. And second, a separation of decisions must be clarified by levels at which decisions are made within an educational system.

Policy making and decision making

Decision making takes place at all levels in an educational organization and at the heart of each decision rests a problem. This problem may be surfaced, stated, and/or refined by anybody having an interest in the educational curriculum. For example, a school board member may express concern about a high dropout rate or an employer may question the competence of certain graduates. Furthermore, problems may or may not have been perceived by educators before these concerns were brought to light. The important factor to keep in mind is that problems will occur at any place and at any time in the educational program and the solutions to these problems will have a direct or indirect effect upon the curriculum. When a problem does arise, then a decision-making situation has materialized and a solution must be formulated. The relationship of decision making to curriculum development is presented graphically in Figure 2-1. Problems that develop may be considered in terms of policy decisions or operational decisions.

Policy decisions are divided into two areas. One set of policy decisions focuses on the formulation of goals and objectives for the educational organization. These goals and objectives should serve as the basis for direction of the educational unit and, therefore, the basis for curriculum development. Another viewpoint would be to think of policy decisions as those decisions affecting long-range planning of the curriculum. For example, a school board may set as a goal that all graduating seniors must either plan to further their education beyond high school or, for those not planning to continue, must have developed a saleable skill before graduation. The other aspect of policy decisions consists of

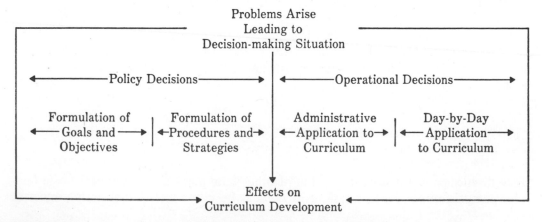

FIGURE 2-1. Decision making affecting curriculum development

problems that must be solved relative to the formulation of procedures and strategies needed for the successful achievement of established goals and objectives. An example of this problem might be that in order for a school to assist graduates in job placement, the school board will provide funds for a placement officer to assist in the placement of graduates. Policy decisions such as this are valuable in giving operational consistency to an education organization.

Operational decisions do not dictate policy formulation of the organization, but serve to apply the established policies to the organization. Decisions at this level are administratively based and should undergird the approved policy procedures and strategies. One such operational decision might be that a vocational director will require all requests for curriculum materials to be in his or her office by a certain date. Day-by-day operational decisions made by administrators and/or teachers serve to move the program smoothly toward the goals and objectives. Decisions at this level tend to be internal, within one segment of an organization, and usually apply only for a specific length of time.

Regardless of where any decision is made, the results will affect all other segments of education and ultimately the curriculum. Policy decisions will affect future operational decisions and operational decisions will support, define, modify, revise, or identify possible changes needed in current policy statements.

Who makes decisions?

The question of who makes decisions is a critical one and the answer is very involved. Some educators in school systems have a great deal of latitude in handling decisions. In other school systems, the control rests primarily with noneducators. The true decision maker in a problem situation depends upon the level at which the problem has occurred. Furthermore, decision makers can be divided into policy decision makers or operational decision makers.

Policy decision makers. Referring again to Figure 2-1, policy decisions revolve around problem situations concerning organizational goals and objectives and setting procedures and strategies for achieving the goals. The final decision made in problem situations involving policy formulation rests with a certain group of individuals. Hamlin (1962) takes the position that professional educators in this country cannot legally make policy; it must be made by citizens or their representatives.* This position is upheld by many others due to the democratic nature of our society and of our school structure.

Policy decisions must rest with boards of education, boards of trustees, or other officially designated groups who represent the people. Members of these groups are spokespeople for the public and work toward the goal of providing the best possible educational program for their community. Although official policy decisions are made by these boards or others, the role that educa-

---

*From *Public School Education in Agriculture*, by Herbert M. Hamlin. Danville, Ill.: The Interstate Printers & Publishers, Inc., 1962, p. 64. Used by permission of the publisher.

tors can and should assume during the process of decision making should not be underestimated or avoided. Membership on these boards may be comprised of individuals who are not accustomed or prepared for full responsibility of decision making in education. This implies that professional educators must be involved in policy decision making by assisting these groups in the consideration of alternatives to problems, the impact of various alternatives, and assembling data needed for decisions, as well as a number of other vital activities. Although boards of education and similar groups are official policy-making bodies, input from others is needed and should be secured from professional educators (administrators and teachers), parents, students, voters, civic leaders, and business and industrial leaders.

Operational decision makers. Decisions made at the operational level are the responsibility of administrators and/or teachers located throughout the educational organization. Once policy formulation has occurred, then the policy must be applied in a professional manner to the educational organization. Policy-making groups depend upon professional educators to take the lead in this task, and in fact, this is why professional educators are hired. Any operational decisions that need to be made must be handled by educators within the school organization. As with policy decision makers, operational decision makers may, in some instances, need input from parents, students, voters, civic leaders, business and industrial leaders, and policy-making groups when arriving at solutions to problems.

Preparing to make decisions

Sound decisions are not made quickly, but require in-depth study by those persons involved. Before arriving at a decision-making stage, the problem to be solved must be stated in clear and concise terms. This is no easy task and one that may determine the degree to which a viable solution is found. Once the problem has been clearly stated and agreed upon by all parties involved, a plan of action or procedure should be outlined to serve as a guide for arriving at possible alternatives and ultimately the final decision. This procedure applies equally well to policy decisions or operational decisions.

In a later section of this chapter, possible models to follow in decision-making situations are presented and discussed in detail. In addition, later discussion will be devoted to the establishment of standards and collection of data needed for making decisions.

Irreversible decisions

The decision-making process in curriculum development must not overlook the magnitude of each decision made. In fact, many decisions made today affect the program tomorrow, next year, and even further into the future. This implies that each decision made must be considered in relation to its future impact on the curriculum. Few decisions are truly irreversible, but nevertheless some decisions may be easier to reverse or change than others.

The extent to which policy and operational decisions can be reversed depends upon the degree to which they have been implemented. For example, decisions can be reversed before money has been spent on equipment or buildings. However, after money or resources have been committed, spent, or buildings constructed, decisions become more difficult to reverse. Money spent on equipment, supplies, or other parts of the curriculum is almost impossible to recover and certainly beyond reason once goods or products have been delivered. This same situation may exist with buildings that are constructed. Reversible decisions regarding the use of buildings depend upon the flexibility that was included in the design of the facility. Laboratories and classrooms constructed with built-in features lower the probability of that space being easily redesigned in the future for other vocational and technical education programs.

Decision makers and curriculum planners must realize that the decision to construct and equip a six-million-dollar facility is a long-term project. This type of decision will influence the curriculum for years to come and may come back to haunt school personnel if it is not made properly. Until technology advances to the point where buildings can be designed and built that will permit total freedom and flexibility for change, the magnitude and irreversibility of policy decisions will be a prime consideration. Furthermore, even operational decisions have a degree of irreversibility—especially decisions that tend to set precedents. For example, permission granted to one vocational department to take their students to a statewide youth organization convention will undoubtedly lead to similar requests from the other vocational departments.

Futuristic decisions

Decisions made by curriculum planners are futuristic, with the true impact not being felt until tomorrow or even ten or twenty years from the time the decision is made. Making realistic and sound decisions today for the future is one of the most difficult dilemmas facing educational decision makers. Factors that are uncertain and unpredictable but that have a strong bearing upon curriculum development are many. Some of the more critical factors concern the economic situation of society, changes in technology that influence the nature of labor market needs, priorities of the local community, and other factors typically associated with the curriculum development. Regardless of this dilemma, decision makers must think in futuristic terms. To do otherwise will only serve to stifle the growth and development of vocational and technical education.

The value of systematic decision making

The value of anything might be said to be based upon those persons who are affected. When a family purchases a new color television, the value that is gained or realized depends upon those who are in the family. The children visualize all the color cartoons that can be seen. Dad may be thinking in terms of those football games and Mom will be looking forward to her favorite program. If thoughtful planning is carried out, a television can be purchased that will meet these expectations and everybody will be pleased. The same thinking might be applied toward an educational curriculum. Developing an effective curriculum is not merely one simple task, but a set of tasks that must be systematically planned, executed, and analyzed.

Why plan for decision making?

The day when decisions in education are made by mere guesswork is past. No longer can decision makers arrive at sound decisions without a professionally prepared plan to follow. Today, schools are larger in terms of student bodies, faculty, and support services. Diversity of program offerings, whether they be college preparatory or vocational programs, should now be considered a part of every curriculum. The delivery systems used to offer curricula and operate school systems are more complex. Funding curricula becomes more complex as federal or state support can be secured for some programs while no support is available for others. Recent emphasis upon career education, disadvantaged, handicapped, and gifted students has added to the already complex situation found in our schools.

   Planning is an absolute essential in our curricula today and in the future. However, just saying that planning is essential is not enough. The planning that needs to be carried out must represent a systematic, purposeful, and professional effort. Taxpayers, students, policy decision makers, and society will not accept anything less.

Impact of effective planning

The ultimate impact of effective planning will be quality curricula that provide the opportunity for student development. Furthermore, graduates will be able to seek and to obtain employment as well as carry on activities that fulfill personal needs in their lives. While this result of effective planning may be thought of by some as an utopian situation, it is nevertheless the underlying purpose and goal of vocational education.

   Effective planning can increase the opportunity for the securement of adequate funds to operate vocational education. For example, an efficient plan that results in tangible data will be more favorably received by decision makers when priorities are established for a curriculum, as compared to verbal requests that lack specific data. Funds, in turn, will aid in securing qualified and competent faculty, adequate levels of consumable supplies and software, equipment and facilities, and curriculum materials to build a good library. Planning in a systematic manner enables vocational educators to better compete with others who are seeking educational dollars. Furthermore, being accountable and establishing a reputation for effective planning will aid in gaining more support for vocational education.

Impact of ineffective planning

Ineffective planning will result in situations occurring that are the exact opposite of those cited previously. For example, curricula could be planned and initiated for students who did not materialize on the first day of class, or students who successfully complete a program may find there are no jobs available that align with their newly acquired skills. An even more far-reaching result of ineffective planning would be the loss of funding for vocational education programs. The impact of such a funding loss could be devastating, whether at the federal, state, or local level. If this situation were to occur, vocational education as we know it today would cease to exist, with both students and society being the losers.

Effect of philosophy on decision making

Decision making in education is quite different from decision making in a commercial organization. In commercial organizations, decisions are typically based upon economic returns of the different alternatives under consideration. In an educational organization, decisions must not only consider the economic aspects but must also take into consideration the philosophies possessed by those associated with the educational process. Unfortunately where philosophy is involved, there are no absolutes, only opinions based upon past experiences of each individual. Since each individual associated in one way or another with vocational education forms his or her own personal philosophy, this gives rise to differences of opinion, differences that must be resolved before meaningful educational decisions can be made.

Whose philosophy is important?

Decision makers may well ask, "Whose philosophy is important to consider when decision-making situations arise?" The initial reaction to a question such as this would be to focus on those persons connected with an educational organization. Philosophies of students, parents, teachers, administrators, state and national educational agencies, and community members are certainly important. However, the philosophy least understood or considered by decision makers and yet the strongest factor affecting decisions is probably the philosophy held by the decision makers themselves. After all data have been carefully gathered, analyzed, conclusions drawn, and recommendations made, the decision maker ultimately faces the time when he or she must choose among alternatives. This responsibility cannot be delegated to anyone else. Thus, all philosophies are important, however the philosophy held by each decision maker must never be overlooked. If a decision maker gives no thought to the influence that his or her own philosophy is having, then decisions may unknowingly be made solely upon the feelings of the decision maker with little or no concern for others who will be affected by those decisions.

Sociopsychological factors affecting decisions

When considering the various sociopsychological factors that may influence decisions, one eventually identifies those attributes which individual decision makers bring with them because they are what they are, or their personalities (Katz and Kahn, 1966).* Katz and Kahn list four of the more important personality dimensions of policy makers that may affect their decisions. These include: 1) their orientation to power versus their ideological orientation; 2) their emotionality versus their objectivity; 3) their creativity versus their conventional common sense; and 4) their action orientation versus their contemplative qualities. Each of these is important in relation to quality of decisions made by curriculum decision makers.

Ideology versus power orientation.   The ideologist brings to the decision-making environment an internalized concept of what the organization should be and if this person is at the extreme point, he or she is unable to compromise on any decision to be made. On the other hand, a decision maker more intent on power is versatile. He or she is able to work with any organization or individual, is less concerned about the program, and is more concerned about staying in power. Certainly each attribute has its advantages. However, of utmost importance is the fact that continual thought must be given to the ideal, otherwise programs would not change or improve. Likewise, compromises must be made by decision makers to the program. An organization driven by power-conscious decision makers will move in the direction of maintaining or increasing their power and not toward building a healthier educational program.

Emotionality versus objectivity.   The biggest concern with emotionality stems from situations where decision makers are influenced by deep, defensive needs (threatening or unpleasant facts) that can block out or distort information being received. This not only applies to decision makers but also to those individuals supplying them with information. For example, if a vocational teacher knows

---

*From *The Social Psychology of Organizations*, by Daniel Katz and Robert L. Kahn, p. 290. Copyright ©1966 John Wiley & Sons, Inc. Reprinted by permission of John Wiley & Sons, Inc., New York, N.Y.

that the school board's current thinking does not include provision for twelve-month teacher employment, that teacher (knowing full well that for an effective program, a twelve-month program is needed) may fail to present a case in favor of a twelve-month program. In other words, the teacher distorts the facts in order to keep in good stead with the school board rather than going against the beliefs of the board and providing more objective information.

Creativity versus common sense.   Some decision makers are gifted with originality and can be quite creative in arriving at solutions to the problems at hand. However, these individuals may not possess the ability to perceive practical outcomes from those solutions. Other decision makers may be thought of more in terms of exercising common sense and good judgment. In the decision-making environment, those individuals possessing common sense should be in the decision-making role. They could reflect upon alternatives identified by the more creative individuals, who could be brought in as resource people when needed.

Action orientation versus contemplation.   Decision makers can vary in their degree of action. While some individuals will form judgments early and will want to act immediately, others will want to think about a decision for an extended period of time. For this reason many organizations do not act on policy matters at the same meeting where a new policy is introduced.*

Influence of national and state philosophy on the local level

As was discussed in Chapter 1, the influence of national and state philosophy on vocational education can easily be pointed out. It might be well to consider briefly the importance of such a force upon local educational programs and upon the decision makers. The basic responsibility for education has been left up to the states, and the degree of latitude that local educational agencies have varies with each state. But it can be stated that each local community must be responsive to provide quality education for its youth. Several observations are well worth noting concerning the relationship and influence between the federal and state level and the local level. On one hand, federal and state educational agencies can influence local decisions by developing statements reflecting national goals and program direction. In addition, incentives such as matching money, one hundred-percent reimbursement, national or state recognition, and other rewards can be offered to help speed up local adoption of ideas. On the other hand, creative programs that had their start in local programs have also served to keep national and state educational agencies from becoming stagnant and

---

*From *The Social Psychology of Organizations,* by Daniel Katz and Robert L. Kahn, p. 290f. Copyright ©1966 John Wiley & Sons, Inc. Reprinted by permission of John Wiley & Sons, Inc., New York, N.Y.

have provided fresh ideas for other states. The one point that must always be kept in mind is that as long as financial incentives are provided from either the national or state level, the philosophy held by the national or state agencies will have a significant role to play in decisions made at the local level concerning curriculum development.

In summary, a decision maker is influenced by many internal and external forces when faced with a decision. Several of these forces have been mentioned in the last few pages. In order to be effective, the curriculum planner must be aware of these forces and must plan to avoid situations where these forces become major blocks to effective decision making.

Decision-making strategies

Thus far, discussion has focused upon factors associated with the decision-making process. These factors may influence the identification of appropriate solutions to the problem. One aspect of the decision-making process not previously discussed deals with the various strategies used to expedite that process. Educators have several unique and well accepted strategies from which to choose as they approach the business of decision making. Although each of the various strategies is useful in its own right, the creative decision maker should strive to develop and perfect a composite strategy that works for his or her educational organization. This strategy might include several of the various concepts to be described. Different decision-making strategies about to be considered include: management by objectives (MBO); decision tree; program evaluation and review technique (PERT); and problem solving.

Management by objectives

The management by objectives (MBO) approach to decision making has been used by many educational organizations in recent years. Briefly, the MBO process in education may be described as the process where administrators and teachers jointly identify common goals of the organization and define each person's role in helping to fulfill those goals. Furthermore, those goals serve to measure the progress of each individual in accomplishing his or her responsibilities and the progress of the organization in fulfilling the goals.

At the heart of a MBO approach is the objective, thus the objective must be carefully derived. A key element of the objective is that percentages, ratios, numbers, averages, and other absolutes are specified so that all concerned know exactly what standard must be met. Once a decision has been made to use a particular standard, educators can then proceed to decide exactly what must be done to aid in meeting that standard. Five sequential steps are followed in developing the objective:

1. Finding the objective;
2. Setting the objective;
3. Validating the objective;
4. Implementing the objective, and
5. Controlling and reporting status of the objective.

Finding the objective.   This initial phase in the MBO approach is critical, since later decisions rest upon the established objective. Individuals seeking out the objective must realize the immediate, short-, and long-range future of the organization. Trends, direction, scope, and other elements that may give rise to the current or future program must be taken into account.

Setting the objective.   This phase serves to formulate and qualify the objective. For example, elements of the objective should point out time lines, should provide results to be achieved and not activities, should be written in positive terms, should be clear to others, and should incorporate facts (e.g., percentages, numbers, averages, and correlations).

Validating the objective.   The need to establish each objective's worth and validity cannot be overlooked. Objectives must reflect the best efforts of those involved and should serve to describe current or future situations accurately.

Implementing the objective.   Implementation of objectives is usually carried out by subordinates. This phase includes activities and events that permit each objective to be implemented within the organization. Congruent values of these objectives must be held by those in the organization.

Controlling and reporting status of the objective.   Each objective must be controlled by indicating time, cost, quantity, and quality associated with that objective. If problems develop in achieving the objective, then corrective measures must be taken to avoid failure.

The real strength of the MBO process may be found within the organizational framework in the educational system. This approach delineates the roles and responsibilities of each member of the organization and what each member must do, by when, as activities of the organization are carried out in order to reach predetermined goals. Thus, if a goal of a vocational program within a school is to place 75 percent of all vocational graduates in jobs related to their educational experiences, decision makers must decide how this might be done. MBO also relates well to the establishment of standards. If a standard is set that at least twenty students must enroll in a particular class, then activities must be carried out to determine the actual number interested in enrolling, and finally, to ensure that a minimum of twenty actually show up the first day of class.

Decision tree

Although the decision tree was basically designed for business executive use, this approach has much value to educators and should be examined by anyone who is actively involved in curricular decision making. This approach is based on the premise that, at different times in the life of an organization, key decision points are reached and decision makers may graphically illustrate these in the shape of tree branches. The decision tree can assist management in clarifying the choices, risks, objectives, monetary gains, and information needs involved in an investment problem (Magee, 1964).* Where investment decisions in the business world may be more concerned with costs and economic returns, the educational field, in addition to these concerns, must also consider the human aspect of the youth and adults whom the educational program is to serve. The decision tree approach does not provide definite answers for the decision makers but it does help to clarify alternatives available at different key decision points. This in itself is a tremendous asset to the curriculum specialist who may be faced with numerous decisions during the curriculum development process.

Magee provides an example of how the decision tree works when a key decision must be made and several alternatives are available. This is illustrated in Figure 2-2. Suppose you are planning to invite seven couples to an evening meal and you have the choice of planning the meal outside on your newly constructed patio or in your house. If it does not rain, a very pleasant time could be had by all outside in the beauty of your surrounding lawn. On the other hand, if it starts to rain during the meal, the food would be ruined and your guests would become damp. At some point, it must also be decided what will be the latest time during the day that the decision can be made to eat inside or outside and still permit time to accomplish all of the needed preparatory tasks. The hostess could then identify possible alternatives and outcomes using the following table form, which can be graphically illustrated by the decision tree approach in Figure 2-2.

The value of considering a decision tree approach in educational decision-making situations comes to light when one remembers that any decision made is not isolated from other aspects of the educational organization. Furthermore, the degree to which decisions made today will have been appropriate ones depends upon how well the alternatives of the different possible decisions were identified when the original key decision had to be made.

---

*From John F. Magee, "Decision Trees for Decision Making," *Harvard Business Review*, July-August 1964, Copyright © 1964 by the President and Fellows of Harvard College; all rights reserved.

CHANCE EVENTS AND RESULTS		
CHOICES	*Rain*	*No Rain*
Outdoors	Disaster	Real Comfort
Indoors	Mild discomfort, but happy	Mild discomfort, but regrets

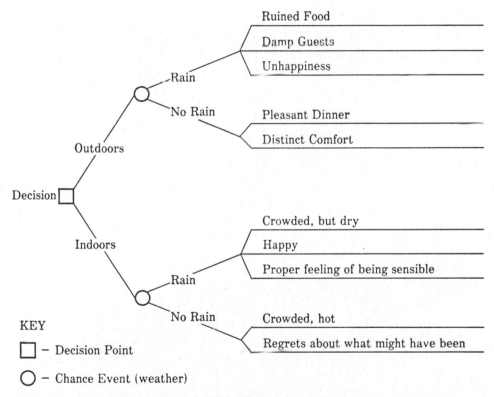

KEY

☐ – Decision Point

◯ – Chance Event (weather)

FIGURE 2-2. Decision tree for a small dinner party

To illustrate the possibilities of how the decision tree approach might be applied to a situation in vocational education, a more realistic example is provided. This situation is typical of key decisions that curriculum planners must make when developing relevant curricula. Figure 2-3 illustrates the decision associated with whether an air conditioning program should be offered, with the chance factor in this situation being the extent to which students will enroll in the course. If a decision is made to offer the program and a high enrollment occurs, the program will operate at high efficiency or a low cost per student en-

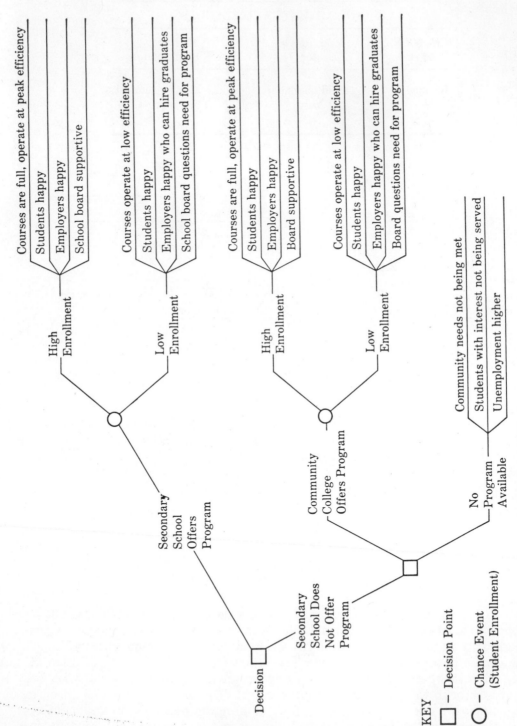

FIGURE 2-3. Decision tree for offering an air conditioning program

rolled, students will be happy to develop skills in an area of interest, employers will be pleased with prospective employees, and the school board should continue to support the program. On the other hand, if a decision is made to offer the program and a low enrollment materializes, the program will operate at a high cost per student, students will be pleased to develop skills in their area of interest, those employers who are lucky enough to hire graduates will be happy while other employers will be displeased, and the school board will begin questioning the need to continue supporting the program.

If the school board chooses not to offer the program, then the possibility exists that a nearby community college will offer the program. If nobody provides the program and student interest is there, community needs may not be met, students with career interests in this area may not be served, and some students may graduate without saleable skills. Of course, if the program is not offered and student interest is not there, money, facilities, and human resources are not wasted, other programs of more interest may then be provided, and everybody is happier.

In this illustration, the chance event was identified as student enrollment. Other chance events that might apply to educational programs are securing qualified instructors, securing and maintaining adequate funding, employment opportunities, cooperative education opportunities, facilities available, offering of courses in other nearby educational institutions, as well as others. A key aspect of the decision tree approach is that all chance events must be identified and the consequences of these events clarified so that they are understood by all who are involved in the decision-making process.

Program evaluation and review technique

The program evaluation and review technique (PERT) focuses on identifying key events and activities leading to the accomplishment of a long-range goal or objective. The strength of this approach is that time lines, activities, and events can be illustrated graphically. Thus, the event and activity are depicted as follows:

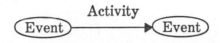

Events are either the start or end of a mental or physical task. Time is not consumed and the event cannot be accomplished until all activities leading to the event are completed. The *activity* describes the work required to accomplish an event. Time estimates for the events can be hours, days, weeks, or whatever the planners choose and time estimates can be made for optimistic (earliest date possible), most likely, and pessimistic forecasts (date likely for completion when unplanned problems arise). In addition, events are numbered sequentially so that they may be easily identified. Figure 2-4 depicts a PERT chart that might be used by decision makers in following a planned course of action to determine if a specific vocational program should be offered. Although this is a simplified version of a decision-making situation involving Program XYZ, the chart illustrates an overall plan of action and the dates when each event is to be accomplished. A supplemental activity assignment sheet might be developed to assign specific activities to certain individuals. The values of using a PERT strategy can be readily identified by reviewing Figure 2-4. First, key events can be identified for reaching a long-range goal. Second, these events can be placed sequentially on a continuum in the order in which the events must occur. Third, a time element can be assigned to each event to serve as a completion date for that event. Fourth, activities needed to complete each event are easier to describe once all events are identified. Fifth, the PERT chart permits an easy assessment of events completed to date and what still needs to be completed. Finally, the PERT strategy permits all who are involved in the decision-making process to be fully aware of the events, times, and the ultimate goal for which the activity is being conducted.

1. Decision made to study feasibility of establishing Program XYZ (1/5)

2. Standards for Program XYZ established (2/15)

3. School-related data identified (3/1)

4. Community-related data identified (3/1)

5. Prospective enrollment figures determined (5/1)

6. Qualified instructors available (5/1)

7. Current facilities assessed (5/1)

8. Current and future budget support determined (5/1)

9. Current and projected employment opportunities determined (6/1)

10. School-related data analyzed (6/1)

11. Community-related data analyzed (6/1)

12. Composite data analyzed and final proposal prepared (8/1)

13. Report reviewed by vocational education advisory council (9/1)

14. Proposal approved by vocational director and school administration (10/1)

15. Proposal presented to school board (11/1)

16. School board makes final decision (12/1)

Problem solving

Another approach to decision making consists of what many refer to as problem solving. In reality, regardless of which decision-making approach may be used by an organization, all involve problem solving. Each approach identifies key points at which a problem or problems must be solved. The basic difference is the manner in which the problem is approached and the degree to which the procedure is formalized. In the approaches discussed thus far, a high degree of

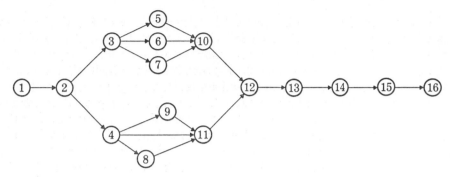

FIGURE 2-4.   PERT network for feasibility study of vocational program XYZ

formal structure is evident by use of charts or a structured format for arriving at decisions. The problem-solving approach is similar to those discussed earlier in that it might deal with one specific aspect of a more complex decision. However, decision makers may not necessarily develop extensive flow diagrams or charts to plot further activities. This would be particularly true, for example, where someone was making a decision regarding a part of a program such as whether or not to use an instructional module.

The approach commonly used when employing problem solving consists of:

1.   Identifying and defining the problem;

2.   Analyzing the problem;

3.   Arriving at appropriate alternative solutions;

4.   Clarifying consequences of the alternative solutions;

5.   Selecting the best alternative solution to the problem, and

6.   Analyzing actual consequences arising from the decision.

Once a problem has been identified, one of the most difficult tasks is that of defining the problem so that everyone clearly understands it. The problem may be brought forth by anybody associated with the educational program; however, the decision-making body must fully agree that the defined problem presented to them is truly representative of the situation. Once the problem has been clearly stated, it can then be fully analyzed, appropriate solutions can be identified, and the problem-solving process is well underway.

Summary of approaches for decision making

In the last few pages, several approaches for decision making have been outlined and discussed. To fully bring this section of the chapter to a close, several general observations need to be made. First, regardless of the decision-making process used by an organization, all individuals must fully understand how the decisions are made and the proper procedures to follow when input is desired. An organization will never establish a procedure in which all individuals involved agree upon the process, but if all understand the process, at least open lines of communications can be maintained. Second, once a procedure for making decisions has been agreed upon, then the process of arriving at any future decisions must adhere to the established written guidelines. Deviation from established policy for decision making will result in a disruptive system and the development of distrust in others who must work with the organization. Third, educational administrators who work directly with the decision-making body must have realistic information and facts about their programs. Subordinates to administrators, teachers, and others who withhold information and present inaccurate pictures will not provide valid data to the decision makers on which to base their decisions. Fourth, all decision-making procedures must provide a system that assures multiple avenues for information to be fed into the decision-making environment. The use of advisory groups, consultants, and a proper atmosphere for individuals volunteering information will assist in helping the decision-making process flow smoothly. Fifth, although not discussed in this chapter but still a vital part of the decision-making process, there must be a follow-up of all decisions made. This would include the consequences observed, how the decision-making process could be improved, and the resulting effect decisions are having on program improvement. Sixth, all decision-making procedures must incorporate within their written policies the roles and responsibilities of all those involved either directly or indirectly with the process. Only in this way will individuals know what is expected of them and what they can expect of others. Finally, no approach is going to be perfect or will provide decision makers with direct answers to a problem under consideration. Decision making ultimately focuses on human judgement, based upon what is thought to be possible, desirable, and—once the decision is made—probable.

Establishing standards for decision making

The need for establishing standards before making decisions cannot be overemphasized. Yet, without a doubt, the establishment of standards before making decisions is usually avoided by curriculum planners and decision makers. For example, if a person were considering the purchase of an automobile, there would be certain minimum standards that automobile should meet before the person seriously considered making a purchase. These standards might be twenty miles per gallon, satisfactory handling qualities, adequate leg and head room, large enough to transport five children, and so forth. The customer would consider these standards and collect the data that could assist him or her in determining which make of automobile would best serve the established purposes.

If a particular car did not meet any of these standards, the customer would then eliminate that make of automobile or reconsider the standard in light of the importance of that standard to the overall satisfaction or degree of dissatisfaction if that automobile was purchased. Standards would then assist this individual in making a sound personal investment in an automobile.

A similar case could be made with regard to standards for educational programs. If standards are not established before program decisions are made, programs might exist where unqualified teachers would be teaching, thirty students might be working in laboratories designed for twenty, programs might be developed and implemented on personal bias of decision makers, or eventually quality programs in vocational education would not exist.

Who establishes standards?

The determination of ultimate standards to be used in deciding whether or not a program or curriculum is developed rests with the decision-making body. This body might be a school board, board of trustees, or similarly designated group. However, the underlying force that has a major impact on the type of standards recommended to this body consists of teachers or representatives of business or industry related to the occupational area under consideration. In most cases, the decision-making body will not have the expertise needed within a specific vocational area to make decisions concerning that area. Thus, they will rely heavily upon school administrators or others to provide standards for them to use in arriving at decisions.

How are standards established?

Standards should be established by those who are best able to develop criteria for quality vocational programs. Individuals who might assume a key role in the establishment of standards include vocational teachers, students, employers, employees in occupations associated with the vocational area under discussion, vocational directors and supervisors, and curriculum planners. In some cases, certain standards could be developed nationally and applied to all state and local programs. Additionally, certain standards might need to be established by state educational agencies, with local agencies needing to use these state standards in developing standards relevant to their locality.

When are standards established?

Once a problem has been identified and the decision-making body defines and agrees upon the problem, standards must then be established to further guide the decision-making process. Data needed by decision makers to help provide a

basis upon which to arrive at decisions cannot be collected until the data collec-
tors know what is needed for the decision. Otherwise, useless data might be collected.

What standards need to be established?

Standards must be established that will provide a framework for quality vocational programs. Although the number of standards may vary with different
vocational programs, there are several common standards that should be established regardless of the vocational area. General categories of standards are:

1. Prospective enrollment;

2. Availability of qualified instructors;

3. Available facilities;

4. Available equipment;

5. Available funding;

6. Employment opportunities;

7. Other similar vocational programs available;

8. Whether vocational programs under consideration support the goals
    and philosophy of the school;

9. Whether delivery of the programs upholds established guidelines,
    and

10. Opportunities for cooperative vocational education programs.

For example, if a vocational course in stenography were under consideration, a standard referring to equipment might be, "That fifteen dictaphones
must be available." Or a standard for masonry might be, "That at least twelve
students per year must express an interest and enroll in the class." An example
of a standard for distributive education might be, "That a cooperative training
station be available for each eleventh and twelfth grade student." In each of
these examples, standards are stated that relate specifically to program quality.
Detailed standards that focus directly on program quality greatly assist decision
makers in arriving at sound decisions concerning curriculum development.

Identifying types of data to be collected

Once standards have been established, the various types of data needed to assist decision makers may then be identified. Using the stenography example, if
one standard indicates that a minimum of fifteen dictaphones are needed to offer

this course, a check of the current inventory would immediately show if fifteen dictaphones were on hand. If the dictaphones were there, then this standard would be met. If they were not on hand, then the cost of securing fifteen dictaphones needs to be reflected in the proposed budget and later it must be determined if funding resources are adequate to provide for their purchase. In addition, other alternatives may be investigated. Donations of equipment from a dictaphone company or equipment loans from local businesses are just two examples of ways that equipment may be obtained. The key factor to keep in mind is that if the minimum standard for a quality program was established as fifteen dictaphones, anything less than this might seriously reduce program effectiveness. Thus, not only must program standards exist, but data must be available to support those standards.

Aligning standards and sources of data

Once standards are established, data collection may now begin. There are two major areas from which data will be needed. The first might be referred to as school-related data, and the second, as community-related data. School-related data basically consist of any type of information directly associated with the school. Several examples might be current facilities available, enrollment trends, and funds available. Community-related data assist in examining the geographical area served by the school. Examples of community-related data might be population trends, labor market demands, and possibilities of cooperative training centers. In some cases, data from several nearby counties would be needed. These might include federal, regional, or state data related to the standard under consideration. For example, a state may have a printing program at a community college to serve the regional needs of that state. Table 2-1 provides a list of data sources that might be used to determine if, in fact, previously established standards could or could not be met. These data sources will be discussed in detail in later chapters; however, the curriculum planner must understand how the various data sources align with basic program standards.

Making decisions in curriculum planning

From the standpoint of curriculum planning, the decision-making process may be viewed as consisting of several stages, each of which builds upon the others and progressively involves the curriculum specialist in data-gathering and decision-making activities. The entire process is represented graphically in Figure 2-5. Note that the stages parallel discussions dealing with areas such as establishing standards, gathering data, and examining the alignment of standards and data. A discussion of each of the five stages illustrated in Figure 2-5 is provided on page 44.

TABLE 2-1. Possible sources of data needed to determine if vocational program standards may be met

General Standard	School-related Data	Community-related Data
Prospective enrollment	Student interest Student ability Enrollment trends Dropout rates Reasons for dropouts Parents' concerns and expectations	Population trends Community goals Industry movement Other vocational education programs available
Availability of qualified instructor	Background of current instructors	Qualifications of local business persons and lay people College graduates
Available facilities	Current facilities Potential for expansion or remodeling Funds available	Local facilities available
Available equipment	Current equipment Funds available	Equipment available in the local area
Available funding	Current and future budget	Current and future budget support Special funding categories from state and/or federal sources
Employment opportunities	Follow-up of graduates Follow-up of adults enrolled in continuing education programs	Population trends Current and projected employment opportunities Current and projected supply and demand of labor Community goals Other vocational education programs available
Other similar vocational programs available	Current and planned vocational programs	Other vocational education programs available
Vocational program being considered that supports goals and philosophy of school	Goals and philosophy of the school	Goals of the community
Delivery of program that upholds established guidelines	Current class schedules	
Opportunities for cooperative vocational programs	Possibility of school-related stations	Number of businesses willing to participate and number of stations Business and industry movement

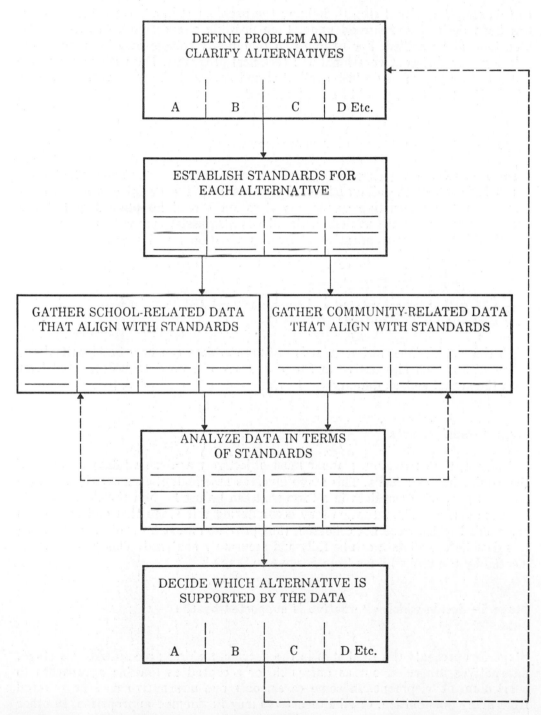

FIGURE 2-5. Making decisions in curriculum planning

Stage 1—define problem and clarify alternatives

In this stage, a critical step is defining the problem at hand. Once the problem has been defined and agreed upon, then possible alternative solutions can be identified and clarified. For example, a community college may be considering offering four different vocational and technical programs. Data concerning each of these four programs could be collected and analyzed simultaneously to decide which, if not all four, should be implemented.

Stage 2—establish standards for each alternative

Once alternatives are clarified, Stage 2 allows for the establishment of standards for each of the alternatives. Standards help the decision maker to determine if the alternative under consideration should be offered and if the necessary resources are available. Standards also assist curriculum planners in the establishment and operation of quality vocational and technical education programs.

Stage 3—gather school-related and community-related data that align with standards

With the establishment of standards in Stage 2, data can now be identified and collected for each alternative in Stage 3. Data will need to be collected from both the school and community.

Stage 4—analyze data

In Stage 4, the curriculum planner must objectively analyze all data in terms of the established standards. This stage involves assembling, summarizing, analyzing, and preparing the data in a form that can be used when the decision-making time arrives. The situation may occur during this stage that additional data are needed which were not collected, thus provision must be made for collecting this data before all data can be fully and accurately analyzed. This process is indicated by the dashed lines from Stage 4 to Stage 3.

Stage 5—decide which alternative is supported by the data

Stage 5 represents the final step in the decision-making process. At this stage, alternatives are ruled out as unfeasible or accepted as feasible approaches to curriculum development. In some cases, only one alternative may be selected from many possibilities, or all alternatives may be deemed appropriate. In other cases, all alternatives may be ruled out. Decision makers may also identify other alternatives not previously considered, and thus the process would be repeated for each new alternative. Repeating the process is represented by the dashed line from Stage 5 to Stage 1.

SUMMARY

The importance of decision making in educational curriculum planning cannot be overemphasized. Of all the activities and elements associated with an educational organization, the instant that a decision is made is one that will have lasting effect upon the future of the curriculum. Hopefully, that effect will be desirable.

Decision making in the educational arena usually involves two major areas, policy decisions and operational decisions. Operational decisions involve day-to-day activities of the curriculum and serve to move the curriculum smoothly ahead. Policy decisions deal with goals, objectives, and some basic structure for achieving these goals and objectives. Curriculum planners must be involved at both levels of decisions. Whereas policy decisions will serve to establish the type of curriculum a school will or will not follow, operational decisions will deal with the management of the approved curriculum. Both of these areas have a direct influence on whether the curriculum will be successful.

The value of systematic planning must be recognized by all who deal with the curriculum. Vocational education curricula must be planned and implemented in such a way to assure that students and societal needs are served. Nothing less than this should be attempted or accepted.

Curriculum planners should be aware of the effect that philosophy and sociopsychological factors have upon those who are in decision-making positions. An understanding of these important elements as they relate to decision making aids curriculum planners as they provide data needed by decision makers to arrive at sound decisions and also provides input as to how curriculum planners can work effectively with those who are in key decision-making roles.

Although many approaches can be useful in guiding the decision-making process, each educational organization must establish a system that is compatible with its particular structure. This procedure should be written and shared with all to ensure a complete understanding of how decisions will be made. Once the procedure is established, a continual review and evaluation should be made to determine how the process can be improved.

Decision makers cannot be expected to reach decisions unless standards are established to help determine whether a program should or should not be offered. Curriculum planners must take the initiative to see that realistic standards are established that reflect quality programs. Once standards have been established, data can then be identified and collected to determine if the program should be offered. These data can basically be thought of as either school-related or community-related.

Although much has been said about sophistication associated with decision making in education, the final decision rests upon human judgement. This judgement must be made by responsible members of society, who are representatives of the community in which a school is located. As society and technology advance, hopefully data provided to these decision makers will become more sophisticated and accurate, and the decisions will represent a higher level of objectivity.

REFERENCES

Braybrooke, David, and Lindbloom, Charles E. *A Strategy of Decision.* New York: Free Press, 1963.

Campbell, Roald F.; Bridges, Edwin M.; and Nystrand, Raphael O. *Introduction to Educational Administration*, 5th Ed. Boston: Allyn and Bacon, Inc., 1977.

Cook, Desmond L. *Program Evaluation and Review Technique.* Washington, D. C.: U. S. Government Printing Office, 1966.

Hamlin, Herbert M. *Public School Education in Agriculture.* Danville, Ill.: The Interstate Printers and Publishers, Inc., 1962.

Katz, Daniel, and Kahn, Robert L. *The Social Psychology of Organizations.* New York: John Wiley & Sons, Inc., 1966.

Magee, John F. "Decision Trees for Decision Making," *Harvard Business Review 42* (July-August, 1964).

Mali, Paul. *Managing by Objectives.* New York: John Wiley & Sons, Inc., 1972.

Malinski, Joseph F. *Planning Techniques for Local Programs of Vocational Education.* Columbus: The Center for Vocational and Technical Education, The Ohio State University, Information Series 63, 1972.

Odiorne, George. *Management by Objectives.* New York: Pitman, 1965.

Taba, Hilda. *Curriculum Development, Theory and Practice.* New York: Harcourt, Brace, and World, Inc., 1962.

Wenrich, Ralph C., and Wenrich, J. William. *Leadership in Administration of Vocational and Technical Education.* Columbus: Charles E. Merrill Publishing Co., 1974.

Young, Robert C.; Clive, William V.; and Miles, Benton E. *Vocational Education Planning: Manpower, Priorities, and Dollars.* Columbus: The Center for Vocational and Technical Education, The Ohio State University, Research and Development Series 68, 1972.

Collecting and Assessing
School-related Data

Introduction

As discussed in the previous chapter, decision making in educational curriculum planning must take many factors into consideration. One factor that must be considered in the curriculum-planning process and yet is often found to be lacking consists of conditions surrounding the school setting. The major goal of vocational instruction is to equip students for successful employment in an occupation of their choice (Allen, 1974).* Many curriculum planners casually mention the student as one factor to consider in the planning processes, but few actually deal with this area in a comprehensive manner. As a result, curricula may be developed with little or no student input and little consideration given to the current situation existing in a school system.

This chapter focuses on the collection of data relating to a school system under study by the curriculum planner. Major points to consider in this regard are the status of current vocational and technical education programs, the current dropout rate and the reasons for it, occupational interests of students, parents' interests and concerns, follow-up of former students, projection of future enrollments, and assessment of current facilities available. The goal of this chapter is to provide the curriculum planner with the capability to take a closer look at what is really happening in the school system as it now exists and to identify data for use in either establishing program standards or determining if established standards can be met. One of the first steps in curriculum development is to study the current program.

---

*From David Allen, "Instruction," *The Philosophy for Quality Vocational Education Programs* (Washington, D.C.: Fourth AVA Yearbook, 1974), p. 113.

Current status of vocational and technical education programs

Before any curriculum-planning decisions can be made, consideration must be given to assessing current programs and developing a basic understanding about them. While some curriculum planners are able to build a vocational and technical education program where none exists, most will be faced with making decisions related to the improvement and/or expansion of ongoing programs. Thus it is imperative that full consideration be given to the current vocational and technical education program.

Structure for offering vocational and technical education

An immediate question to consider deals with the manner in which current vocational and technical education programs are offered. The purpose of this chapter is not to discuss issues such as the pros and cons of area vocational schools vs. comprehensive high schools at the secondary level, but one must at least keep basic school system frameworks such as these in mind. Many curriculum planners have been involved in developing area vocational schools to expand existing offerings or provide new ones. However, once area schools have been built, educators have been reluctant to revert to the local high schools as the main delivery system for vocational and technical education programs. The point here is that curriculum planners should have a thorough understanding of the type of arrangements that current programs are operated under in the school system or attendance area being studied, as well as alternatives that are available based on previous decisions that have become binding.

   Another major consideration at this time would be provisions for postsecondary vocational and technical education. Is the current high school or area vocational school providing vocational and technical education beyond high school? Are there community colleges or two-year schools accessible to students living in the school district? Curriculum planners must have these types of information available as curriculum decisions are made at the secondary and postsecondary level.

Current vocational and technical programs, enrollments, and capacity

The assessment of current programs begins with identifying and listing individual courses that are presently being offered. While this may seem a trite step to some, the listing will help to eliminate some future problems and misunderstandings, especially with those involved in curriculum planning who do not have vocational education backgrounds.

The use of a form, such as that in Figure 3-1, enables the curriculum planner to produce a clear, concise picture of current vocational and technical education programs. Column 1 is used to list specialty program areas and the courses offered under each program area. State department of education approved titles should be used in listing program areas or courses. The use of abbreviated names or nicknames will often lead to confusion and misunderstanding in communications between curriculum planners. If the state department of education has assigned code numbers to approved courses, these could also be used and placed in parentheses after each course offering. The second column is designed to help identify the location in which a course is currently being offered. This would be of special value when vocational courses are offered in different buildings or when students are bused to different locations for their vocational and technical courses.

Columns 3, 4, 5, and 6 deal with the course enrollment status. In planning any educational program, planners must be aware of the current capacity of courses in the school system. Capacity could be interpreted as either state-established levels or maximums set for the current facility being used. Columns 4 and 5 help the curriculum planner to determine whether current program offerings are operating at maximum capacity. Listing the grade level of students enrolled in each course in Column 6 assists planners in assessing whether students are enrolled in vocational and technical courses designed for their grade level. Thus a standard may be established that in order for course X to be offered, the facility must be of sufficient size to permit twenty-two students to enroll. Information collected on the form in Figure 3-1 can assist a curriculum planner in determining if that program standard will be met.

Assessing current dropout rates

What is a good dropout rate? Of course, a zero percent would be ideal. But school officials come up with figures such as 20.0 percent, 10.7 percent, 5.4 percent, or some other vague number. As curriculum planners begin to develop educational programs, some attention must be directed to the current dropout rate being experienced in the school or school system. Not only must planners look at percentages, but they must also attempt to assess the reasons why students are dropping out of school. A summary and analysis of the dropout information should provide valuable data for curriculum planners. Decision makers who finalize curriculum goals, objectives, and program standards without first considering current dropout rates and reasons behind these rates may develop programs that do not address real world concerns.

Calculating dropout rates

Referring back to the figures mentioned earlier of 20.0, 10.7, or 5.4 percent, what do these figures mean? In other words, how were these percentages calcu-

FIGURE 3-1. Current vocational and technical programs, enrollments, and capacity for ——— [school district, community college, etc.]

Date: ———

Vocational and Technical Programs and Courses [1]	Room number or Name & Facility [2]	Enrollment		Over or Under Enrollment [5]	Number of Students by Grade Level [6]									Special Remarks [7]
		Capacity [3]	Current [4]		6	7	8	9	10	11	12	13	14	

lated? Six of the more common methods of calculating dropout rates are outlined in Figure 3-2. Before discussing the different methods of calculating dropout rates, several rules or procedures need to be mentioned. To calculate any dropout percentage, a base period must be established. This base period could be any point in time as determined by the individual calculating the dropout rates. Students comprising the figures used for the base period should then represent the students for which any future calculations should be made. Furthermore, an understanding must be formed as to what constitutes a dropout. A dropout is a student who leaves the school system before graduation and who does not enter another school system. With these assumptions or parameters outlined, attention can now be turned to Figure 3-2.

True dropout rate.   Cases 1a and 1b in Figure 3-2 would be classified as a True Dropout Rate. Referring to Case 1a, students entering the first grade numbered 300, but of these 300, 240 graduated from high school. This represents **60** students who dropped out sometime in the twelve-year span (we will assume that they did not reenter another school system). Thus the True Dropout Rate is 20 percent.

A more realistic example is Case 1b. Three hundred students entered the first grade and 50 dropped out of school before graduation. Ten students left the school system and reenrolled in another school system. Thus the base period figure must be readjusted to 290. This now gives a True Dropout Rate of 17.2 percent. Another point to make when setting the base period figure is that student transfers into the school system should not be added to the base period figure or the current enrollment figure. If student transfers were added in, an inaccurate percentage figure would be obtained.

High school dropout rate.   Some schools use dropout rates reflecting only what has happened since the students entered the ninth grade. Case 2 illustrates what might be called the High School Dropout Rate. In this example, 280 students enter the ninth grade and 250 graduate from that school. This leaves 30 dropouts, for a percentage of 10.7. If a situation existed similar to the one described in Case 1b, where 5 of the 30 entered another school system leaving 25 dropouts, then the readjusted base period would become 275 and the dropout rate would be 9.1 percent.

Yearly dropout rate.   In Case 3, 280 students entered the eighth grade in August and the following August, 265 entered the ninth grade. Assuming that no student failed and none moved to another school, 15 students were classified as dropouts. The dropout rate on a yearly basis was 5.4 percent for the eighth grade. Although the example here is for the eighth graders, a person could select any grade level except the twelfth grade for calculating a Yearly Dropout Rate. Another variation would be to add all grades together and arrive at a total percentage for the school on a yearly basis.

FIGURE 3–2.   **Methods for calculating dropout rates**

	Base Period	Current Enrollment	Number of Dropouts	Percent of Dropouts
True Dropout Rate				
Case 1a	300 enter first grade	240 graduate from high school	60	20.0
Case 1b	300 enter first grade 290 (Readjusted Base Period)	240 graduate from high school (10 entered another school system)	50	17.2
High School Dropout Rate				
Case 2	280 enter 9th grade	250 graduate from high school	30	10.7
Yearly Dropout Rate				
Case 3	280 enter 8th grade in August	265 enter 9th grade the following August	15	5.4
School Year Dropout Rate				
Case 4	250 enter 11th grade in August	240 complete 11th grade the following June	10	4.0
Transfer Dropout Rate				
Case 5	50 transferred in to date	45 still remain	5	10.0
Course Dropout Rate				
Case 6	15 enter vocational course in August	14 complete the vocational course the following June	1	6.7

School year dropout rate.   Some of the lowest dropout rates that are used reflect what might be called a School Year Dropout Rate. In Case 4, 250 students enter the eleventh grade in August and of these 250 students, 240 are still in school when the school year ends in June. Assuming that no students left school and entered another school, ten students were classified as dropouts. Thus the dropout rate was 4.0 percent. Any person using this procedure must keep in mind that students who do not reenter school in the fall after the summer break are not reflected in this dropout percentage, but in reality, these students are dropouts.

Transfer dropout rate.   Since students transferring into a school system could represent a sizeable portion of the school body, some accounting of these students must be made. If the transfer students were added to other procedures for calculating dropout rates, inaccurate percentages would result. With reference to Case 5, the base period would represent all students who have transferred into the school system at the time of the calculation. The current enrollment would reflect those transfers who are still in the school system. For example, if the assumption is made that 50 students have transferred into the school system, and of these 50, 5 have dropped out, then the Transfer Dropout Rate is 10.0 percent.

Course dropout rate.   One approach in considering dropout rates that has special implications to vocational educators would be the figures obtained through a Course Dropout Rate. Although this type of percentage has not been discussed much in the past, the figure is one that curriculum planners should consider. In Case 6, 15 students entered a vocational and technical course in August and 14 students were still in the course the following June. With one dropout, the percentage is 6.7.

Again, several variations for a course dropout rate might be considered. One variation would be the establishment of a base period at the time students enter the first course in a sequence of courses spanning two or more years. The current enrollment figure would then be either the number of students in the program at the time of the calculation or the number of students who complete the vocational course at some later date.

Analyzing different dropout rates

Once a curriculum planner has calculated dropout rates that seem important, other types of data might be obtained and used in curriculum planning. Thus far, calculations have dealt with all students who dropped out of school, regardless of their courses of study. However, more specific information could be obtained if the dropout rate for vocational and technical students were compared against other students in the school system. This should be done with extreme caution, since there may be a number of factors that affect students leaving school.

Vocational and technical dropouts vs. academic dropouts.   Educators have maintained and research has indicated that vocational and technical education programs have a strong holding power of students enrolled. The wise curriculum planner should determine just where the current dropout rate is occurring. Is the dropout rate higher for students enrolled in the academic, general, or vocational curriculum? Furthermore, an assessment of dropouts by grade levels may also provide valuable planning information. Gathering the data mentioned in the last few pages will not provide direct answers, but when considered in relationship with reasons why students dropped out of school, they should provide some meaningful input for curriculum planning.

Student withdrawal from a vocational and technical course. Another type of dropout category to consider consists of students who do not drop out of school, but do withdraw from a vocational and technical course. Every time that a student withdraws from a course, time, energy, and money have been committed that could have been utilized to help another student. If the withdrawal rate is excessive, serious questions need to be raised with either the student selection process, the course being offered, the content of the course, or the competency of the teacher.

The calculation of a percentage of withdrawals could be taken on an academic year basis for those vocational and technical courses designed to be completed in a year. For those courses with a sequence spanning more than one year, a base period should be established when students enter the program. Only in this way will curriculum planners have a sound perception of the holding power of ongoing vocational and technical courses. Although it is difficult to say that a certain percentage of withdrawals is either good or bad, the fact remains that if the withdrawal rate is too high, the last course in the sequence may have a small number of students. When this happens, the cost per graduate rises substantially and program efficiency becomes questionable.

Determining reasons for dropping out

The calculation of dropout rates is not sufficient data by itself to assess a current picture of the dropout situation in a specific school system. While percentages may lead curriculum planners to the conclusion that a problem exists, the figures will not provide reasons why the dropout rate is at a certain level.

Reasons for dropping out. The reason for which a student drops out of school should be obtained before he or she officially leaves the school. This type of information could be obtained through a short questionnaire or through a personal conference with the student. Reasons will vary, but they might include the following:

Adverse school experience

Courses not interesting
Courses do not relate to career goals
Teachers do not like me

Marriage

Work

Military service

Adverse home circumstances

Health

Attainment of mandatory age limit (for high school students)

Other

Collecting and analyzing this data may employ several different methods. Students could be separated into the types of curricula offered in the schools to determine if a certain pattern emerges concerning the reasons given for dropping out. Another method would be to divide the dropouts by sex. Females may, in some cases, have different reasons for dropping out as compared to males. Regardless of the procedure used in calculating dropout rates and the reasons used to determine why students drop out, the ultimate concern of curriculum planners should be the collection of data that will be of value to them as decisions are made about future program development resulting in improved educational curricula.

Assessing student occupational interest

The story is told of how a new program was added to the school curriculum and the most up-to-date facility was constructed; but when it came to enrolling students, no one wanted to take the program. Although this story may be more fiction than fact, administrators and teachers have no doubt wondered from time to time if students were really interested in the courses being offered. Planners must take into account the occupational interests of students when measuring program standards. The specific learning goals for each student should be based upon an understanding of the wide differences in personalities, interests, backgrounds, and abilities (Allen, 1974).*

Standardized tests

One approach to assessing the occupational interests of a large group of students is through the use of standardized tests. This is especially helpful if several different grade levels are to be surveyed. Such tests are available to educators and can be an effective tool in curriculum planning. But it must be kept in mind that no test is available that specifically identifies into which occupation a person should go. Vocational interest tests are intended to point out general vocational interests of students and should not be interpreted beyond this point.

---

*From David Allen, "Instruction," *The Philosophy for Quality Vocational Education Programs* (Washington, D.C.: Fourth AVA Yearbook, 1974), p. 127.

Interest inventories.   Students will be more highly motivated to investigate occupations and firm up career decisions if they have a good understanding of
themselves. Interest inventories not only help students to learn more about
themselves, but also aid curriculum planners in making generalizations about future program direction.

The following factors should be kept in mind by students and curriculum
planners when using standardized interest inventories:

1. Interest inventories do not indicate ability. A student may be inter-
    ested in an occupation but not have the ability to succeed in it.

2. Interest inventories may help students recognize interest in occupa-
    tions that they did not know existed.

3. Interest inventories may help students confirm what they thought
    were their interests.

4. Interest inventories should never be used as the only method of as-
    sessing student occupational interests. Other factors to consider are
    stated interests, individual observations, and activities in which the
    student has participated.

Several interest inventories are currently available. Two of the more
common tests are the KUDER GENERAL INTEREST SURVEY and the OHIO
VOCATIONAL INTEREST SURVEY. The KUDER FORM E is a general interest survey designed to be administered to grades six through twelve. The test
requires thirty to forty minutes for administration. The survey measures an individual's preferences for activities grouped into the following areas: outdoor,
mechanical, scientific, computational, persuasive, artistic, literary, musical, social service, and clerical. The survey can be either machine- or hand-scored.

The OHIO VOCATIONAL INTEREST SURVEY (OVIS) is designed for
grades eight through twelve and requires sixty to ninety minutes to administer.
This survey measures an individual's preferences on the following twenty-four
interest scales: manual work, machine work, personal services, caring for people
or animals, clinical work, inspecting and testing, crafts and precise operations,
customer services, nursing and related technical services, skilled personal service, training, literary, numerical, appraisal, agriculture, applied technology,
promotion and communication, management and supervision, artistic, sales representative, music, entertainment and performing arts, teaching, counseling and
social work, and medical. This survey must be machine-scored.

Standardized aptitude tests

Scholastic aptitude tests are also available and can give a rough estimate of a
student's ability to learn from books or from tasks required in school. Several
aptitude tests that may be administered are: CALIFORNIA TEST OF MEN-
TAL MATURITY; OTIS-LENNON MENTAL ABILITY TEST; SRA PRIMARY
MENTAL ABILITIES TEST; and the LORGE-THORNDIKE INTELLIGENCE

TEST. To prevent the branding or labeling of students, educators should refrain from using specific test scores or IQ scores. The recommended practice is to use test scores in general terms.

Another aptitude test is the GENERAL APTITUDE TEST BATTERY (GATB), which is administered by the branches of the state employment service. Nine factors included in this test are: general reasoning ability, verbal aptitude, numerical aptitude, spatial aptitude, form perception, clerical perception, motor coordination, finger dexterity, and normal dexterity.

Standardized achievement tests

Tests such as the STANFORD ACHIEVEMENT TEST and the CALIFORNIA ACHIEVEMENT TESTS are also used by many school systems. Achievement tests measure what a student has already learned, while aptitude tests are used more for predicting future performance.

Selecting standardized tests

With the multitude of tests on the market, the curriculum planner may wish to review current listings in EDUCATION INDEX. However, he or she must eventually decide which test to administer to students. A review of the different types of standardized tests may lead the planner to eliminate some tests immediately, since the purpose for which a particular test is to be administered may not be appropriate for curriculum planning.

In addition to the purpose for which a test is to be used, several other factors should be considered regardless of the type of test desired. Information regarding the following factors is usually found in the booklet describing each test. *Reliability* refers to the ability of the test to give the same results if administered to the same student at a later time. *Validity* refers to the ability of the test to measure what it purports to measure. Several other items should be considered to determine if the test is practical to administer. One factor to consider is the time required to administer the test. The time should be reasonable and it is helpful if the test can be administered within a single class period. Another factor is the cost. Although curriculum planners would not want to select a test solely because it is the least expensive one available, tests that entail a higher cost per student could run into a sizeable figure if administered to a large group of students. The last factor to consider deals with the ease of administering, scoring, and interpreting the results. A test should be selected only if it gives understandable and useable results.

Specialized interest scales for specific vocational and technical program areas

Although some research and interest test development have been initiated, curriculum planners will not, in general, be able to use standardized tests to any great degree for determining occupational interests of students within specific program areas. For example, Hamilton (1967) has developed an AGRICULTURAL OCCUPATIONS INTEREST SCALE for secondary students and has obtained some norms. The test consists of 100 items and relates interests to five agricultural occupational groups: agricultural production, ornamental horticulture, agricultural business, agricultural mechanization, and conservation and recreation. Further research and development need to be carried out in each of the vocational program areas before interest tests can be used with any degree of accuracy for program planning.

Teacher-made surveys

Many planners have relied upon teacher-made surveys for use in specific program areas. Although these surveys are not as sophisticated as standardized tests, teacher-made surveys can prove valuable to curriculum planners. Each survey must be developed with a purpose in mind. If the need arises for determining the occupational interests of students in the area of distributive education, then occupations or situations that lend themselves to occupations found in distributive education must be identified and incorporated into the survey.

The format and length of such surveys can vary widely, depending upon the degree to which a curriculum planner desires to pinpoint occupational interests. The survey should be relatively short and easy for the students to complete. Short answers or questions that students can check or circle will aid in maintaining student interest throughout the survey. An example of a teacher-made survey is included in Appendix A.

Administering tests and surveys

One important factor to determine is when a test should be administered. Typically, standardized tests are administered to all students in a school system to assess their current occupational interests. If a program is being planned that will go into effect two years from the time a survey is administered, instruments should be administered to students in the lower grades who will be able to select vocational and technical courses two years hence.

Although teacher surveys are usually developed for specific vocational program areas and are used with students already enrolled in those areas, administration of the survey to other students has some merit. The standardized instruments discussed earlier indicate student interest in occupational groups. Teacher-made surveys, however, assist students in identifying specific interests within a certain area. To administer any interest survey or test to a certain group of students and not to others assumes that the students not provided the opportunity to express their interests do not possess occupational interests in that area. This is often a false assumption and one that curriculum planners cannot afford to make.

Obtaining assistance

Curriculum planners who are unfamiliar with the administration and interpretation of test results may want to seek professional assistance. Most colleges and universities with vocational and technical education programs have personnel who can provide assistance to local schools in collecting and interpreting data related to educational decision making. Specialists in state departments of education also have expertise in this area. Furthermore, private consultants are also available to local school systems on a fee basis; however, the cost for this type of service may prove to be prohibitive.

Interpreting test results

Once the tests have been administered and the data summarized, the task is now one of interpreting or analyzing the data in light of established program standards. As mentioned earlier, test scores should never be the only source of information to the curriculum planner. Data received through the administration of tests or interest surveys should only be one factor to consider.

Standardized tests come with booklets or other aids for use in interpreting test results. However, curriculum planners must realize that the final decision regarding a priority listing of courses to be offered must come from them. In addition to data collected from either standardized or teacher-made tests, curriculum planners should conduct personal interviews with as many students as possible. This not only helps to further refine data to be used in the decision-making process, but also provides a source of input from students that cannot be readily collected during the administration of standardized tests.

Characteristics of students

Another type of assessment that can be carried out by curriculum planners is the comparison of student characteristics with those types of characteristics possessed by people holding certain occupations in society. Compton (1969) found that the characteristics of clothing and textile students were similar to those characteristics found in people employed in clothing and textile occupations. While this is an area in which more research is needed, curriculum planners may find in the future more research showing a positive correlation between students in a certain curriculum and people who are employed in occupations relating to that curriculum. Or curriculum planners may desire to conduct their own research on the local level to determine the benefits of such an approach to matching students with a curriculum and thus matching a vocational program to the needs of a community.

Soliciting parents' interests and concerns

The involvement of parents in the local school system is vital to the planning and conducting of a sound educational program. Parents, whether overtly expressing their feelings or not, are vitally concerned and interested in the education of their children. Curriculum planners must take the initiative to see that input from parents is received prior to the decision-making step in curriculum development. Even though this source of input has been traditional at the secondary level, there is no reason why the process should not be extended to the postsecondary level, if appropriate.

Identifying types of parent input

In curriculum planning, certain types of information can be contributed by parents and can aid the planners in decision making. For example, parents always possess certain expectations of the vocational program in their local school. To help clarify what is meant by an expectation, it is an anticipation or hope of what a vocational and technical program should provide to the student. Furthermore, parents will always have certain concerns about the program. A concern is an interest, feeling, or responsibility characterized by uneasiness or apprehension about the vocational technical education program. This could be a concern about a current program or about a program being planned for the future.

A list of possible concerns and expectations of parents relating to vocational and technical education programs can be found in Appendix B. Curriculum planners may find this list helpful in securing input from parents. Parts I and III of Appendix B contain statements that are more applicable to a comprehensive high school offering vocational education courses. Parts II and IV are additional statements reflecting concerns and expectations relating to area vocational schools and the home high school. Provision has also been made for parents to express the degree to which their expectations have been met.

Collecting input from parents

Appendix B is set up so that use can be made of the statements in obtaining input from parents. If a large number of parents are to be contacted, sufficient room can be provided in the right-hand margin of the questionnaire for coding and keypunching.

Two approaches may be used in identifying the population from which to draw a sample. One approach would be that all parents of students enrolled in a vocational or technical education course comprise the population. The other approach would be to identify the population as the parents of all students in the local school. This might include the high school, junior high school, middle school, elementary school, or the entire school system. In many cases, the population may be a much larger group than can be feasibly handled. Thus the random selection of parents by use of a table of random numbers should provide reliable data at a lower cost. The questionnaire could be a mailed, self-administered type with a follow-up letter sent to those not responding. Personal contacts or telephone calls could be used as additional follow-up procedures.

If any personal contact with parents is to be made, providing them with advance notice of the purpose and reasons for the study will yield a greater response. Use of radio announcements, newspaper articles, and advance letters would also be well worth the effort. The best time of day for any personal contact is in the evening or during the day on Saturday. Since curriculum planners, teachers, and administrators are usually quite busy with teaching and administrative responsibilities, seeking assistance to conduct a personal parent contact would be advisable. Usually volunteer assistance can be obtained from mature students, retired individuals, housewives, members of PTA's, or other interested groups or individuals.

Interpreting data results

The nature of the results obtained from any parent survey or input solicited by curriculum planners will naturally depend upon the purpose and nature of the questionnaire. In reference to the value of identifying the concerns or expectations of parents, several distinct implications can be made for curriculum planners as they assess the extent to which program standards can be met.

Influence of identified concerns.   The identification of distinct parent concerns can give direction for future activities of curriculum planners. If it is evident that parents are concerned about certain aspects of a vocational program, alternatives should be sought out that would help to diminish those concerns. This is especially critical if results of a survey indicate that parents are uninformed about vocational or technical programs.

Influence of identified expectations.   The true expectations that parents hold of vocational or technical education programs can also be of significant value to curriculum planners. If parents have unrealistic expectations for the program, efforts need to be made that will bring parents' expectations in line with what is possible. Furthermore, parents may provide ideas that have been previously overlooked.

Following up former students

Follow-up studies are designed to evaluate the product of career programs—the graduate. The primary goal of such education—the preparation of individuals for employment—can best be assessed by examining the placement records of graduates and gathering job performance data from employers. In addition, very important information regarding the strengths and weaknesses of a program may be gathered from the former students, who are in the best position to judge such characteristics (Wentling and Lawson, 1975).

Identifying and locating former students

The identification of students should pose no special problems to curriculum planners. Most schools maintain files of former graduates and students and this can serve as a basis for composing a follow-up list. Locating former high school or community college students may be more of a problem. This points up the need for placement coordinators to provide leadership in the placement of students and maintenance of files to keep abreast of students for follow-up situations. If no records have been maintained, usually parents, relatives, or teachers can provide addresses of students.

Contacting former students

The best practice to follow in order to assure a high response rate from students is personal contact. Again, selected mature students, retired individuals, PTA members, or other interested individuals can greatly assist in the collection of data. Telephone calls could be made to those living out of the community. Another approach would be through a mailed questionnaire; however, the rate of return would not be as high as that from personal contact.

Regardless of the approach used, curriculum planners must demand a high rate of return from former students. Otherwise, the validity of the study may be seriously questioned.

Information to gather from former students

The type of information to gather from former students depends upon what the student has done or is currently doing since leaving school. Activities can usually be separated into two categories, employed or continuing education.

Students who are employed. There is basic information that should be collected from students who have been employed since leaving school. An example of a format developed by Krebs (1969) for use in soliciting employment information from former students is found in Figure 3-3. This form should be completed for each former student. The student's name and address, student number, and year of graduation are placed at the top of the form. A chronological listing of jobs held since leaving school is listed under Column 1. Employment held is listed by job titles. The second column permits the identification of employers. This information has special significance for information needed by curriculum planners for decisions identified in Chapters 4, 5, and 6.

FIGURE 3-3. Individual student: employment*

Student Name _____   Student No. _____

Year Graduated _____

Student Address _____

Jobs Held—Titles[a] [1]	Employer Name and Address [2]	Date Took Job [3]	Date Left Job [4]	Hrs. Per Week [5]	Wages[b] Start End[c] [6]	Satisfaction[d] [7]
1.						1 2 3 4 5
2.						1 2 3 4 5
3.						1 2 3 4 5
4.						1 2 3 4 5
5.						1 2 3 4 5
6.						1 2 3 4 5

Note: Use additional forms as needed to list all jobs held.

Military Service Dates: From _____ To _____

[a] List jobs in chronological order.
Report each change of position or job within the same business as a new job.
[b] Show wages by amount per hour.
[c] Record current wage for job now held. Record best estimate of wages individual can provide.
[d] Circle according to scale:
1 = Highly satisfied;   2 = satisfied;   3 = noncommittal;   4 = dissatisfied;   5 = highly dissatisfied

Source: A. H. Krebs, *Model for Evaluation of Secondary School Programs of Vocational Education in Agriculture.* College Park, Md.: University of Maryland, Agricultural Experiment Station, MP 733, July, 1969.

Columns 3 and 4 provide information relating to job stability and unemployment periods. The hours of work per week give an indication of full- or part-time employment. In addition to the job titles listed, wages received provide insight as to advancements made. The identification of wages also gives an idea as to the starting pay of former students. Level of job satisfaction can be ascertained in Column 7. This type of information could also prove valuable in making decisions brought forth in Chapters 4, 5, and 6.

Students who are continuing their education. Krebs (1969) also developed a form that can give curriculum planners data relating to those students who have continued their education since leaving school. Information gathered by this form (Figure 3-4) relates to the identification of institutions enrolled in, courses of study, personal objectives, and if appropriate, why the student left the program.

Individuals enrolled in adult classes. If valuable information can be obtained by following up former high school or community college students, then the assumption can be made that a follow-up of adult students would also prove to be valuable. Figure 3-5 is an example of a form suggested by Krebs (1969). Information can be secured as to why adults enrolled in courses, and whether they were able to accomplish their goals after completing them.

The information discussed in the last few pages can provide valuable data for curriculum planners. For example, discussion may be underway as to whether a vocational program should be continued, thus a standard may be established that at least 75 percent of the graduates from a particular vocational service area either must be employed in a job related to their training or must be continuing their education. Data collected by use of the forms in Figures 3-3 and 3-4 will provide this information.

Projecting future enrollments

The need to project into the future is vital to the effectiveness of any educational program and is basic to any curriculum planning. Many times programs developed are not available to students until two, three, four, or more years in the future. Therefore curriculum planners need to establish standards concerning potential enrollments for an educational program in order to balance the program with the number of students in the school system or attendance area.

Community data

Most projections begin by considering only those students currently enrolled in school, although it would not be too premature to look even further. Securing data about the current birth rates in any one county or school district may give

---

FIGURE 3–4.   Individual student: continuing education*

Student Name_____ Student No._____

Student Address_____Year Graduated _____

1. Name of institution in which enrolled_____

2. Address of institution_____

3. Dates of enrollment: Starting_____Ending_____

4. Program (or course) in which enrolled_____

5. Program major (if not same as program)_____

6. Enrollment status: full-time student _____
                               part-time student _____

7. Length of the program (months)_____

8. Objective for which enrolled: (check all that apply)

    _____ a. Preparation for job (specify)_____

    _____ b. Upgrading in present job

    _____ c. Maintaining competency for present job

    _____ d. No occupational objective

    _____ e. Other reason (specify)_____

9. If no longer enrolled in the program named, check all of
    the following that apply:

    _____ a. Completed program or course

    _____ b. Transferred to another school program

    _____ c. Took a job

    _____ d. Entered military service

    _____ e. Academic dismissal

    _____ f. Other reasons for leaving (specify) _____

Source: A. H. Krebs, *Model for Evaluation of Secondary School Programs of Vocational Education in Agriculture.* College Park, Md.: University of Maryland, Agricultural Experiment Station, MP 733, July, 1969.

FIGURE 3–5. Individual student: Adult education*

Name _____ Student No. _____

Address _____

Highest grade completed: (circle) Under 7, 7, 8, 9, 10, 11, 12, 13, 14, 15, 16, over 16

Present occupation _____

Adult courses in which enrolled	Year[a]	Purposes for which enrolled			Evidence of accomplishment of purpose — record any evidence available[b]
		Improve in present occupation	Prepare for new occupation	Other reasons [specify]	

[a]For the year or years offered by School Division.

[b]Evidence such as: job or salary promotions; employment in new occupation; recognition for work performed; comments regarding increased job satisfaction; increase in net income and net worth.

*Source: A. H. Krebs, *Model for Evaluation of Secondary School Programs of Vocational Education in Agriculture.* College Park, Md.: University of Maryland, Agricultural Experiment Station, MP 733, July, 1969.

curriculum planners leads as to trends that might occur in the future. Tentative answers can be found for such questions as: "Will school enrollments increase or decrease in the future?"; "What will be the sex ratio?"; "Will the educational programs and facilities be adequate to meet future needs?" Seeking answers or at least tentative answers to questions such as these through the use of census data might have prevented some of the critical enrollment situations that schools have found themselves involved in today.

Projecting school enrollments

Once students begin to attend school, more accurate data can be secured for use in projecting trends. A format such as the one presented in Figure 3-6 will provide curriculum planners with a quick and concise look at what they might expect as far as enrollments in the future and the composition of the student body are concerned. This form could be used for any class for which curriculum planners may wish to collect information. In addition, the projected year column can be readjusted to reflect the future years under discussion. The one point which needs to be remembered is that curriculum planners must continually keep abreast of population shifts in the community, industry movement, or other factors that could greatly affect the size of the community and the number of students.

Assessing facilities

In an earlier section of this chapter, a form was suggested that would help to indicate to planners the use made of current facilities by the vocational and technical program. While this will provide some data about the use of facilities, several other points also need to be made.

School facilities

Curriculum planners must always be working toward a more efficient use of current facilities. With the increased cost of building construction and the reluctance of taxpayers to spend more money on education, decision makers in the future must spend more time identifying new and creative ways of using current facilities. Remodeling schools and adding new sections to existing ones may become more common in the future. With elementary grade enrollments on the decrease nationwide, local schools would be wise not to overbuild at the elementary level. In fact, over the next twenty years, planners need to place more emphasis upon facilities for junior and senior high schools and postsecondary education.

FIGURE 3-6. Description of school population—current grade level _____

Information	Current Year 19 _____	Projected Enrollment		
		Year _____	Year _____	Year _____
Sex				
1. Male				
2. Female				
Ethnic Groups				
1. Black				
2. White				
3. Native American				
4. Asian				
5. Hispanic				
Disadvantaged				
1. Academic				
2. Economic				
3. Social				
4. Cultural				
Handicapped				
1. Deaf				
2. Blind				
3. Speech defect				
4. Crippling condition				
5. Convulsive seizure				
6. Mentally retarded				
7. Emotionally disturbed				

SUMMARY

The importance of understanding the school system and related data cannot be underestimated when vocational and technical education curricula are being planned. Many curriculum planners will not be developing programs from scratch, thus the current school situation and its existing programs may have a great impact on decisions that must be made in the future.

One of the first factors that must be assessed is the status of the current program. This includes the listing of all vocational and technical courses as well as an understanding of all courses offered by the school system. Course capacity and current enrollments must be studied. The current dropout rate must be examined in detail to determine where dropouts are occurring and why students are dropping out, in order to provide some insight as to what may be done to improve the situation. Soliciting and obtaining the input of students and parents are vital to sound educational planning. Students can provide valuable ideas and suggestions if provided the opportunity. Parents also have a moral right to express their feelings, and planners must assure that input from parents is secured in order to promote acceptance of new and different programs.

Without a doubt, the follow-up of former students is a must if planners and decision makers are to have sound and realistic data of what is happening to former students of their school system. Distinct trends can be identified that have strong implications for planners. The projection of future enrollments and the assessment of facilities will serve to provide planners with input to help avoid critical problems in the future.

Finally, school-related data will help provide curriculum planners with information to determine if established, quality program standards can be met. If such standards can be met, the opportunity for development of new vocational programs or expansion of current programs will become more of a reality.

REFERENCES

Allen, David. "Instruction," *The Philosophy for Quality Vocational Education Programs*. Washington, D. C.: The Fourth Yearbook of the American Vocational Association, 1974.

Barlow, Melvin L., ed. *The Philosophy for Quality Vocational Education Programs*. Washington, D. C.: The Fourth Yearbook of the American Vocational Association, 1974.

Braden, Paul V., and Paul, Krishan. *Occupational Analysis of Educational Planning*. Columbus: Charles E. Merrill Publishing Company, 1975.

Compton, Norman H. "Characteristics of Clothing and Textile Students," *Journal of Home Economics* (March, 1969), pp. 183-188.

Crunkilton, J. R., and Bail, J. P. *Area Occupational Education Programs in a Selected Twelve-County Area in New York: Concerns and Expectations*. Albany: The Bureau of Occupational Education Research, The New York State Education Department and Agricultural Education Division, Department of Education, Cornell University, Final Report 454, 1969.

Education Index. Cumulated Volume 27. Bronx, N. Y.: H. W. Wilson Company, July, 1976-June, 1977.

Elson, Donald E. *Annual Local Evaluation of Vocational and Technical Education*. Richmond: Virginia Polytechnic Institute and State University, Division of Vocational and Technical Education and the Division of Vocational Education, State Department of Education, February, 1977.

Hamilton, W. H., and Hill, C. W. *Development of a Scale to Measure Interests in Agricultural Occupations*. Ithaca, N. Y.: Cornell University, Project Number 6-8304, Grant Number OEG-1-6-08304-0814, February, 1967.

Johnson, Norbert. *Occupational Orientation: An Introduction to the World of Work*, Teachers Edition. Jackson, Miss.: Mississippi State University, Curriculum Coordinating Unit for Vocational and Technical Education and the Division of Vocational and Technical Education, Mississippi State Department of Education, 1973.

Krebs, A. H. *Model for Evaluation of Secondary School Programs of Vocational Education in Agriculture*. College Park, Md.: University of Maryland, Agricultural Experiment Station, MP733, July, 1969.

————, ed. *The Individual and His Education*. Washington, D. C.: The Second Yearbook of the American Vocational Association, 1972.

Kuder Form E—General Interest Survey. Chicago: Science Research Associates, 1970.

Ohanneson, Greg, and Vaughn, Glenn. "The Collection and Use of Vocational Program Information," *American Vocational Journal* (May, 1975), pp. 36-37.

Ohio Vocational Interest Survey [*OVIS*]. New York: Harcourt Brace Jovanovich, Inc., 1972.

Vocational Education and Occupations. Washington, D. C.: U. S. Government Printing Office, July, 1969.

Wentling, Tim L., and Lawson, Tom E. *Evaluating Occupational Education and Training Programs*, Boston: Allyn and Bacon, Inc., 1975.

Young, Robert C.; Clive, William V.; and Miles, Benton E. *Vocational Education Planning: Manpower, Priorities, and Dollars*. Columbus: The Center for Vocational and Technical Education, The Ohio State University, Research and Development Series No. 68, 1972.

4

Collecting and Assessing Community-related Data

Introduction

The development of vocational education curricula cannot be discussed without some consideration being given to the community in which a school is located. The community surrounding a school has a major influence on the type of curriculum offerings, since local labor supply and demand, program resources, and existing educational programs will aid curriculum planners in determining if established quality program standards can be met.

Labor supply and demand data reflect the current employment situation in a community; resources aid in determining the level of funding available, personnel on hand, and facilities and equipment feasible; and existing educational programs point to voids in current curricula offerings. Thus the discussion to follow focuses upon various aspects of the community and how they affect the curriculum planner.

The community

Curriculum planners cannot develop realistic educational programs if they do not first obtain a valid picture of the community in which a school is located. Thus an important aspect of curriculum planning is familiarity with the community. If an understanding of the community is lacking, the planner must devote sufficient professional energy to bringing himself or herself up to date. Only then is one able to speak and react knowledgeably about the community during curriculum development activities.

Community boundaries

A major question that the curriculum planner must answer (if it has not already been defined) is, "What are the geographical boundaries of the community?" To solve this problem accurately, he or she must take into account several considerations. For example, in one situation, the community might represent the same geographical area contained in the established school district's lines. In another situation, the word "community" must take on a broader concept, especially if graduating students tend to migrate out of a local area into surrounding areas for employment. Thus the community might include two or more counties or sections of counties surrounding the school. However, it might be appropriate and necessary in special situations to think in terms of regional and statewide areas. An example of this might be a postsecondary institution that offers a program for farriers with graduates being prepared to fill the labor needs within a particular region of the state.

The curriculum planner must use established standards as a focal point in determining geographical lines of a community. In fact, one may need to readjust community boundaries for different types of data collection. For example, in assessing current occupational education programs available to students, a planner may need to consider a smaller geographical area than if attempting to assess labor demands that might influence the type of curricula offered within a local school.

Population trends

The number of people within a community will vary over the years, and the curriculum planner must be aware of any shifts in population. One such shift that may occur would be immigration or emigration. Either population shift has major implications for developing vocational curricula. An emigration of people would cause curriculum planners to look outside their traditional community lines to discover the types of jobs taken by their graduates. An immigration could result in increased school enrollments and thus result in a demand for greater diversity of vocational education offerings. One of the most popular methods of determining population trends is the use of census data. A curriculum planner could also study other indicators of population trends, such as school enrollments, housing starts, and new businesses or factories coming into the area.

Another aspect of the population would be its makeup. For example, number of people by age groups, number of students reaching high school age (ninth grade), or number of graduating seniors. Statistics such as the number of citizens reaching retirement age each year will give some indication of openings each year and type of occupational openings. Some national statistics now indicate that the increase in number of students in the lower grades is beginning to level off or even decrease. This implies that in the future, curriculum planners will need to determine how the shift in school enrollments will affect the vocational education student's needs.

Community goals

A discussion in Chapter 2 concerned the philosophy held by members of the decision-making groups and the effect that their philosophy might have on decisions. Associated with this philosophy are community goals. Whether the goals are for an entire community, individual members of that community, or state, they are nonetheless an important source of community-related data.

> The vocational education planner is faced with a broad array of goals in pursuit of which he/she must design the vocational training program. There is little reason to believe that all of his/her goals will be mutually consistent in terms of policy implications. Conflict among goals—as well as between the goals and procedural constraints, such as implementation of resources—is inevitable. Somewhere in the planning process, implicitly or explicitly, consciously or unconsciously, choice between conflicting goals becomes inevitable, and consequently, rational planning demands explicit delineation of goals. (Young, Clive, and Miles, 1972)

The logical place to begin the formulation of community goals would be the development of a manpower or labor policy, or as some individuals would state it, a written set of priorities for a particular community based upon political, social, and moral values. Examples of local situations that might give rise to community goals are: 1) reduce unemployment; 2) reduce unemployment in target groups (i.e., teenagers, 20-30–year age group); 3) provide qualified labor for new and expanding businesses; 4) retrain the underemployed; 5) prepare all graduating seniors for some type of entry level employment; or 6) provide more educational opportunities for females. These six examples are not intended to be all-exclusive and any particular community may identify similar or different goals. For example, one community might place a higher priority on helping disadvantaged students to obtain employment rather than helping those who are unemployed.

If the curriculum planner discovers that goals do not exist for a community, steps must be taken to assure that decision-making groups (i.e., school boards) take the lead, and in cooperation with lay people in the community, develop these goals. The important point to keep in mind is that before any decision is made to establish a vocational program, standards should be established which, when met, should indicate that the program will indeed serve to meet a community's priority in vocational education. (Chapter 7 treats goal development in greater depth.)

Obtaining assistance in data collection

Identifying the data needed to make effective decisions is only the beginning in data collecting. A necessary next step is the actual collection of data. The curriculum planner will not usually have time to travel about a community collecting needed data. Alternate methods of either collecting or identifying current information about the community must be considered. In fact, many times the data may already exist; the problem is finding out which individual, agency, company, or other group has this data.

Referring back to Table 2-1 in Chapter 2, much community data may be found in one central location. For example, census data would be a source to utilize when assessing population trends, characteristics of the population, educational level of the community, and other related information. State employment commissions or agencies would have current information available about industry movement, current job openings, projected employment opportunities, and types of businesses and companies in the community. Many times the Chamber of Commerce, Better Business Bureau, and similar organizations conduct surveys in the local community and collect data that may prove useful to the curriculum planner. State, regional, or local planning commissions may also provide valuable data about the community.

However, from time to time, the curriculum planner may discover that needed data have not been collected, and thus must proceed to gather the data from sources in the community. When this situation occurs, assistance may be obtained from students, retired individuals, or other community members who want to volunteer their time to a worthy cause. In some cases, schools might consider hiring individuals who, for a reasonable cost, may be able to collect ample data to aid in the decision-making process.

Current and projected sources of employment

Before an assessment can be made of the projected supply and demand for labor, sources of employment must be identified. While some curriculum planners may see this as a minor item, the identification of every possible source of employment within a community is critical to the development of relevant vocational education curricula. Therefore curriculum planners must be sure that all areas of employment are identified.

Identifying current sources of employment

Several approaches to identifying current sources of employment may be utilized by curriculum planners. These approaches may be used individually; however, alert planners will use several approaches to ensure that all areas are identified. A brief discussion of each approach follows.

State employment commissions.   The two basic roles of employment commissions are to assist employers in finding employees and to help those seeking jobs to find openings. Thus employment commissions are an important source in identifying sources of employment. However, curriculum planners should not rely only on them, since only those businesses and industries who seek help from employment commissions may be identified by the planners. Larger businesses tend to hire their own personnel managers to recruit new employees and small businesses may choose to seek and hire their own employees. Thus some businesses will not be identified if a planner only relies upon employment commissions for information.

Chamber of Commerce. The Chamber of Commerce, as well as similar civic organizations, will usually be knowledgeable about businesses and industries within a community. Many times, these organizations prepare fact sheets or brochures that highlight local firms.

Planning commissions. Planning commissions may exist at the state, regional, or local level. In some instances, electric power companies have planning commissions in certain geographical areas to plan and project population growth and business expansion in order to meet electrical demands.

Yellow pages in telephone books. A telephone book may yield valuable data that might otherwise have been missed. For example, students in a class were surprised to learn that by checking the Yellow Pages, seventy-three service stations, fifty-five retail groceries, and fifty-four restaurants existed within a small community under study. When all businesses such as these are added together, a sizeable number of occupations can be identified in any community.

Products produced in the area. Another approach to identification of employment sources in a community is to list the products or types of materials and goods produced in the community. The end product of any business or industry will give strong indication to types of employment. For example, the following items might be identified:

Dresses	Concrete products
Nightwear	Campers
Animal food	Powder
Torque motors	Processed cheese

These items would indicate that sewing machine operators, electricians, and dairy farmers are among the occupations existing in the area.

Students enrolled in school. A teacher once remarked that the best assistance received in the identification of employment sources was through his own students. In fact, businesses were identified that the teacher did not realize existed. Within two short class periods, the entire class had constructed a valuable list of employment sources. Furthermore, this exercise proved to be a beneficial learning experience for the students.

Identifying emerging areas of employment

The curriculum planner must be able to project into the future regarding employment trends. While any long-range projections run the risk of being inaccurate, efforts must still be devoted to identification of emerging occupations. Furthermore, the development of vocational programs should not be based solely upon today's labor market, since the time span between the original program idea or concept and the first student graduate may be five years or more.

Even with future uncertainties, selected elements of a community can be studied to help predict employment sources. For example, if population is on the increase, certain services must be expanded. Hospitals, utilities, food services, and housing contractors are just a few areas in which increased employment may occur. Close contact should be made and maintained with Chamber of Commerce organizations, since one of their efforts focuses upon attracting new businesses to the community. Other people to maintain contact with would be key political figures, business leaders, and those individuals holding leadership positions.

In addition to identifying emerging areas of employment, one must also be alert to areas that are tending to experience a decrease in employment. Some communities may find that as inflation and/or recession affects our society, certain businesses may relocate or reduce the number of employees. Very few communities are stable in size of the work force and employment sources, thus curriculum planners must continually reassess local sources of employment.

Projecting labor supply and demand

One of the crucial stages in the development of relevant vocational programs deals with the labor supply and demand. The major thrust of vocational education is to prepare individuals for employment and certainly for opportunities that exist. To be an effective curriculum planner, he or she must be knowledgeable as to the different vocational education service areas and the occupations most closely related to those areas. For example, when distributive education is mentioned, people immediately think of sales persons, agricultural education such as farming, and so forth. However, a close search of the literature will point up many other occupations. The point is that a curriculum planner must be open-minded as he or she goes about the job of assessing labor supply and demand.

One publication that should be in the library of every curriculum planner is *Vocational Education and Occupations*. This publication, resulting from a combined effort of the U. S. Department of Health, Education, and Welfare and the U. S. Department of Labor, identifies occupations by vocational education service areas. For further details as to what each job involves, the *Dictionary of Occupational Titles* or other publications such as the *Occupational Handbook* can be consulted.

Assessing current and future labor demands

The Vocational Education Acts of 1963 and 1968 were explicit in pointing out that vocational education must focus upon education which is realistic in terms of opportunities for gainful employment. These legislative actions imply that the curriculum planner must develop vocational education programs based on employment opportunities. Fundamental to this implication is that planners must assess current and future labor demands in their communities if they expect to develop relevant programs.

The first problem faced by curriculum planners is that accurate and guaranteed approaches to use in projecting precise labor demands do not exist. Labor demands projected beyond four years are often inaccurate and could lead decision makers in the development of inappropriate curricula. As economists have pointed out:

> ...the period over which we can usefully forecast the demand for manpower in the present state of knowledge is much more limited than is usually admitted. All the evidence shows that we do not yet know how to forecast beyond three or four years with anything remotely resembling the 10 percent margin of errors that are regarded as just tolerable in general economic forecasting. (Young, Clive, and Miles, 1972)

Types of labor forecasts. Curriculum planners have several different approaches to choose from when preparing to assess labor demand. Realistically, several of the following approaches may be used rather than relying on data collected by a single approach. The four approaches consist of employer surveys, extrapolation, the econometric approach, and job vacancy.

Employer surveys. Probably the most widely used approach in assessing labor demand data is through what many educators refer to as employer surveys. This approach basically involves contacting the employer in order to assess current and projected labor demands. The strength of such an approach is that meaningful data can be obtained at a relatively low cost. Employer surveys are easy to administer and can provide labor demand data in a reasonably short time. In addition, employers' short-range plans can be assessed as to their influence on possible emerging employment opportunities. Finally, educators may feel the direct contact between employers and the school will lead to further cooperation between the two.

Curriculum planners using the employer survey approach must also be aware of certain limitations. First, employers may be reluctant to share employment data with strangers who come to their business, and sometimes may not even share information with individuals they know. Thus, when using this approach, it is helpful to contact employers before the actual personal interview to make them aware of why information is needed and how it will be used. Another limitation in using this approach is that businesses moving into the area may not be reflected in the final data. The best that planners can do in this situation is to stay alert to business and industry movement, and through a brief reassessment of the community, be able to identify areas of key employment opportunities or possibly the decrease in opportunities.

If the curriculum planners intend to use employer surveys, a data-collecting instrument must be developed that will assist in determining if established program standards in the area of labor demands can be met. Since data should be collected regarding the current and projected labor demands, the instrument used should accomplish both purposes. The form illustrated in Figure 4-1 is designed to accomplish that task. Figure 4-2 provides an example of how this form will appear once it has been completed. Using this example, the curriculum planner can readily see that here is a business currently employing twenty-two people, with the projection of thirty-three employees three years hence and, in six years, forty-four. Furthermore, the projected demand for each job title can be assessed.

Once data have been collected from businesses and companies in the community, information can then be summarized using the form shown in Table 4-1. Sample data have been included to illustrate how this form could be used by the curriculum developer. Using the forms provided in Figure 4-1 and Table 4-1, the planner can begin to determine if established standards may be met regarding labor demand and occupational experience training program stations. In addition to the information collected by use of the form depicted in Figure 4-1, the planner may identify other relevant data needed for a particular school and provide for the collection of this data. It should be kept in mind that data collection instruments must be as short as possible in order to help ensure an employer's cooperation and assistance.

Several approaches may be used in the collection of data from employers. Mailed questionnaires, personal interviews, and telephone calls constitute the most common approaches. The personal interview approach is by far the best to use, since a high rate of response may be obtained. If the telephone approach is to be used, a letter and sample form should be sent to the employer in advance in order to ensure cooperation and also to assist in collecting data during the conversation.

Extrapolation. This approach to projecting future labor demands is based on the assumption that past and current trends will give an indication as to what will happen in the future. The strength of this approach is that it is relatively easy to perform and can be done in a short time. Additionally, the

FIGURE 4–1.   Employer labor demands*

Date_____

1.   Name of company or business_____

2.   Address_____

3.   Person interviewed and title_____

Telephone_____

4.   *Functions of company or business:*
(Check all that apply)

_____ Manufacturing
_____ Purchasing
_____ Service
_____ Constructing
_____ Retailing
_____ Warehouse
_____ Processing
_____ Wholesaling
_____ Contractor
_____ Other (specify)
_____ _____

5.   List of products or services involved in
functions checked in Item 4

_____

_____

_____

6.   Available as training station for
occupational experience program

_____ Now being used
_____ Interested in possibilities
_____ Need more information
_____ Not interested

7.   Job titles, number of workers, and projected demand.

Job Titles	Number Employed	Percent Annual Replacement Demand	Number of New Workers Needed by 19___ 19___
_____	_____	_____	____ ____
_____	_____	_____	____ ____
_____	_____	_____	____ ____
_____	_____	_____	____ ____
_____	_____	_____	____ ____
_____	_____	_____	____ ____
_____	_____	_____	____ ____

Signature of Interviewer

*Adapted from A. H. Krebs, *Model for Evaluation of Secondary School Programs of Vocational Education in Agriculture.* College Park, Md.: University of Maryland, Agricultural Experiment Station, MP 733, 1969.

FIGURE 4–2.   Employer labor demands*

Date *Jan. 14, 19X0*

1.   Name of company or business *Ajax Company*

2.   Address *1234 Delaware Street, Anywhere, USA 12345*

3.   Person interviewed and title *Joe Brown, Supervisor*

Telephone *555-3322*

4.   *Functions of company or business:*
     (Check all that apply)

     _____ Manufacturing
     _____ Purchasing
     ___✓___ Service
     _____ Constructing
     _____ Retailing
     _____ Warehouse
     _____ Processing
     _____ Wholesaling
     ___✓___ Contractor
     _____ Other (specify)
     _____ _____

5.   List of products or services involved in
     functions checked in Item 4

     Houses
     Excavating, Plumbing
     Electricians

6.   Available as training station for
     occupational experience program

     _____ Now being used
     ___✓___ Interested in possibilities
     _____ Need more information
     _____ Not interested

7.   Job titles, number of workers, and projected demand.

Job Titles	Number Employed	Percent Annual Replacement Demand	Number of New Workers Needed by 19X3	19X6
Electricians	4	0	2	4
Electrician Helper	1	100	1	3
Carpenters	10	10	5	10
Bulldozer Operator	2	0	1	1
Power Shovel Operator	2	0	1	1
Plumbers	2	0	1	2
Supervisor	1	0	0	1

Judy Allen
Signature of Interviewer

*Adapted from A. H. Krebs, *Model for Evaluation of Secondary School Programs of Vocational Education in Agriculture.* College Park, Md.: University of Maryland, Agricultural Experiment Station, MP 733, 1969.

TABLE 4–1.   Number of workers and projected demand by job title

		Plumbers		
		Job Title		
Name of Company	Number Employed	Percent [1] Annual Replacement Demand	Number of New Workers Needed in	
			3 Years	6 Years
Ajax Company	2	0	1	2
Brown's Hardware	2	0	0	1
Harry's Plumbing	4	25(1)	2	2
Hale's Enterprises	10	10(1)	2	3
Smith's Home Builders	3	0	1	3
Joe's Hardware	1	0	0	0
Total	22	2	6	11

[1] Numbers in parentheses indicate numbers of workers needed per year based upon current replacement data.

cost of extrapolating is quite low. An example of this procedure as applied to the occupation of child care assistants is provided below:

1960	1965	1970	1975	1980	1985
5	8	11	21	34	54

In this situation, a community may have had five individuals employed as child care assistants in 1960, and by 1965, the number had increased to eight. By 1975, the number employed had reached twenty-one, or about a 160-percent increase every five years. Extrapolating into the future, and making the assumption that the number of child care assistants will continue to increase at approximately the same rate, the curriculum planner may project that by 1985, fifty-four child care assistants will be needed within that community. Further analysis of this data indicates that about four new positions of child care assistant would occur each year, thus giving the curriculum planner a basis for determining if this type of vocational education program should be initiated. However, the planner must realize that the further into the future projections are made, the greater likelihood that projections will be inaccurate.

The econometric approach.   The econometric approach to labor forecasting appears to be the most sophisticated labor forecasting in use today. This approach is utilized by the Bureau of Labor Statistics of the U. S. Department of Labor and results in ten-year forecasts of labor demands.

Briefly, the steps taken in generating the Bureau of Labor Statistics forecasts have been outlined by Young, Clive, and Miles (1972). They are as follows:

1. Projection of the population by age, sex, color, and geographical distribution.

2. Projection of the labor force by age, sex, color, educational level, and state.

3. Based on the assumption of minimal unemployment, an estimate is then made concerning future levels of gross national product, based on trends in productivity, hours of work, and consumer expenditures.

4. These estimates of final demand are then examined for their implications in terms of industrial output at both the final stage of production as well as among the intermediate and basic industries that provide the inputs to the final production process.

5. Given the final output expected from the various industrial sectors, estimates are then made of the manpower or occupational structure within each industry required to produce that output.

6. These estimates of occupational employment by industry, based on the industry/occupational matrix or the B. L. S. matrix, may then be summed to provide the total estimated employment by occupation.

7. In addition to changes in requirements as a result of growth or decline in occupational employment, estimates are made of those leaving the work force through withdrawal, death, and retirement. These two components of future occupational need-growth and occupational losses are then summed to provide the estimate of new openings for labor force entrants. Net interoccupational mobility is allowed for only roughly, due to the *inadequacies* of empirical data.

While the econometric approach as used by the Bureau of Labor Statistics yields data that is more relevant at the state and regional levels, curriculum planners may find implications for using this approach at the local level. For example, data concerning a population's age, sex, race, and geographical distribution could be easily obtained for a community. Furthermore, labor force projections by age, sex, race, and educational level are available by regions or counties within a state. As with other labor demand forecasts, the econometric technique has several limitations. Among the major drawbacks is that economic activity in our society fluctuates widely; thus projections may be inaccurate. Other limitations center around the unpredictable rate of technological advances and the attempt to predict the educational requirements for occupations that now are few in number, but in the future may represent a sizeable share of the work force.

Job vacancy.   This approach to labor demand forecasting is based upon current job vacancies existing for thirty days or more within a community. The job vacancy approach depends heavily upon information obtained and compiled by state employment agencies. The strength of this approach is that immediate needs of an area can be quickly ascertained. Furthermore, curriculum planners can easily rank job vacancies by priority of importance or number of vacancies. If any ranking occurs, reasons as to why these openings continue to appear must be considered. For example, do the openings exist because of the lack of qualified people, low wages, or poor working conditions, or are qualified people available but reluctant to go into the occupation? Job vacancy as a means of labor demand forecasting does have some limitations. First, are the jobs listed by this approach permanent jobs or seasonal jobs? Answers to this question must be provided before job vacancy information becomes of value to curriculum planners. The second consideration when vacancies continue to appear for the same job would be to ascertain whether the actual job entry qualifications are similar to traditional competencies required for that specific occupation. For example, employers may actually have a higher standard of employment for a particular occupation than may be the established standard, due to other internal factors (say, promotional opportunity) within their organization. A third limitation to the job vacancy approach is that if one vacancy was filled, it might lead to three other vacancies or jobs becoming available that complement the original vacancy. An example would be the hiring of a carpenter, which would lead to a need for a carpenter's helper. Finally, vacancies related to contract or government work may be duplicated, especially where companies or businesses within a community are competing for the same labor. Another way to look at this last limitation is that the number of vacancies identified is not the same as the total number of individuals who could be hired.

Summary of labor demand forecasting

The four labor demand approaches treated in this section are just several of those curriculum planners may choose from to collect labor information. The selection of an approach depends upon the resources and time available to the planner. Furthermore, selection of approaches depends upon whether the planner needs information about the current labor demand or about future labor demands. For example, the employer survey can provide data on both current and projected labor demands. The collection of data by this method may take longer and the cost would depend upon the manner in which information was obtained. Extrapolation procedures would be faster; however, past and current data are needed in order to project into the future. Thus an employer survey or a job vacancy approach would need to be used if current information about vacancies were not available. The econometric technique is based upon detailed information concerning characteristics of the population and work force. While this information may be available, curriculum planners may be reluctant to use it due to lack of specific information about a local school district or community in which a school is located. The job vacancy approach is relatively fast, easy, and reflects more of the current situation rather than what might be the situation in the future. All four approaches have distinct advantages and limitations and the relative accuracy of information obtained by each approach has not been determined or agreed upon by economists or educators. Thus the final selection a planner makes in determining the labor demand for his or her school district must be based upon the established standard to be met. Another way to view the situation is, "What data collection approach will yield the type of information needed to determine if the standard can be met?"

Assessing current and projected labor supply

Projecting labor demand is not complete unless an effort is made to assess the current labor supply. By projecting labor demand in conjunction with the assessment of current labor supply, the planner is able to estimate fairly accurate labor needs within the community. Assessment of the real labor supply in any community is illustrated in Figure 4-3, and a discussion follows related to various segments of this supply.

Additions to the current labor supply

Additions to the current labor supply in any community occur continually. These additions may come from several different sources and the curriculum planner must be able to assess the influence of these new job-seekers on the labor market. Each of these sources of new entrants is treated in the following sections.

Graduates of vocational programs.   Graduates of existing vocational education programs enter the labor market each year. These individuals may come from comprehensive high schools, area vocational schools, adult programs, postsecondary institutions, technical institutes, four-year colleges, trade schools, manpower development centers, or other similar vocational education programs. Data about the number of graduates by vocational service area can easily be obtained from each respective source.

Immigration.   People in the United States tend to be mobile and this creates population fluctuations in any community. Immigration implies that people will be moving into communities and thus creating an impact on the labor supply. Since it is difficult to obtain a general estimate of immigrating numbers that the curriculum planner might expect for his or her particular community, each planner must attempt to calculate expected immigration on a community-to-community basis. U. S. census data and state employment commissions are two sources that should be investigated for current information pertaining to specific communities.

Other occupations.   People included in this category are individuals who transfer from one job to another. While these individuals will not alter the total supply figure, they affect the number of individuals available for any one specific occupational title. For example, a carpenter's helper may become sufficiently skilled to become a carpenter, thus a shift occurs within the labor supply by oc-

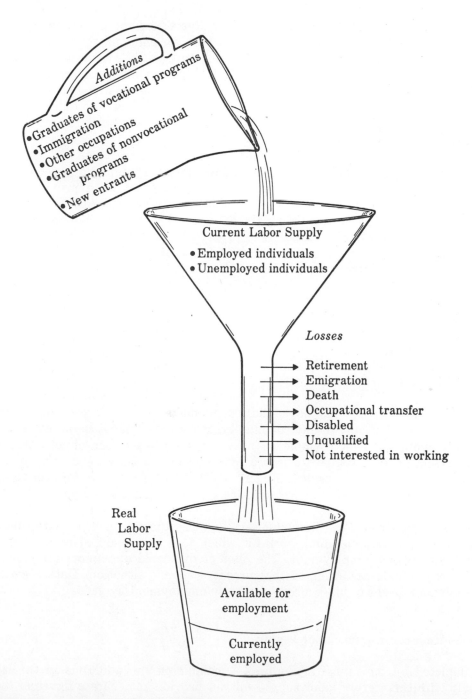

FIGURE 4-3.   Assessing real labor supply

cupational title. Data about occupational transfers is difficult to obtain, and thus the curriculum planner may not be able to reflect this change in labor supply accurately.

Graduates of nonvocational programs.   Individuals included under this category are graduates of nonvocational programs who have changed their career plans and accept positions for which they were not necessarily prepared. This might include graduates from academic curricula in high schools, postsecondary institutions, four-year colleges, or other nonvocational programs. Information about the number of graduates from these schools should be easy to obtain; however, it is more difficult to project the number of graduates who may go into jobs requiring less than a bachelor's degree.

New entrants.   A new entrant into the labor market is one who is not included in any of the four previous categories and who has not been previously employed. This category consists primarily of dropouts from educational programs and spouses who are now entering the labor market rather than remaining in the home. The number of dropouts from educational programs in any community can be obtained quite readily, while it is more difficult to assess the number of spouses entering the labor market.

Current labor supply

Two major categories serve to make up the current labor supply. Included are individuals who are currently employed and those who are available but are not employed for some reason.

Employed individuals.   Employed individuals make up the largest proportion of the current labor supply in any community. However, it must be noted that the current number of people employed never equals the number of jobs that are filled. Some people hold two or more jobs and others may be employed part-time. A curriculum planner desiring data on those employed by types of occupations can easily secure this information from state employment agencies.

Unemployed individuals.   Individuals in this classification are persons who are able to work but cannot find work for which they are qualified or are not aggressively seeking employment. The number of people unemployed at any one time will fluctuate according to the current economic situation. Data regarding those unemployed can be secured from state employment agencies.

Losses from the current labor supply

As depicted by the funnel in Figure 4-3, combining the additions to the labor supply with the current labor supply will not provide an accurate figure of those available for employment. From this labor supply must be subtracted individuals who will not be available for employment.

Information concerning losses to the labor supply will be reflected in data provided by state employment agencies or employers. Losses to the labor market will occur due to retirement, emigration, death, and occupational transfer and will be given as percentage of replacements needed each year. Any one of these categories by itself will not usually represent a sizeable loss to the current labor supply. However, when all losses are added together, the current number of individuals available for employment will be influenced. In addition, there will be individuals who would like to work but who are disabled in some way that prohibits them from entering the labor market. Unqualified individuals are those who do not possess sufficient knowledge of the basic skills to permit them to seek employment. Finally, there will be those individuals who are able and qualified to work, but who choose not to work for some reason.

Real labor supply

Real labor supply represents individuals who are available for employment. This includes persons who currently hold jobs and those individuals unemployed but actively seeking employment.

Interfacing labor demand and supply

There remains one last critical step the curriculum planner must carry out in determining net labor needs. Net labor needs may be defined as the estimated number of individuals needed to fill a specific occupation but who are not available at that time. This involves an analysis of information obtained during a labor demand study in relation to information obtained during a labor supply study. The form contained in Figure 4-4 will help in determining if established standards can be met in regard to labor needs. This form should aid with the analysis process when the curriculum developer is determining where curriculum priorities should be placed. A brief treatment of the various information to be placed in this form follows.

Occupational title

The occupational titles that are placed in this column should reflect titles for which a local school and the curriculum developer wish to assess the labor demand and supply. Specific titles would be those occupations identified by the use of a form such as that contained in Figure 4-1.

Occupational Title	Labor Demand				Labor Supply			Net Labor Needs
	Number Currently Employed	New Positions	Replacement[1]	= TLD[2]	Grad. of Voc. Prog.	+ Others[3]	= TLS[4]	
		+	=		+	=		
		+	=		+	=		
		+	=		+	=		
		+	=		+	=		
		+	=		+	=		
		+	=		+	=		

[1] Annual Replacement
[2] Total Labor Demand
[3] Estimate of others who may be available for that occupational title
[4] Total Labor Supply

Number employed

This column is used to indicate the number of people currently employed in each particular job title within a community. The procedure used to identify the number employed within a job title may be accomplished by using appropriate labor demand approaches discussed earlier in this chapter or by other means available within a community. The value of this figure becomes important when calculating the annual need for a specific occupation based upon annual replacement percentages. This figure is also valuable when past employment numbers are available for a specific occupation such that projection for labor demands can be made by extrapolation.

Labor demand

The labor demand column enables identification to be made of demand figures for each occupational title under study. The subcolumn indicated by "New Positions" represents positions to be added during the year(s) under consideration. The replacement column provides the opportunity to calculate the number of individuals needed to replace people lost for any reasons outlined as "Losses" in Figure 4-3. The replacement calculation must be made on the projected number to be employed during the year under study and not the current employed number. The end result is the Total Labor Demand (TLD), which indicates the total demand for a specific occupational title beyond the current number of employees. A local community can decide if this should be done for a specific year or years and project into the future to a year congruent to its local philosophy and goals.

Labor supply

The labor supply column has been divided into two subcolumns, representing vocational graduates coming into the labor market and others representing a source of employees. The vocational graduates represent those individuals coming into the labor market possessing the skills necessary for entry level employment in that occupation. The figure placed in the column headed "Others" represents an estimate of those individuals who might be coming into the labor market. As was pointed out earlier in this chapter, the figure in this latter column would be influenced by immigration, transfer from other occupations, graduates from nonvocational programs, and new entrants, for all of which absolute figures may not be available. The ultimate value of this column is the "Total Labor Supply" (TLS). This figure represents (for each occupational title) the total number of individuals available for new or replacement positions identified in the Total Labor Demand (TLD) estimated for the year or years under study.

Net labor needs

The net labor needs column reflects the estimated total number of individuals needed for a specific occupational title who are not available. This figure is obtained by subtracting the Total Labor Supply (TLS) from the Total Labor Demand (TLD). The figure obtained as the Net Labor Needs reflects the year or years for which the TLS and TLD were projected. As discussed earlier, Net Labor Needs are, at best, an estimate. The economic situation existing in society, technological advance, human judgment, error, and individuals changing career choices, all influence the accuracy of the Net Labor Needs. However, if those individuals responsible for collecting data develop a systematic approach to assess Net Labor Needs, the projections developed should be more accurate and provide a much firmer base upon which decisions affecting curriculum programs can be made.

An example of how the form appearing in Figure 4-4 can be used is provided in Figure 4-5. This example is for a local school district with the projection being made for five years into the future.

Example 1. After an employer survey was conducted, it was found that 362 adjustment clerks were currently being employed. No new positions were projected in the next five years and the typical annual replacement rate is 10 percent. After surveying vocational programs in the community, it was found that twenty seniors graduate each year with competencies in this area and an estimate was made that ten individuals per year would seek employment as adjustment clerks in addition to vocational graduates.

At a 10-percent replacement per year, this would result in thirty-six individuals being hired each year for five years, for a Total Labor Demand (TLD) of 180. The twenty seniors graduating each year would add to a total of 100 in five years, with fifty additional individuals being available from other sources. Thus the Net Labor Needs for the next five years was placed at thirty, or six per year on the average.

Example 2. Farm equipment mechanics number thirty-five, with five to be added in the next five years. The annual replacement percentage was found to be 5 percent. No vocational programs were found to exist in the community and it was estimated that no individuals would be qualified to seek employment of this type.

With this example, the replacement percentage indicates that about two replacements would be needed each year, or ten for the five years. In addition, five new positions would be added, giving a TLD of fifteen. The TLS was zero, with the resulting Net Labor Needs for the next five years as fifteen.

Example 3. Social secretaries were found to number 475, with twenty new positions to be added each year. The replacement percentage is estimated to be 10 percent per year. In obtaining data from vocational programs in the community, approximately sixty individuals in secretarial programs are graduated each year and it was estimated that an additional twenty individuals per year would be qualified to seek employment as social secretaries.

Occupational Title	Number Currently Employed	Labor Demand			Labor Supply			Net Labor Needs for Five Years
		New	Replace-ment	= TLD[1]	Grad. of Voc. Prog.	+ Others	= TLS[2]	
1. Adjustment Clerk	362	0	+ 180	= 180	100	+ 50	= 150	30
2. Farm Equipment Mechanic	35	5	+ 10	= 15	0	+ 0	= 0	15
3. Social Secretary	475	100	+ 260	= 360	300	+ 100	= 400	−40
4. Dishwasher	150	0	+ 375	= 375	0	+ 100	= 100	275

[1]Total Labor Demand
[2]Total Labor Supply

In this example, the size of the group currently employed and the current replacement percentage require additional calculations. The following table helps to detail this procedure:

	Employed	New Positions	Replacements
Year 1	475	20	48
Year 2	495	20	50
Year 3	515	20	52
Year 4	535	20	54
Year 5	555	20	56
Total		100	260

This provides an estimate for the TLD as 360 for the next five years. In calculating the TLS, the graduates entering the labor market total 300 (60 × 5) and the 100 others who may enter give a TLS of 400. The Net Labor Needs is —40 (360—400), or an estimated oversupply of social secretaries.

Example 4. A high turnover rate of 50 percent was found for dishwashers, with no new positions predicted. About 100 individuals were estimated to be available for this position over the next five years.

In this case, with seventy-five (50 percent of 150) replacements needed each year, a total of 375 replacements would be needed over the next five years, for a total TLD of 375. The TLS was 100, resulting in the Net Labor Needs for the next five years of 275.

Summary of projecting net labor needs

The procedure followed to arrive at the Net Labor Needs for a specific occupation is, at best, an estimate. As pointed out throughout this section, certain information is lacking that has an influence on the accuracy of the final projection of Net Labor Needs. First, whether employers or some other source provides information for predicted labor demand, opportunity for variation from these predictions exists. Economic situations in society, technology, rapid growth, recession, or other unforeseen variables may create a change in expected new positions to be added or in the precentages of replacements experienced. When projecting labor supply, the numbers of graduates from vocational programs can be predicted with some degree of accuracy. The problem arises as to how many persons will actively seek employment in the area for which they were trained. Some may go into military service or change their career plans, and other situations may develop that lower the number actually seeking employment in a specific occupation for which they were trained. Combined with these variables is the unpredictable source of new entrants. Thus when a number is obtained for Net Labor Needs, this represents the best estimate considering what is known at the time the data were collected.

Estimates for Net Labor Needs must be carefully analyzed with regard to established standards. Referring again to Figure 4-5, let us assume that a standard was established as follows: "If twelve farm equipment mechanics would be needed in the next five years, a course should be initiated in Agricultural Machinery Service." Following the Net Labor Needs formula, a curriculum planner would have determined that, in fact, the estimated need for farm equipment mechanics met the established standards.

The Net Labor Needs formula may also provide data that are useful in establishing standards for future curriculum development. For example, a situation may occur that a Net Labor Need is found to be fifty for an occupation in which no vocational program exists. Thus the curriculum planner may further study this situation to determine if standards should be established in deciding whether vocational courses should be offered that would prepare individuals for employment in that occupation. One note of caution needs to be mentioned if a large Net Labor Need develops for a specific occupation. The example of dishwashers in Figure 4-5 is an excellent illustration. There are certain jobs that experience a high turnover rate, thus resulting in a high job vacancy. The problem may not be a lack of people available to fill such a position, but the shortage may exist due to low wages, poor working conditions, or other undesirable aspects of the job that keep people from seeking employment in it. Another example would be sewing machine operators in a clothing factory. This job tends to become extremely monotonous for some employees and as a result, a high turnover rate often occurs.

Even with limitations that may exist with forecasting labor supply and demand, vocational education curriculum developers must continue to forecast and predict labor needs for various occupations. Only in this way will vocational education programs remain relevant to the needs of a community. Until the techniques and procedures for predicting labor supply and demand become more sophisticated and data used to make these predictions become more reliable, one must continue to use approaches that will provide the best opportunity to determine if established program quality standards can be met.

Projecting program costs for use in decision making

Treatment of the subject of costs of proposed programs may, at first glance, appear as if it should have been covered in the preceding chapter. However, when considering funding of proposed programs, the curriculum planner must eventually consider resources available in that community to determine if standards relating to financial support are indeed available. Thus the following section deals with projecting program costs, with the remaining section concerned with identification of resources.

Determining program costs to estimate

When considering program costs, there are two basic types that will need to be examined. One type of cost involves the introduction of a vocational curriculum not currently available in the school; and the second, the cost to incorporate or expand a course offering within a vocational service area that is already a part of the curricular offerings within a school. Discussion of each type of cost follows.

Costs for new programs. Projecting costs for a new program may begin by using the outline contained in Figure 4–6.

Instructional and support staff. Estimates for hiring staff vary widely from state to state and even within states. Curriculum planners contemplating the development of new vocational programs should have little trouble in projecting the cost needed to obtain staff associated for the program under consideration.

Instructional materials and supplies. Estimated costs for materials and supplies cannot be accurately accomplished unless the curriculum content has been determined. Once the content has been determined (treatment of this topic is found in Chapter 6), it then becomes easier to assess what the costs will be. The forms contained in Figures 4–7 and 4–8 may assist in projecting costs for materials and supplies for any program(s) under consideration; an example has

---

FIGURE 4–6. Projecting costs for new vocational programs

Item	Support Needed Total	Per Student
Staff		
Instructional	$_____	$_____
Support	$_____	$_____
Instructional		
Materials & Supplies	$_____	$_____
Equipment	$_____	$_____
Travel	$_____	$_____
Facilities	$_____	$_____
Other (specify)	$_____	$_____
Totals	$_____	$_____

FIGURE 4-7.   Projecting costs for materials and supplies

Course _____

Project or Activity	Material	Size	Quantity per Student	Number of Students	Total Quantity Needed
Machine Bolt	Round iron	½"	6½"	40	21.6 feet
	Hex. nuts	½" NC	2	40	80
Wiring Single Pole Switch	Programmed instruction	–	1	40	40

FIGURE 4-8.   Summary sheet for projecting costs for materials and supplies

Course or Vocational Service Area Machine Shop

Material	Size	Quantity Per Class			Total Quantity Needed	Price Per Unit	Total Cost
		Class XYZ	Class ABC	Class EFG			
Round iron	½"	21.6'	50.0'	—	71.6'	$0.15ft.	$10.74
Hex. nuts	½" NC	80	300	65	445/20box	1.44/box	$31.68
Programmed Instruction Manual—single pole switch	—	40	—	—	40	3.50 ea.	$140.00

TOTALS

been included on each form. In summarizing costs on the form in Figure 4–8, cost per vocational service can be obtained, cost per vocational course can be determined, and costs per student per course and/or per vocational service area can be projected. All of these total cost figures can be transferred to the form in Figure 4–6, where they may be used to assist planners in arriving at the projected instructional materials and supplies cost for a course under consideration.

Equipment. The cost to equip a new facility will vary widely and is largely dependent upon the vocational service area and type of equipment needed. While it is difficult to provide an estimate that will be accurate for all situations, curriculum planners must rely upon equipment lists available for each vocational service area from state departments of education or teacher education institutions.

Travel. Expenses for the travel of teachers and field trips for students should be provided. In vocational education, supervised occupational experience projects are a part of the programs, thus teachers must be provided ample travel expenses in order to supervise and establish educational occupational experience projects for each student. Costs of field trips may also be included under this category.

Facilities. Projecting the cost of new facilities is similar to the equipment costs. Construction costs vary widely throughout the United States, thus for each locality one will need to check closely with local contractors as to costs. Plans and blueprints for vocational service areas are usually available from state departments of education.

Costs for expanding current vocational programs. Estimating costs for expanding or adding programs or courses to a vocational service area already in existence would be similar to the process followed for a new program. The form referred to in Figure 4–6 would need to be revised slightly and an example of this revision is provided in Figure 4–9. The major difference is that provision is made for indicating current support available and an estimate of support needed if the expansion of a vocational service area is to take place.

Following the procedures presented in the last few sections, the curriculum developer may estimate the amount of resources needed to offer a quality vocational program. For example, a figure of $285 per student is determined as the amount of financial support needed in order to offer a quality vocational course. Thus a standard must be established to that effect, then data must be obtained to determine if financial support is available. The standard may also be applied in terms of equipment, facilities, or other relevant items.

Obtaining assistance in projecting costs

The task of identifying and projecting costs is not an easy one, and this type of activity must usually be carried out over a long period of time. The curriculum planner must, therefore, seek the assistance and cooperation of others who can provide pertinent information. Individuals who might be contacted would in-

FIGURE 4-9. **Projecting costs for expansion of a vocational service area**

Item	Present Support		Support Needed	
	Total	*Per Student*	*Total*	*Per Student*
Staff				
Instructional	$_____	$_____	$_____	$_____
Support	$_____	$_____	$_____	$_____
Instructional				
Materials & Supplies	$_____	$_____	$_____	$_____
Equipment	$_____	$_____	$_____	$_____
Travel	$_____	$_____	$_____	$_____
Facilities	$_____	$_____	$_____	$_____
Other (Specify)	$_____	$_____	$_____	$_____
TOTALS	$_____	$_____	$_____	$_____

clude vocational teachers aligned with the program or course currently under study, vocational directors, specialists in vocational service areas, or other individuals who have direct knowledge of the service area. Advisory councils can be of particular help, especially when projecting costs of equipment, supplies, and materials. In addition, schools that have recently initiated new programs can be of tremendous help to schools that are just starting a curriculum development study.

Inflation considerations

The need to consider inflation rates must be considered, since the time from which a program is first conceived to the actual building construction may be three to five years. Failing to account for rising costs due to inflation may place a school in a situation of having to cut back on some of the facilities, equipment, supplies, or staff when the expense occurs. If this situation materializes, then realizing established quality program standards may be impossible.

Special considerations in projecting costs

As society and technology advance, those individuals responsible for developing vocational curricula must be alert to elements of our environment that have an influence on vocational education programs. *Energy* and its conservation appears to be a major concern to all. The construction of buildings and the conservation of needed utilities are areas that planners must consider as new buildings are constructed or older buildings renovated. *Safety* and the passage of the Occupational Safety and Health Act will have an impact on planning vocational curricula. Facilities and equipment designed for safety of students, teachers, and others will become a greater concern in the future. *Handicapped* individuals are now being recognized as one group of students overlooked in the past. Many older buildings did not take into account the handicapped individual. The construction of new facilities and renovation of older facilities will need to accommodate the handicapped. *Flexibility* is the key to vocational programs in the future. Never before in history has the type of jobs changed so rapidly and, in the future, changes will be occurring at an ever-increasing rate. Construction of new facilities must incorporate flexibility so that as programs and courses become obsolete, changes for emerging courses and programs needed for job entry skills can be initiated with a minimum of expense.

Identifying and assessing available resources

Once standards have been established for resources needed in a quality vocational program, plans must be made to collect data that will indicate if resources are indeed available at the level required. Four basic areas of resources to be examined include funds, facilities and equipment, human resources, and cooperative training stations.

Funds

The monetary resources for vocational programs may originate from local, state, or federal sources. While the percentage of funds for each source may vary from state to state or locality to locality, those individuals planning vocational programs must determine just how much is available and from what source. While the treatment of this topic is not lengthy, funds are, nonetheless, one of the most critical factors in achieving program quality. *Furthermore, as funds are identified for educational programs, curriculum planners must determine just how much of those funds will be used for vocational education programs.* With there being more possibility that distribution of funds obtained for any one vocational program might be different than for other vocational programs, a slight revision to the form in Figure 4–9 permits information about any one vocational course or service area to be analyzed with relative ease. The revised form is included in Figure 4–10 and provides the planner with an opportunity to designate the source and amount of funds received from each funding level.

Facilities and equipment

The assessment of school facilities and equipment was discussed in an earlier chapter; however, curriculum planners must not overlook facilities and equipment that may exist in a community. An assessment of community facilities and equipment could take place while an employer survey is being conducted to determine labor demand. The value derived from an awareness of community resources could be pointed out, for example, if an employer owned a piece of equipment valued at $3,000 and the school were able to rent or borrow the equipment. This arrangement might be more economical than investing $3,000 in this equipment and leaving it idle for fifty weeks out of the year.

Human resources

Effective and quality vocational programs do not rely only on adequate equipment, funds, and materials, but also on competent teachers to conduct the programs. Human resources include support personnel as well as administrators. Thus a standard must be established regarding the specification of human resources needed for a quality program and data need to be collected to measure whether this standard can be met.

Cooperative training stations

The value of cooperative training stations to student development is frequently supported in the literature. Schools may well desire to establish a standard in

FIGURE 4–10. **Projecting costs for new or expanding vocational service areas and source of funds***

	Present Support		*Support Needed*	
Item	*Total*	*Per Student*	*Total*	*Per Student*
Staff Instructional	$_____	$_____	$_____	$_____
Support	$_____	$_____	$_____	$_____
Instructional Materials				
and Supplies	$_____	$_____	$_____	$_____
Equipment	$_____	$_____	$_____	$_____
Travel	$_____	$_____	$_____	$_____
Facilities	$_____	$_____	$_____	$_____
Other (specify)	$_____	$_____	$_____	$_____
TOTALS	$_____	$_____	$_____	$_____
Source of Funds				
Local	$_____	$_____	$_____	$_____
State	$_____	$_____	$_____	$_____
Federal	$_____	$_____	$_____	$_____

**Source:* Adapted from A. H. Krebs, *Model for Evaluation of Secondary School Programs of Vocational Education in Agriculture.* College Park, Md.: University of Maryland, Agricultural Experiment Station, MP 733, July, 1969.

this area. Information collected from employers with the use of the form shown in Figure 4–1 permits a school to assess whether or not sufficient training stations are available. Information collected via this form might also be useful for developing a list of those employers who need more information about cooperative programs, and this may lead to further contact and cooperation between the school and community.

SUMMARY

The Vocational Education Acts of 1963 and 1968 were based upon preparing youth and adults for placement in entry level jobs, and with this concept, the need to collect and analyze community-based data for use in decision making in vocational education programs is vitally important. One of the first tasks of curriculum development is to define community boundaries, and these boundaries might fluctuate depending upon the standard being measured. Once standards and geographical boundaries are firmly defined, collection of data can be achieved.

Data are usually needed regarding the types of industries and businesses existing in the community as well as the number of people employed by occupational title. In addition, attempts to determine new and emerging sources of employment will aid in keeping vocational programs relevant. Labor demand and supply must be assessed to establish net labor needs. The net labor needs reflect the number of individuals not available who are needed to fill newly created jobs or to replace those leaving their occupations. While many uncontrollable variables will influence the estimates made for future labor demand and supply, vocational educators, especially those responsible for curriculum development, must continue their efforts to arrive at realistic projections.

Vocational education program quality will not be achieved unless adequate resources can be identified and committed to the program. Funding, facilities and equipment, human resources, and cooperative training stations are just a few such resources. Projected costs for initiating new or expanded programs must be assessed to determine if established standards can be met. Consideration must also be given to energy conservation, safety, the handicapped, and program flexibility.

Established program standards related to community-based information have a great influence on the success of quality vocational education programs. Therefore every effort must be made to collect accurate data, so that decisions which affect curriculum development will be based on the best available information.

REFERENCES

Braden, Paul V., and Krishan, Paul. *Occupational Analysis of Educational Planning.* Columbus: Charles E. Merrill Publishing Co., 1975.

Copa, George H., and Irvin, Donald E., Jr. "Manpower Information Versus Decision-Making Needs," *American Vocational Journal* (October, 1975), pp. 41–42.

Dictionary of Occupational Titles, Definitions of Titles, Volume I. Washington, D.C.: U. S. Government Printing Office, 1965.

Dictionary of Occupational Titles, Occupational Classification, Volume II. Washington, D.C.: U. S. Government Printing Office, 1965.

Evans, Rupert N. *Foundations of Vocational Education.* Columbus: Charles E. Merrill Publishing Co., 1971.

The Guide to Vocational Education in America: Trends to 1978. Westport, Conn.: Market Data Retrieval, 1975.

Kidder, David E. *Review and Synthesis of Research on Manpower Forecasting for Vocational-Technical Education.* Columbus: The Center for Vocational and Technical Education, The Ohio State University, Information Series No. 54, 1972.

Krebs, A. H. *Model for Evaluation of Secondary School Programs of Vocational Education in Agriculture.* College Park, Md.: University of Maryland, Agricultural Experiment Station, MP 733, 1969.

Kruger, Daniel E. "Manpower Planning and the Local Job Economy," *American Vocational Journal* (May, 1975), pp. 32–35.

Lewin, David; Horton, Raymond; Shick, Robert; and Brecher, Charles. *The Urban Labor Market—Institutions, Information, Linkages.* New York: Praeger Publishers, 1974.

Mager, Robert F., and Beach, Kenneth M., Jr. *Developing Vocational Instruction.* Belmont, Calif.: Fearon Publishers, 1967.

Norris, Carol A. "Job Market Philosophies and Voc. Ed. Curriculum," *American Vocational Journal* (May, 1977), pp. 55–56.

Occupational Outlook Handbook, Department of Labor. Washington, D.C.: U. S. Government Printing Office, 1976–1977.

Ohanneson, Greg, and Vaughn, Glenn. "Collection and Use of Vocational Program Information," *American Vocational Journal* (May, 1975), pp. 36–37.

Poland, Robert. "Manpower Planning and Curriculum Construction," *American Vocational Journal* (October, 1975), pp. 51–52.

Sources of Occupational Information. Jefferson City: State of Missouri, Guidance Services Section, Department of Education, 1965.

Strong, Merle E., ed. *Developing the Nation's Work Force.* Washington, D.C.: American Vocational Association, Yearbook 5, 1975.

Vocational Education and Occupations. Washington, D.C.: U. S. Government Printing Office, 1969.

Wentling, Tim L., and Lawson, Tom E. *Evaluating Occupational Education and Training Programs.* Boston: Allyn and Bacon, Inc., 1975.

Young, Robert C.; Clive, William V.; and Miles, Benton E. *Vocational Education Planning: Manpower, Priorities, and Dollars.* Columbus: The Center for Vocational and Technical Education, The Ohio State University, Research and Development Series No. 68, 1972.

Establishing
Curriculum
Content

The initial section of this book has served to provide a meaningful planning base for the vocational and technical curriculum. School- and community-related data are thoroughly examined to determine whether or not the curriculum should be offered and, if so, what its general scope should be. While decisions associated with planning are a fundamental part of the curriculum development process, they are not designed to pinpoint content essential to the curriculum. Thus the planning base must be expanded to include specific content a curriculum will contain.

This section deals with the processes used to establish meaningful curriculum content. Whether a curriculum is just being formulated or is undergoing revision, it becomes vitally important to ensure that content is identified which reflects needs of the work world. The section provides curriculum developers with a means of establishing relevant content while placing particular emphasis on approaches that can be used in applied settings (e.g., high schools, area vocational schools, community colleges, technical institutes, or manpower centers).

The three chapters in this section each deal with a key dimension of the content establishment process. While the chapters may be used independently, they have been designed to project a sequence of events in the process of establishing meaningful content. Initially, it is important to determine the range of content that has potential to be included in a curriculum (Chapter 5). This process aids in clarifying what might constitute curriculum content. After potential content has been identified, the curriculum developer must make decisions regarding which content may be used in a particular educational setting (Chapter 6). Constraints such as time, facilities, personnel, and students can affect the amount of content that can be covered. Thus the useable content is typically less than that initially identified. An additional element in the establishment of meaningful content deals with developing curriculum goals and objectives (Chapter 7). While it would be possible first to establish goals and objectives and then move on to the identification of content, the end result might be a lack of content relevance. When content derived from the world of work precedes the formal establishment of goals and objectives, the result will be more tangible, meaningful curriculum outcomes.

The reader should be mindful that this section is not meant to be prescriptive. While some persons may be able to follow the sequence suggested in Chapters 5, 6, and 7, others may find that content has already been derived for their teaching areas. However, regardless of a curriculum developer's particular needs, the information contained in Section II should provide substance for the establishment of meaningful curriculum content in vocational and technical education.

Determining
Curriculum Content

Introduction

Determining curriculum content for vocational and technical education is very
rewarding and yet extremely frustrating. The rewarding aspect is the final product: content that may be actually used in the instructional environment to aid
vocational students in achieving their fullest potential. The frustrating aspect of
determining curriculum content consists of identifying that which is truly relevant to *both instructional and occupational settings*. The paragraphs that follow
focus directly on these concerns. Initially, consideration is given to the factors
associated with curriculum content determination including constraints placed
upon the curriculum developer. Next, areas of concern associated with selecting
a meaningful content derivation strategy are discussed. Finally, a number of
strategies are presented, each of which serves as an alternate route to the determination of meaningful curriculum content.

Factors associated with determining curriculum content

While it might appear that one could just sit down and decide which content is
most important to include in a curriculum, this impression is far from reality. In
a typical educational setting, the curriculum developer is confronted with a
variety of factors that may affect the task of determining what should actually
be taught. These factors may have great impact on the direction one takes when
establishing a content framework. Idealistically, the developer may have unlimited resources and flexibility to shape content in the ways he or she wants to;
however, real world considerations often dictate the scope of the content de-

termination process. Factors such as time and dollars available; internal and external pressures; federal, state, and local content requirements; and the particular level of content all have potential to affect the means by which content is determined for a particular curriculum.

Time and dollars available

Time becomes a critical element in the entire curriculum development process and is obviously a key concern when content is to be determined. The curriculum developer typically is not able to spend an unlimited amount of time deriving content to be taught. Instead, he or she is usually given a prescribed amount of time within which to establish content. This may be a day, a week, a month, or a year but time is, nonetheless, a finite figure that impacts on the content determination process. A developer who is given two weeks to establish content for a curriculum will, in all likelihood, use a content determination strategy that can be executed in a relatively short period of time. On the other hand, an individual who is able to spend a year at this same effort has a variety of options available as far as strategies are concerned.

The dollars a developer has at his or her disposal to use in the content determination process can, likewise, affect the scope of a particular effort. Time and money are often considered synonomous in education, since professional salaries constitute such a large portion of the overall budget. Within this context, however, money may be considered in connection with the purchase of items such as travel, printing, postage, secretarial assistance, and the hiring of temporary personnel and/or consultants. When one is examining the ways content might be determined, money is a key factor, since the amount actually available tends to dictate which content derivation strategy is used. Some strategies require no additional funds over what may be available in a typical educational institution's budget. Others require extensive travel or mailings to gather information and, consequently, demand that additional dollars be made available. Thus the curriculum developer must be very much concerned about time and dollars available in support of content determination activities. Each of these areas is a constraint placed upon the developer that must be dealt with logically and thoroughly as content is being determined.

Internal and external pressures

Another factor related to determining curriculum content consists of the subtle (and sometimes not so subtle) pressures exerted by individuals and groups from within as well as outside the educational environment. Certain individuals or pressure groups may feel it is in the best interests of themselves or others to support inclusion of certain content in the curriculum. The reasons behind this sort of support are numerous, since local situations and personalities often enter into the process. Reasons may range from honest concern for students' welfare to quasi-political tactics. Regardless of the reason behind this pressure, the curriculum developer must recognize that in some cases the cause supported by certain individuals or groups may not be in the best interests of students. For example, emotional concern about content that might be included in a curriculum is no substitute for systematic content derivation. This is not to say that concerns of this type should be ignored. The contemporary curriculum developer must maintain an open mind and search for meaningful curriculum concerns that individuals and groups might possess.

Pressure in support of certain content might be exerted from within an educational environment by several sources. Administrators, vocational and technical teachers, academic teachers, guidance counselors, students, and placement specialists may each feel that certain content must be included in a curriculum and strongly support that conviction. A major responsibility of the curriculum developer is to sort out these concerns and determine which are valid and which are not. If this critical analysis is not accomplished, an invalid concern might receive widespread support and actually be included as content in a curriculum. When a situation such as this occurs, students as well as the school may suffer the consequences.

Pressures from outside the educational environment may emanate from areas such as businesses, industries, self-employed persons, professional organizations, unions, and advisory committees. Since every vocational curriculum must be responsive to the world of work, concerns from these areas cannot be ignored. In certain situations where pressure for specific content is applied from an individual or group outside the educational environment, the validity for a claim must be established. It might be that a particular business firm supports the inclusion of curriculum content dealing with word processing, since they have need for competent workers in this area; or an occupational advisory committee might believe that metrication should be an integral part of a building construction curriculum. In either case, such concern might be valid and should, therefore, be verified during the content derivation process. Working with the public is an ongoing responsibility of vocational educators and handling the concerns of lay persons is just one part of this responsibility. The curriculum developer must be responsive to public concerns and pressures by examining their implications and determining which claims are valid and justifiable.

Federal, state, and local content requirements

Curriculum content determination is seldom made solely by a curriculum developer or teacher group. In numerous occupational areas there are content requirements specified that serve as a basic framework for curricula. These requirements, which may already be established at the federal, state, or local level, tend to limit the extent to which a curriculum developer can become involved in the content determination process. For example, the Federal Aviation Agency (FAA) specifies the content and hours of instruction required of a person before that individual may be qualified as an aircraft mechanic. This content has been established through national surveys of the occupation. Obviously, major departures from prescribed FAA content might affect not only graduates' competence but also their licensure as aircraft mechanics.

A similar situation exists at the state level with regard to certain occupations. State regulations often specify the content and hours of instruction that must be included in nursing and cosmetology programs, and examinations administered at the state level tend to focus on this content. Consequently, there may be few changes one can make in curriculum content in areas such as these.

State level content requirements may also be seen in the general education area. The specific general education courses required for completion of an associate degree or high school diploma may be contributing or limiting factors in the design of a relevant curriculum. Excessive general education requirements can limit the extent to which vocational and technical content is provided. Likewise, requirements for extensive vocational and technical content may adversely affect students' general educational development through restriction of course selections.

Local content requirements tend to parallel job opportunities in the particular area. If industries in a locale are heavily involved in the production of textiles, providing relevant core content for all students planning to enter this occupational area would be appropriate. Arrangements might be made with local unions to give credit toward the completion of apprenticeship programs if certain content requirements are met while students are still in school. The content ties between school and work not only benefit the graduate but the employer, the school, and the community. While local content requirements are of a more informal nature, they are equally as important to curriculum building as state and national requirements.

Level at which content will be provided

A final factor related to curriculum content determination is the level at which that content will be provided (i.e., secondary vs. postsecondary). These different levels have direct impact on content, with the impact being felt in rather subtle ways. At the secondary level, students' educational needs tend to be more basic. While some students may progress more rapidly to advanced studies in technical areas, the majority focus on developing those competencies associated with the entry level work. Instruction is generally geared toward preparation for a specific occupation or closely related family of occupations. At the postsecondary level, students are typically those who have completed high school and have chosen to pursue education beyond that level. The postsecondary student is usually older and more mature. Thus content must focus on the needs of this type of student. In many instances, postsecondary vocational and technical education prepares students for an occupational field rather than for a specific occupation. If this is the situation curriculum developers find themselves in, content needs to be identified that has high transferability to a number of occupations within a field.

Selecting a curriculum content determination strategy

The actual selection of a curriculum content determination strategy appears simple. However, the selection process can be quite complex, with the degree of complexity dependent upon a variety of concerns. Of immediate concern to one who is selecting a strategy are the aforementioned factors (time and dollars available; internal and external pressures; federal, state, and local content requirements; and level of content) that may impact on the content determination process. Each of these factors can affect the decision that is ultimately made and, therefore, all factors should be examined closely and information about them saved for future reference. Once the various factors associated with determining content have been examined, the developer may focus on three additional areas of concern. These involve the educational setting, the occupational setting, and the content determination strategies available. Each of these concerns is discussed in the paragraphs that follow.

The educational setting

The setting in which curriculum content will be implemented is most important to study. This enables the curriculum developer to determine which aspects of the setting may affect selection of one strategy over another. Although there are a multitude of questions one might ask about how the educational setting relates to curriculum content, some likely examples might be: What is the current educational philosophy of the school and the attendance area? What support for vocational and technical education emanates from the educational community? To what extent will teachers and administrators assist in the content determination process? How well will educators accept the results of systematic curriculum content determination? These are several questions a curriculum developer should pose.

The occupational setting

The occupational setting represents another area of concern for the curriculum developer. As with the educational setting, those aspects of the occupational setting that may result in a better strategy choice must be identified. Several of the questions one might ask about relationships between the occupational setting and curriculum content include: Is the occupation clearly identifiable or is it emerging? Can workers in the occupation be interviewed by telephone or face-to-face? Will permission be granted for workers to complete survey forms and questionnaires? To what extent will businesses or industries assist with data gathering? These are the types of questions that should be asked by the developer as he or she begins to focus on the ways content may be determined.

Content determination strategies

. final and most important concern is with strategies that may actually be used to determine curriculum content. While each of the various strategies will be described in detail later in this chapter, one must first see how these strategies are similar to and different from each other. If we were to draw a straight line and place "more subjective" at one end and "more objective" at the other, we would have a continuum along which each of the strategies could roughly be placed. The *philosophical basis* for determining content is perhaps the most subjective strategy, since a specific philosophy or set of philosophies serves as a foundation for content decisions. This strategy is most typically used to develop curriculum content in academic areas. *Introspection* is used by an individual or group to examine personal experiences and knowledges and incorporate these into a framework for the vocational curriculum content. This strategy may be classed as quite subjective, since very little (if any) "hard" data is used in the decision-making process. The *function approach* to curriculum content determination focuses on systematically identifying and unifying the functions and activities performed across an entire business or industry. The methodology associated with this strategy, which requires systematic data gathering, enables more objective curriculum content information to be acquired. *Task analysis* focused on the identification and verification of tasks performed by workers in a certain occupation or cluster of occupations. Its procedures enable this strategy to produce quite objective data related to worker tasks. Several other meaningful strategies may be considered by the curriculum developer. These include the *critical incident technique* and the *Delphi technique*. The critical incident technique is useful in identifying curriculum content related to worker values and attitudes. Content in emerging occupations may be identified via the Delphi technique.

The observation may be made that the more objective curriculum content strategies are, the more costly they are to use. For example, task analysis is a very objective process but this objectivity is obtained at a high cost, since one must send materials or travel to locations where workers are employed. While the philosophical approach is very inexpensive, the small investment yields a meager return in terms of objectivity. Realistically, the curriculum developer should *consider using several strategies*, since each has its own particular strengths and weaknesses. When several strategies are used, there is a much greater likelihood that the content developed will be valid.

Philosophical basis for content determination

Philosophy appears to have had the greatest history of affecting curriculum content decisions. Before more sophisticated means of determining content were established, philosophy served as the guiding light for curriculum developers. Even today, the philosophy of vocational education espoused by a particular school, school district, or community college may provide a framework for the various curricula offered. Most of the general education offerings found in our schools today are based solely upon teachers', administrators', and/or school board members' personal philosophies of education. Thus, the fact that philosophy can and often does serve as a foundation for curriculum content is quite evident.

Establishing a philosophy

While a detailed discussion dealing with philosophical foundations of vocational education is beyond the scope of this volume, focusing on some examples of philosophy is certainly appropriate. These serve to illustrate the ways that a philosophy might be specified. One must keep in mind that a person's philosophy is basically that which he or she believes. We may say that a philosophy is composed of several belief statements, each of which contributes in some way to the overall makeup of the philosophy. Philosophy tends to vary from individual to individual and group to group just as might be expected of such a value-laden area. Therefore a group may have difficulty reaching consensus regarding some belief statements while other statements may be agreed upon unanimously with little or no discussion.

The establishment of belief statements is a rather straightforward activity. Various sources are examined to identify statements that might align with one's personal philosophy. Textbooks, articles, and speeches can all serve as useful sources of information. Philosophies developed by professional associations, community colleges, school districts, and similar units provide a wealth of potential belief statements. Whatever sources may be used, it is important to recognize that these statements represent a potential philosophy. Eventually, a group of concerned and knowledgeable persons must examine each belief statement and agree as to which ones will constitute a philosophical base for the curriculum.

A literature search might serve first to clarify the characteristics of vocational education. For example, a review of numerous sources that included individuals, organizations, agencies, and federal legislation served as a basis for the following statements about vocational education's character (Finch and Sheppard, 1975):

1. Education of less than college grade or baccalaureate degree;

2. More emphasis on fitting a person for a job and less emphasis on exploring and establishing one's self in a career;

3. Preparation for gainful employment;

4. Preparation for careers that require less than a baccalaureate degree;

5. Emphasis on skill development or specific job preparation;

6. Focus of attention at the upper middle grades, senior high, two-year college, and adult levels.

The foregoing serves to illustrate how a basic curriculum framework may evolve. If, for example, we believe that vocational education involves "preparation for gainful employment," our belief should certainly have impact on the curriculum that is established. Based upon this belief, any vocational curriculum content that does not relate in some way to the work environment should be seriously questioned.

Belief statements may take many forms. The following represent a range of possibilities in this regard and, in some cases, serve as sources of other belief statements:

1. Vocational and technical education is an integral and inseparable part of a total educational program, whether on the local or regional scene or in state or national levels of government (Olivo, 1971).

2. Vocational education has a significantly different social environment than other program areas (Miller, 1974).

3. Instruction should be based on broad core curricula characterized by flexibility in offerings (Allen, 1974).

4. The students enrolled are those who can profit from the instruction and who can qualify for placement upon graduation or completion of a particular curriculum (Olivo, 1971).

These statements are but a few of the many to be gleaned from the literature and used as a foundation for the vocational curriculum. Dedication to the task of identifying belief statements such as these will ensure that a comprehensive philosophy is developed.

Philosophy as related to curriculum content

Once belief statements have been identified, agreed upon, and molded into a philosophy, content may then be identified that aligns with this philosophy. As this process begins, it is almost immediately realized that belief statements are rather broad and tend to cut across several content areas, whereas the technical content appears to be more specific to the individual curriculum. This, perhaps, points up a basic strength and weakness of the philosophical approach to content determination. The strength has to do with the way a philosophy can permeate an educational institution. A philosophy can, for example, direct the focus of curricula within a school to better meet the needs of groups such as women, minorities, and the handicapped. If those who oversee the operation of a school firmly believe in the statement that "vocational education should be available to all those who can profit by it," their actions should be directed toward the establishment and maintenance of curricula for these groups. This does not mean merely providing a few token offerings but actually aligning curricula with students' needs on a large-scale basis. If it is stated in a philosophy that "a comprehensive placement service should be provided to both currently enrolled and former students," then action should be taken to establish the type of service to align with each curriculum.

These few examples serve to illustrate the broad impact that a sound philosophy can have on curriculum development. However, this impact is not as great in the area of specific technical content, and here is where problems tend to arise in relating philosophy to content. The general nature of a belief statement may not describe specific competencies needed by an individual in the work environment. Thus the curriculum developer must speculate about what specific competence should be and hope that this speculation results in the identification of appropriate content.

Introspection

The introspection process basically consists of examining one's own thoughts and feelings about a certain area. However, within the context of curriculum content determination, this strategy may involve either an individual or a group. The person or persons engaged in introspection are typically vocational teachers who each ask themselves the basic question, "What do I feel should constitute the content of this curriculum?" Then a search is made of one's personal employment, teaching experiences, and education to identify what might be most appropriate to include as curriculum content.

The introspection process

Introspection typically begins with an examination of ongoing vocational programs and literature related to them. This serves to remind the developer of what content might possibly be included that he or she would not otherwise recall from past experiences. The examination of literature and observation of programs might include traveling to other locations and talking to those who are involved with relevant curricula or examining course catalogs and outlines from other institutions. Concurrent with this, magazines and other related sources are reviewed to identify "ideas" for curriculum content.

Once the examination is complete, the developer considers what content might be best for students, using subjective judgement as the decisive element. Consideration is given to both the education process and the result of that process from the perspective of an experienced vocational teacher. Eventually, a content outline is developed that serves as the basis for the curriculum.

Introspection often becomes a group process where several teachers develop their individual thoughts regarding curriculum content and then meet to decide collectively what form the curriculum should take. This procedure has the advantage of providing a variety of inputs from persons with differing backgrounds and experiences. Teachers who have had different exposure to an occupational area will most likely be in a better position than one individual to determine which content is most relevant to a particular occupation or occupational area. The group process can also serve as a means of keeping personal bias to a minimum. If the group must agree collectively on curriculum content, one person's biases become more difficult to be accepted; unless, of course, all group members share the same bias with this individual.

The foregoing points to a major shortcoming of the introspection process. While changing the curriculum decision-making process from one teacher to a group of teachers may make these decisions more reliable, using introspection does not mean that the content will be any more valid (i.e., relevant and realistic). For example, even though a group of electronics instructors unanimously agrees that curriculum content should consist only of studying vacuum tubes, this still does not make the content exactly relevant to employment in our transistorized society.

Therefore the curriculum developer must recognize that introspection is not always the most valid content determination process. To come up with truly realistic content by this process is often quite difficult, particularly when one considers the nature of individual instructors and the scope of many occupations.

One means of at least partially overcoming this validity problem is through use of occupational advisory committees. The advisory committee is, by its very nature, supposed to be in close touch with reality. Committee members should be able to distinguish between relevant and irrelevant content and provide the curriculum developer with the sort of guidance needed. A basic assumption being made is that committee members are, in fact, close to the occupation, can determine what content is most relevant and, therefore, should be included in the particular curriculum. However, if this assumption cannot be met, the curriculum developer is not much better off than he or she would be with a teacher group.

The DACUM approach

A most useful variant of introspection is the DACUM (*D*eveloping *A C*urriculum) approach. The DACUM approach utilizes some basic ideas associated with introspection but shares few of its shortcomings. The reason for this is that DACUM relies on experts employed in the occupational area to determine curriculum content and allows them to be guided through a systematic content determination process. While the approach has some commonalities with other content determination strategies, DACUM will be examined in a singular fashion because of the success Canadian curriculum developers have had using this approach in content determination.

DACUM was initially created as a joint effort of the Experimental Projects Branch, Canada Department of Manpower and Immigration, and General Learning Corporation. The idea was later adopted and used by Nova Scotia New

Start, Inc. and utilized in the determination of vocational curriculum content for disadvantaged adult learners (Adams, 1975). DACUM was felt particularly useful for the New Start activity because immediate action needed to be taken on curriculum development and limited dollar resources were available.

DACUM may be defined as "a single sheet skill profile that serves as both a curriculum plan and an evaluation instrument for occupational training programs" (Adams, 1975, p. 24). A unique aspect of the DACUM approach is the way that curriculum content is displayed. A single sheet skill profile is used to present the skills of an entire occupation, thus reducing the chance of treating one element of an occupation separately from the others. The profile provides an independent specification of each of the behaviors or skills associated with competence in the occupation. These behaviors are stated in a rather simple manner so that the student can understand them and are organized in small blocks on the chart in such a manner that each can be used as an independent goal for the student. The profile also contains a rating scale that facilitates evaluation of achievement for each of the behaviors. In this manner, the profile may be used as a record of achievement for both student and teacher. As the example in Figure 5–1 indicates, a profile need not only serve as a record of achievement in school, but may also be used as a sort of diploma or documentation of skill development in an occupation.

The development of a DACUM profile involves using a committee of ten to twelve resource persons who are experts in the particular occupation. These resource persons are nominated by employers as being skilled in the occupation and currently serving as a worker or supervisor in the area. Experiences with this approach have revealed that instructors in the occupation usually *do not* contribute effectively to the DACUM process. Vocational instructors, therefore, *should not* be utilized as committee members.

The DACUM committee functions as a group with all developmental activities taking place when the members are together. Time required to complete a DACUM profile generally ranges from two to four days. A coordinator from outside the committee works with the group to facilitate the development process. Examples of previously developed DACUM charts and related materials are provided to committee members so that they may see what the end product will look like.

Following committee orientation, the facilitator guides the group through a series of steps that includes:

1. Reviewing a written description of the specific occupation;

2. Identifying general areas of competence within the occupation;

3. Identifying specific skills or behaviors for each general area of competence;

4. Structuring the skills into a meaningful learning sequence;

5. Establishing levels of competence for each skill as related to realistic work situations.

FIGURE 5-1.

FIGURE 5-1. Example of a DACUM profile*

ELECTRONICS TECHNOLOGY

Duty	Tasks
IDENTIFY AND HANDLE ELECTRONIC COMPONENTS	IDENTIFY AND SELECT WIRE AND CABLES · IDENTIFY AND SELECT CONNECTORS AND TERMINALS · IDENTIFY, SELECT, STORE AND HANDLE CLEANING MATERIALS · IDENTIFY AND SELECT RESISTORS · IDENTIFY, SELECT, HANDLE AND STORE CAPACITORS · IDENTIFY AND SELECT INDUCTORS
SELECT AND APPLY TOOLS AND TESTING EQUIPMENT	APPLY SOLDERING TECHNIQUES FOR ELECTRONIC ASSEMBLY · SELECT, CARE FOR AND OPERATE HAND AND POWER TOOLS · SELECT AND APPLY ALIGNMENT TOOLS · MEASURE PHYSICAL QUANTITIES · SELECT AND APPLY VOLT OHMMETERS · SELECT AND APPLY VACUUM TUBE AND TRANSISTOR VOLTMETERS
ANALYZE ELECTRONIC CIRCUITS AND SYSTEMS	ANALYZE PASSIVE DC CIRCUITS · ANALYZE PASSIVE AC CIRCUITS · ANALYZE ACTIVE DC CIRCUITS · ANALYZE ACTIVE AC CIRCUITS · ANALYZE TUNED AND RESONANT CIRCUITS · ANALYZE FILTER CIRCUITS · PERFORM TRANSIENT ANALYSIS OF RCL CIRCUITS
TEST, MAINTAIN AND CALIBRATE ELECTRONIC EQUIPMENT	FOLLOW DETAILED TEST PROCEDURES · MONITOR AND RECORD ROUTINE SYSTEM PERFORMANCE · INSPECT EQUIPMENT FOR MECHANICAL FAULTS · CHECK PERFORMANCE AND MAINTAIN COOLING SYSTEMS · SELECT AND APPLY LUBRICANTS · SERVICE BATTERIES · CALIBRATE EQUIPMENT USING RECOMMENDED PROCEDURES · ANALYZE MECHANICAL FUNCTIONS TO DETERMINE ACCEPTABLE PERFORMANCE · MAINTAIN AND TEST MOTORS AND GENERATORS · MAINTAIN AND TEST TRANSFORMERS · ADJUST AND MAINTAIN PRESSURIZED SYSTEMS · MEASURE RETURN LOSS · MEASURE SINGING POINT · CONDUCT TDR TESTS
TROUBLE SHOOT, ISOLATE AND REPAIR DEFECTIVE UNITS	REPLACE COMPONENTS AND CIRCUIT MODULES · REPAIR PRINTED CIRCUIT CARDS · INSPECT ELECTRICAL CONNECTIONS · CONDUCT OHMMETER TESTS ON CIRCUIT COMPONENTS · ISOLATE FAULTS TO MODULE OR CIRCUIT LEVEL · ANALYZE SYMPTOMS TO ISOLATE FAULTS · ANALYZE VOLTAGE AND CURRENT MEASUREMENTS TO ISOLATE FAULTS
INSTALL, INTERFACE AND DESIGN SYSTEMS	INTERPRET AND FOLLOW INSTALLATION SPECIFICATIONS · PRE-PLAN INSTALLATION AND SELECT TOOLS AND EQUIPMENT · INSTALL AND TERMINATE SHIELDED CABLE · WIRE COMMON CONNECTORS · PLAN WIRE AND CABLE ROUTING · INSTALL WAVE GUIDE · INSTALL ANTENNAS, GROUND PLANES AND FEEDERS
CONSTRUCT AND TEST MODEL AND PROTOTYPE ELECTRONIC EQUIPMENT	ASSEMBLE PROTOTYPE TO SPECIFICATIONS AND DRAWINGS · CHECK PROTOTYPE EQUIPMENT TO ASSEMBLY DRAWINGS · PREPARE AND ASSEMBLE CABLE HARNESSES · FABRICATE AND ASSEMBLE PRINTED CIRCUIT BOARDS · SELECT AND PREPARE WIRE AND HARDWARE · ASSEMBLE MECHANICAL PARTS TO CHASSIS · ASSEMBLE ELECTRONIC COMPONENTS TO CHASSIS
DESIGN AND DEVELOP ELECTRONIC CIRCUITS AND EQUIPMENT	DETERMINE DESIGN MODIFICATIONS · PREPARE DESIGN CHANGE NOTES · DESIGN INDUCTORS AND TRANSFORMERS · DESIGN TEST JIGS AND FIXTURES · SELECT COMPONENTS TO MEET ENVIRONMENTAL AND RELIABILITY REQUIREMENTS · ASSESS COMPONENT ACCEPTABILITY FOR CIRCUIT APPLICATION · DETERMINE REQUIREMENTS AND SELECT PRINTED CIRCUIT MATERIALS
PERFORM ELECTRONICS MATH CALCULATIONS	CALCULATE USING SLIDE RULE · CALCULATE USING CALCULATORS · SOLVE SIMPLE EQUATIONS · USE AND SOLVE QUADRATIC EQUATIONS · USE AND SOLVE SIMULTANEOUS EQUATIONS · SOLVE LINEAR SIMULTANEOUS EQUATIONS FOR CIRCUIT ANALYSIS · CALCULATE USING LOG AND EXPONENTIAL FUNCTIONS · ANALYZE VECTOR DIAGRAMS IN RECTANGULAR AND POLAR COORDINATES
PLAN AND CONTROL WORK METHODS	MAINTAIN CLEAN AND ORGANIZED WORK ENVIRONMENT · INTERPRET AND APPLY SAFETY CODES AND PROCEDURES · RECOGNIZE AND HANDLE HAZARDOUS EQUIPMENT AND SYSTEMS · EVALUATE ENVIRONMENT TO DETECT HAZARDOUS CONDITIONS · ANALYZE CONDITION AND APPLY FIRE EXTINGUISHING TECHNIQUES · APPLY FIRST AID · DETERMINE CONDITION OF EQUIPMENT RELATIVE TO CSA STANDARDS
INTERPRET AND COMMUNICATE TECHNICAL INFORMATION	INTERPRET MANUALS TO DETERMINE MAINTENANCE PROCEDURES · INTERPRET CATALOGUES TO SELECT EQUIPMENT AND COMPONENTS · INTERPRET SPECIFICATIONS TO DETERMINE PERFORMANCE PARAMETERS · INTERPRET SCHEMATICS TO DETERMINE PRIMARY CIRCUIT FUNCTION · ORDER COMPONENTS, SUPPLIES AND EQUIPMENT · PREPARE SIMPLE MECHANICAL DRAWINGS · PREPARE PARTS LIST

Name _____

Rating Legend

C	CAN PERFORM THIS SKILL WITHOUT SUPERVISION OR ASSISTANCE AND CAN LEAD OTHERS IN PERFORMING IT.
4 B	CAN PERFORM THIS SKILL WITHOUT SUPERVISION OR ASSISTANCE WITH INITIATIVE AND ADAPTABILITY TO SPECIAL PROBLEM SITUATIONS.
A	CAN PERFORM THIS SKILL WITHOUT SUPERVISION OR ASSISTANCE WITH PROFICIENCY IN SPEED AND QUALITY.
3	CAN PERFORM THIS SKILL SATISFACTORILY WITHOUT SUPERVISION AND/OR ASSISTANCE.
2	CAN PERFORM THIS SKILL SATISFACTORILY BUT REQUIRES PERIODIC SUPERVISION AND/OR ASSISTANCE.
1	CAN PERFORM SOME PARTS OF THE SKILL SATISFACTORILY, BUT REQUIRES INSTRUCTION AND SUPERVISION TO PERFORM THE ENTIRE SKILL.
0	HAS SOME KNOWLEDGE AND LIMITED EXPERIENCE, BUT NOT SUFFICIENT FOR PARTICIPATION IN A WORK ENVIRONMENT.

Ratings on the chart are based on industrial performance standards. They are confirmed by an instructor (a skilled and experienced person from this occupation) who views and evaluates performance as he would in the role of an employer or supervisor.

Instructor _____

Date _____

A letter of reference attesting to the individual's attendance, punctuality, and work habits, is available from the Registrar's office.

*Used by permission of Holland College, Charlottetown, P.E.I., Canada (May, 1974).

FIGURE 5-1. [continued]

IDENTIFY AND SELECT TRANSFORMERS	IDENTIFY, SELECT AND HANDLE DIODES AND RECTIFIERS	IDENTIFY, SELECT AND HANDLE TUBES	IDENTIFY, SELECT AND HANDLE TRANSISTORS AND FETS	IDENTIFY AND SELECT SEMI-CONDUCTOR GATING DEVICES	IDENTIFY, SELECT, HANDLE AND STORE BATTERIES	IDENTIFY, SELECT AND HANDLE HIGH FREQUENCY MEASUREMENT TRANSDUCERS	IDENTIFY, SELECT AND HANDLE ACOUSTIC SYSTEM TRANSDUCERS	IDENTIFY, SELECT AND HANDLE COMMUNICATIONS EQUIPMENT TRANSDUCERS	IDENTIFY, SELECT, AND HANDLE FUSES AND PROTECTIVE DEVICES	IDENTIFY, SELECT, HANDLE AND STORE METER MOVEMENTS
APPLY TUBE TESTERS	APPLY TRANSISTOR TESTERS	SELECT AND APPLY POWER SUPPLIES	SELECT AND APPLY LOW FREQUENCY OSCILLOSCOPES	SELECT AND APPLY HIGH FREQUENCY OSCILLOSCOPES	SELECT AND APPLY LOW FREQUENCY SIGNAL GENERATORS	SELECT AND APPLY HIGH FREQUENCY SIGNAL GENERATORS	SELECT AND APPLY SWEEP GENERATORS	SELECT AND APPLY FUNCTION GENERATORS	SELECT AND APPLY PULSE GENERATORS	SELECT AND APPLY POWER METERS
ANALYZE FUNCTION GENERATOR CIRCUITS	ANALYZE LOGIC SWITCHING CIRCUITS	ANALYZE CONTROL SWITCHING CIRCUITS	ANALYZE POWER SUPPLY CIRCUITS	ANALYZE COUPLING AND DECOUPLING CIRCUITS	ANALYZE AUDIO CIRCUITS AND SYSTEMS	ANALYZE FEEDBACK CIRCUITS	ANALYZE OSCILLATOR CIRCUITS	ANALYZE PULSE CIRCUITS	ANALYZE DEMODULATOR CIRCUITS	ANALYZE NONLINER AMPLIFIER CIRCUITS
PERFORM RECOMMENDED CLEANING PROCEDURES	ALIGN AND BALANCE SERVOMECHANISMS	CONDUCT FREQUENCY MEASUREMENTS	CONDUCT POWER OUTPUT MEASUREMENTS	CONDUCT PHASE MEASUREMENTS	ANALYZE AND INTERPRET WAVE FORMS	INTERPRET ASSEMBLY DRAWINGS TO DETERMINE LOCATION OF COMPONENTS	CONDUCT FREQUENCY RESPONSE MEASUREMENTS	MAINTAIN STANDARDS FOR CALIBRATION	CONDUCT MODULATION TESTS	CONDUCT FREQUENCY SPECTRUM MEASUREMENTS
PERFORM T.V. COLOUR ALIGNMENT AND ADJUSTMENT	RUN DIAGNOSTIC COMPUTER PROGRAMS									
UTILIZE CALIBRATION AND MAINTENANCE PROCEDURES TO ISOLATE FAULTS	ISOLATE FAULTS TO COMPONENT LEVEL	ISOLATE FAULTS BY SIGNAL TRACING AND INJECTION	CONDUCT IN-CIRCUIT TESTS OF COMPONENTS	ADAPT TESTING PROCEDURES FOR IN-SERVICE MEASUREMENTS	TRACE CIRCUITS TO GENERATE CIRCUIT DIAGRAM	TRACE CIRCUITS TO IDENTIFY AND ISOLATE FAULTS	DETERMINE COMPONENT EQUIVALENCY	CHECK COMPONENTS BY PATCHING		
PERFORM INSTALLATION CHECKOUT ROUTINE	DETERMINE & INCORPORATE SHIELDING, GROUNDING & DECOUPLING REQUIREMENTS	SELECT EQUIPMENT AND COMPONENTS TO MEET REQUIREMENTS OF SPECIFICATIONS	DETERMINE CONDITION OF LOAD & BALANCE ON PRIMARY POWER SOURCE	ASSESS ENVIRONMENTAL CONDITIONS	ANALYZE ENVIRONMENTAL REQUIREMENTS AND RECOMMEND CONTROL	ANALYZE SHOCK AND VIBRATION TO DETERMINE MOUNTING TECHNIQUES	ANALYZE SPECIFICATIONS TO DETERMINE EQUIPMENT COMPATIBILITY	DETERMINE CAUSE OF INCOMPATIBILITY	ANALYZE USER REQUIREMENTS TO DEVELOP TECHNICAL SPECIFICATIONS	CONDUCT FEASIBILITY STUDY
FABRICATE AND ASSEMBLE CHASSIS	PERFORM ENVIRONMENTAL TESTS	WIND SPECIAL COILS AND TRANSFORMERS	BUILD TEST JIGS AND FIXTURES	PERFORM TEST AND EVALUATION OF PROTOTYPE EQUIPMENT	PREPARE PROTOTYPE TEST PROCEDURES					
DETERMINE REQUIREMENTS AND SELECT ENCAPSULATING MATERIALS	DETERMINE REQUIREMENTS AND SELECT INSULATION MATERIALS	DETERMINE REQUIREMENTS AND SELECT CONDUCTIVE MATERIALS	DETERMINE REQUIREMENTS AND SELECT HEAT SINKS	DESIGN CHASSIS	LAYOUT ELECTRONIC COMPONENTS	LAYOUT PRINTED CIRCUITS	LAYOUT HIGH FREQUENCY CIRCUITS	LAYOUT HIGH GAIN AND HIGH IMPEDANCE CIRCUITS	SELECT COMPONENTS TO PROVIDE CIRCUIT PARAMETERS	PARTICIPATE IN COST REDUCTION ANALYSIS
SOLVE PHASOR PROBLEMS USING COMPLEX NUMBERS	EXPRESS ABSOLUTE POWER & VOLTAGE LEVELS IN DECIBELS	PERFORM GRAPHICAL ANALYSIS OF MEASURED DATA	FIT CURVES TO RECORDED DATA	INTERPRET AND CONVERT UNITS OF MEASUREMENT	INTERPRET AND DETERMINE ACCURACY OF MEASUREMENTS	DETERMINE CUMULATIVE ERROR OF MEASUREMENTS AND CALCULATIONS	CALCULATE MEDIAN AND STANDARD DEVIATION	UTILIZE NOMOGRAMS TO DETERMINE DESIGN OR SYSTEM VALUES	PLOT SMITH CHARTS FOR IMPEDANCE CALCULATIONS	PERFORM DECIMAL, OCTAL AND BINARY CONVERSIONS AND CALCULATIONS
PREPARE MATERIAL COST ESTIMATES	MONITOR PROGRAM TO CONTROL COSTS	ESTIMATE TIME AND LABOUR REQUIREMENTS	PREPARE COST ESTIMATES	PROVIDE INPUT TO PROJECT CPM PLANNING	PREPARE DELIVERY ESTIMATES	PLAN AND CONTROL PROGRAM OF WORK	ESTABLISH AND MAINTAIN STOCK CONTROL SYSTEM			
PREPARE DETAILED BLOCK DIAGRAMS	SKETCH ELECTRICAL DRAWINGS	PREPARE LAYOUT AND ASSEMBLY DRAWINGS	LAYOUT WIRING DIAGRAMS	PREPARE WIRING ROUTE SHEETS	PREPARE TECHNICAL REPORTS	MAINTAIN TECHNICAL LOG BOOK	PREPARE DEFECT AND FAILURE REPORTS	PREPARE DATA TABLES, GRAPHS AND CHARTS		
PREPARE DETAILED CIRCUIT DIAGRAMS								RECORD MEASUREMENTS AND RESULTS		

FIGURE 5-1. [continued]

Block A

IDENTIFY, SELECT HANDLE & STORE MAGNETIC & FERRO-MAGNETIC MATERIALS & COMPONENTS	IDENTIFY, SELECT, HANDLE AND STORE MAGNETIC TAPE	IDENTIFY, SELECT AND HANDLE RELAYS	IDENTIFY, SELECT AND HANDLE MECHANICAL SWITCHES	IDENTIFY, SELECT AND HANDLE LINEAR INTEGRATED CIRCUITS	IDENTIFY, SELECT AND HANDLE DIGITAL INTEGRATED CIRCUITS	IDENTIFY, SELECT AND HANDLE DISPLAY DEVICES	IDENTIFY AND SELECT AC AND DC ROTATING MACHINES	IDENTIFY, SELECT AND HANDLE SYNCHRONOUS CONTROL ELEMENTS	IDENTIFY, SELECT, HANDLE AND STORE MICROWAVE COMPONENTS	IDENTIFY, SELECT AND HANDLE SPECIAL PURPOSE TUBES
SELECT AND APPLY FREQUENCY COUNTERS AND TIMERS	SELECT AND APPLY AC AND DC BRIDGES	SELECT AND APPLY DISTORTION ANALYZERS	SELECT AND APPLY SPECTRUM ANALYZERS	SELECT AND APPLY X-Y AND CHART RECORDERS	SELECT AND APPLY NETWORK ANALYZERS	SELECT AND APPLY CURVE TRACERS	SELECT AND APPLY FIELD STRENGTH METERS	SELECT AND APPLY ABSORPTION METERS		
ANALYZE MIXERS AND MODULATORS	ANALYZE RECEIVER SYSTEMS	ANALYZE TRANSMITTER SYSTEMS	ANALYZE AFC, AVC, AND AGC CIRCUITS	ANALYZE R.F. AMPLIFIER CIRCUITS	ANALYZE EQUALIZATION CIRCUITS	ANALYZE VIDEO CIRCUITS	ANALYZE CONTROL SYSTEMS	ANALYZE AC AND DC MACHINERY	ANALYZE MICROWAVE CIRCUITS AND SYSTEMS	ANALYZE ANTENNA AND TRANSMISSION SYSTEMS
CONDUCT INTERMODULATION MEASUREMENTS	CONDUCT TRANSIENT RESPONSE MEASUREMENTS	ALIGN AND ADJUST FILTERS	CONDUCT NOISE MEASUREMENTS	CONDUCT INSULATION TESTS	CONDUCT VOLTAGE AND POWER GAIN MEASUREMENTS	ALIGN OSCILLATORS, DISCRIMINATORS AND RATIO DETECTORS	CONDUCT VSWR MEASUREMENTS	CONDUCT FIELD STRENGTH MEASUREMENTS	CONDUCT DIFFERENTIAL PHASE AND GAIN MEASUREMENTS	ANALYZE SYSTEM FUNCTIONS TO DETERMINE ACCEPTABLE PERFORMANCE

Block B

DESIGN SYSTEM LAYOUT	INTERFACE ANTENNAS WITH TRANSMITTERS AND RECEIVERS	CALCULATE PROPAGATION CHARACTERISTICS	ANALYZE AND PREDICT SYSTEM RELIABILITY	DETERMINE CONDITION AND CONTROL GALVANIC CORROSION	PREPARE INSTALLATION SPECIFICATIONS

Block C

INITIATE DESIGN FROM BASIC CIRCUIT CONCEPTS	INITIATE DESIGN FROM DESIGN SPECIFICATION	ASSESS HUMAN ENGINEERING ASPECTS OF DESIGN	ANALYZE AND PREDICT EQUIPMENT MTBF	IMPROVISE TEMPORARY TEST EQUIPMENT	MAINTAIN DESIGN NOTES AND SKETCHES

Block D

APPLY BOOLEAN ALGEBRA TO SOLVE LOGIC FUNCTIONS	UTILIZE COMPUTER PROGRAMS	DIFFERENTIATE SIMPLE FUNCTIONS	DETERMINE POINTS OF MAXIMUM AND MINIMUM RESPONSE USING DERIVATIVES	INTEGRATE SIMPLE FUNCTIONS	SIMULATE CIRCUIT FUNCTIONS USING ANALOG COMPUTER	ANALYZE WAVE FORMS WITH FOURIER SERIES	APPLY LAPLACE TRANSFORMS TO LINEAR CIRCUIT ANALYSIS

Block E

PREPARE ILLUSTRATIONS FOR TECHNICAL REPORTS	PREPARE TIME AND WORK RECORDS	CONDUCT LITERATURE SEARCH	PREPARE EXPERIMENT AND TEST PROCEDURES	PARTICIPATE IN TECHNICAL DISCUSSIONS AND PRESENTATIONS	PREPARE BUSINESS CORRESPONDENCE	PREPARE MAINTENANCE SCHEDULE AND ANALYSIS CHARTS	PREPARE SYSTEMS TEST SHEETS	DISCUSS AND INTERPRET PROBLEMS AND SYMPTOMS WITH CUSTOMERS	COORDINATE SERVICE AND MAINTENANCE WITH USER NEEDS	LOCATE AND APPLY STANDARDIZED SPECIFICATIONS

Once the DACUM profile has been developed, the product may serve as a basis for developing instructional content and materials that focus on student attainment of specified skills. It should be noted that teachers become involved *after* the profile has been produced. This procedure has the advantage of identifying only those skills that are most relevant to the work setting.

The DACUM approach to curriculum development has some distinct advantages. First, the committee procedure results in a relatively low development cost. The major expense would be payments to committee members and, in many cases, a business or industry will gladly release an "expert" from his or her duties to assist in this process. Second, the time frame for conducting the DACUM activity is quite short. Thus, in a relatively brief time, instructors may use the profile to prepare for their classes. No time is spent waiting for forms to return or worrying about nonrespondents. Third, and perhaps most important, is the way that DACUM enables curriculum content to be derived without academic intervention. DACUM's advantage over the traditional introspection process is quite clear. The process allows more relevant content to be identified and incorporated into a curriculum. At first glance, the DACUM approach appears no different from the traditional trade and job analysis process (e.g., Fryklund, 1970; Mager and Beach, 1967). One should note, however, that these approaches rely on the instructor to determine what the content should be with little direct consideration given to input from persons employed in the actual work setting.

Function approach

While introspection and the philosophical basis for content determination tend to lean in the direction of subjective judgement, there are other strategies of a much more objective nature. One of those which has received more attention from professionals in agricultural education is the function approach. This strategy focuses on the functions of a business or industry that may be defined as "the operations that *must* be performed somewhere in the total business or industry in order for it to be successful or to continue in operation" (Clark and Meaders, 1968).

Characteristics of the function approach

The function approach focuses on identification of content in terms of unifying characteristics across a particular industry or business. Whether it be the agricultural equipment industry, the garment industry, or some other business or industry, the whole is examined to determine which parts, as expressed in functions, are performed throughout.

There are several inherent features in this approach. Perhaps most obvious is its ability to unify functions across an entire business or industry, and thus identify curricular inputs from an extremely broad base. For example, an examination might be made of the feed industry. In this case, as well as others, numerous functions might be identified that cut across traditional vocational service area lines. These could include growing, processing, transporting, purchasing, and selling. Ultimately, an identification is made of that which constitutes performance of a function rather than what might be taught in one particular service area. This sort of information is particularly important if there is a desire to build a curriculum that is truly relevant, regardless of traditional program categories associated with vocational education.

A second feature of the function approach is its focus on a broadly based business or industry rather than on a specific job title. Even though examination of certain occupations may be important, other considerations can warrant the examination of curricular content from a much broader base. While the task analysis approach, as described later in this chapter, might identify work that a greenhouse grower performs, the function approach identifies contributions that greenhouse grower employees make to other functions in the industry. These might include sales, office practices, public relations, and others (Clark and Meaders, 1968).

Conducting the function study

Utilizing the function approach requires a great deal of time and effort. Additional factors such as the breadth of an industry and the number of contacts to be made typically make this a regional rather than a locally-based activity. Several examples of industries examined via the function approach are described by Clark and Meaders (1968). Notable among these are studies by Gleason (1967) and Berkey (1967), while an additional study by Berkey and others (1972) describes a variant of the function approach. Essentially, a step-by-step procedure is followed that is relatively simple to execute (Gleason, 1967).

Initially, the purposes of the industry are defined and then essential functions to be performed in line with these purposes are identified. Clark (1965), for example, identified functions performed somewhere in the total feed industry to include processing, sales, service, office practices, public relations, purchasing, transportation, research, and maintenance.

After functions have been identified, a list of activities is developed for each function. Assistance in the development of this list is obtained from people who are familiar with the industry. These might include representatives from industry, cooperative extension specialists, and teachers. Examples of activities for the feed industry sales function might include the following:

Assists farmers and ranchers in planning feeding programs and trouble-
    shoots feeding problems;

Sells directly to producer;

Sells directly to customer across the counter;

Recognizes abnormal animal health conditions.

Next, a list of the various competencies needed by persons performing the activities of a function is developed. Assistance with list development is obtained from people familiar with the industry, such as cooperative extension specialists, industry representatives, and teacher educators from the particular areas. Competencies are usually stated in terms of knowledge, understanding, and ability at different levels of performance.

Fourth, the activities and competencies are grouped into compatible areas for the purpose of developing the proper educational mix required to prepare personnel for the industry or business. After this step is complete, a jury of experts including persons from business, industry, and education examines the curriculum content that has been identified and verifies its appropriateness.

While the function approach does require a considerable amount of time and resources to execute, its strength lies in the potential to cut across traditional teaching area lines and bring together a variety of experts to build a curriculum. Sales functions in the feed industry, for example, require worker competence that is a melding of agriculture, business, and distributive education. Other functions such as service might encompass trade and industrial education as well. Thus it is important to recognize that function analysis has potential to better link the various teaching areas into a more relevant, cohesive curricular thrust.

Task analysis

Few content determination strategies have seen such widespread use as task analysis. This particular approach has been employed by vocational educators in varying forms for a number of years. However, during the mid-1960s, several developments occurred that resulted in major refinements to the task analysis process. These refinements have enabled curriculum developers to make more objective decisions regarding content that should be included in various curricula. Of particular note was research conducted at the Personnel Research Laboratory, Lackland Air Force Base, Texas, which resulted in the development of a procedural guide for conducting occupational surveys (Morsh and Archer, 1967). This guide has enabled educators to study systematically the behavioral aspects of job requirements. Further refinement and use of the task analysis process by groups such as the Vocational-Technical Education Consortium of States (V-TECS) has shown this approach to be quite applicable to public vocational and technical education (Lee, 1976).

Task analysis fundamentals

Basically, task analysis may be defined as the process wherein tasks performed by workers employed in a particular job are identified and verified. The worker's *job* consists of duties and tasks he or she actually performs. *Duties* are large segments of work done by an individual that typically serve as broad categories within which tasks may be placed. Examples of duties would be: organizing and planning; typing; maintaining equipment and tools, and loading and hauling. *Tasks*, on the other hand, are units of work activity that form a significant part of a duty (Morsh and Archer, 1967). Each task has a definite beginning and ending point and usually consists of two or more definite steps. Examples of tasks performed by workers would be: planning menus; filing materials; computing depreciation, and winterizing vehicles. Basic to the task analysis process is the gathering of information directly from workers. Obtaining information from this source ensures that workers are actually providing input for curriculum content decisions. Just as the name "task analysis" implies, potential tasks are identified and then verified by job incumbents, with the resultant analysis serving to determine which tasks are actually associated with the particular job.

Conducting the task analysis

While there are several possible ways that a task analysis may be conducted, the key to success lies in being both thorough and systematic. For this reason, much of the discussion that follows is drawn from procedures utilized by the Vocational-Technical Education Consortium of States (V-TECS) in the conduct of their task analyses. V-TECS is a cooperative effort among a number of state agencies to develop catalogs of performance objectives, criterion referenced measures, and guides in selected occupational areas. The Consortium is administered by the Southern Association of Colleges and Schools, Commission on Occupational Education Institutions, Atlanta, Georgia. Catalogs based on task analyses are completed or underway for over 280 job titles ranging from child care to turf management (Lee, 1976). The experience of this Consortium over the past several years has enabled V-TECS to develop a set of task analysis procedures that is extremely functional. There are, of course, other sources of information for persons who are planning to conduct task analyses (e.g., Moss and Smith, 1971; Melching and Borcher, 1973). However, most references are, at least in part, based upon Morsh and Archer's work.

What, then, are the basic steps involved in task analysis? Typically they include reviewing relevant literature, developing the occupational inventory, selecting a worker sample, administering the inventory, and analyzing the collected information.

Reviewing relevant literature

The first step in conducting a task analysis consists of examining literature in the occupational area. This review is useful in determining the extent to which other analyses may have already been conducted. If meaningful analyses have been completed, there is usually no reason to go any further with the analysis process. A second use of the literature review is to develop lists of potential tasks and equipment associated with the occupational area. Tasks may be listed for one or several jobs, with the exact scope of the analysis being determined by the curriculum developer. Thus an occupational area typically consists of two or more jobs in a related area or cluster. Equipment lists serve to identify the extent to which equipment is used and, once verified, serve as meaningful aids in laboratory planning and similar areas.

Developing the occupational inventory

After task and equipment lists have been gleaned from the literature, duplicate items are deleted and, wherever appropriate, relevant items are added. Lists are then incorporated into an inventory that will eventually be completed by incumbent workers. The equipment list is generally placed on a separate sheet of the inventory, together with spaces for workers to check items used in their current assignments. An equipment list from food management, production, and services is provided in Figure 5-2.

In order to keep track of the various jobs examined in a task analysis, standard numbers and job titles provided by the *Dictionary of Occupational Titles* (D.O.T.) may be used. The D.O.T. classification scheme is utilized by the U.S. Department of Labor (1965) and might prove especially helpful when an instructor is eager to know what tasks are appropriate to various jobs in an occupational area.

Tasks are grouped under appropriate duty headings, with the exact number of headings being dependent on the particular occupational area. Duties provided in a V-TECS occupational inventory for plumbing include:

A. Organizing and Planning

B. Directing and Implementing

C. Inspecting/Evaluating

D. Training

E. Joining Pipe

F. Installing Hangers and Supports

G. Building Distribution Lines

H. Building Drains

I. Installing Traps and Cleanouts

J. Installing Vents

K. Installing Fixtures

L. Installing Hot Water/Steam Systems

M. Maintaining Plumbing Systems*

*Used by permission of Vocational-Technical Education Consortium of States (V-TECS).

FIGURE 5-2.   **Example of an occupational inventory equipment list***

CHECK THE EQUIPMENT YOU USE IN YOUR CURRENT ASSIGNMENT

(1) _____ Bain-marie	(29) _____ Fire extinguisher
(2) _____ Band saw	(30) _____ Food chopper, electric
(3) _____ Blender	(31) _____ Food mixer, electric
(4) _____ Broiler	(32) _____ Freezer
(5) _____ Bun fillet steamer	(33) _____ French knife
(6) _____ Butcher knife	(34) _____ Frying pan, electric
(7) _____ Can opener, electric	(35) _____ Garbage disposal
(8) _____ Can opener, manual	(36) _____ Gas broiler
(9) _____ Carving set	(37) _____ Grill, griddle
(10) _____ Cash register	(38) _____ Hot top
(11) _____ Charcoal broiler	(39) _____ Measuring cups and spoons (pints, quarts, gallons)
(12) _____ Chicken fryer	
(13) _____ Cleaver	(40) _____ Meat grinder
(14) _____ Coffee pot, electric	(41) _____ Meat slicer
(15) _____ Coffee pot, regular	(42) _____ Microwave oven
(16) _____ Cold food server	(43) _____ Mixer, electric
(17) _____ Compartment steamers	(44) _____ Oil stone
(18) _____ Deep fat fryer	(45) _____ Pans, assorted
(19) _____ Deep freezer	(46) _____ Paresian cutter
(20) _____ Dipper, ice cream	(47) _____ Peeler
(21) _____ Dishwasher, electric	(48) _____ Potato masher, hand
(22) _____ Double boiler	(49) _____ Power meat saw
(23) _____ Egg poacher	(50) _____ Power mixer
(24) _____ Egg slicer, hand-operated	(51) _____ Range, electric (institutional)
(25) _____ Electric grinder (meat)	(52) _____ Range, gas
(26) _____ Electric juice extractor	(53) _____ Refrigerator
(27) _____ Electric slicing machine	(54) _____ Roasting pans
(28) _____ Emery wheel	(55) _____ Saucepans

*Used by permission of Vocational-Technical Education Consortium of States (V-TECS).

FIGURE 5-2. [continued]

CHECK THE EQUIPMENT YOU USE IN YOUR CURRENT ASSIGNMENT

(56) _____ Scales	(67) _____ Two-deck baking ovens
(57) _____ Slicer, power-driven	(68) _____ Two-deck steam cooker
(58) _____ Stack ovens	(69) _____ Vacuum cleaner
(59) _____ Steam-jacketed kettles	(70) _____ Vegetable peeling machine
(60) _____ Steam kettle	(71) _____ Waffle iron
(61) _____ Steam table	(72) _____ _____
(62) _____ Strainers	(73) _____ _____
(63) _____ Teapots	(74) _____ _____
(64) _____ Tenderizing machine	(75) _____ _____
(65) _____ Toaster, conveyor	(76) _____ _____
(66) _____ Toaster, individual	(77) _____ _____

For this particular inventory, a total of 293 tasks was included. In this manner, a comprehensive picture of the job is provided so that meaningful reactions are obtained from workers. After task and equipment lists have been developed in preliminary form, they are reviewed by a sample of incumbent workers and supervisors to obtain reactions directly "from the field." Feedback from these individuals may result in anything from technical and grammatical refinements to the addition of relevant items. This is obviously an important part of the task analysis process, since validity of the inventory can be verified.

An equally important aspect of inventory development deals with the areas marked by incumbent workers. These consist of scales to check whether or not tasks are done in the present job and they permit the indication of time spent doing the tasks. Data collected from workers are used to determine whether or not a particular task is of sufficient importance to warrant its inclusion in the curriculum. Figure 5-3 contains one task list page from an inventory for secretarial, stenographic, typing, and related occupations.

Since it may be helpful to obtain additional data about workers in the occupational area, the inventory includes a page devoted to background information. The items in Figure 5-4 are representative of information usually gathered. Workers' names and addresses may be needed in the event that some responses require clarification, whereas "total months in career field" may be used to categorize workers' responses in accordance with their work experience. A curriculum developer using this approach is advised to keep informational items to a minimum and only include those items which are absolutely essential.

FIGURE 5–3. Page from an occupational inventory task list for secretarial, stenographic, typing, and related occupations*

Inventory [Duty-Task List] *Page 29 of 32 pages*

---

1. Check tasks you perform now (✓).
2. Add any tasks you do now that are not listed.
3. In the "Time Spent" column, rate checked (✓) tasks on time spent in your present job.

Time Spent Scale

1. *Very Much Below Average*	5. *Slightly Above Average*
2. *Below Average*	6. *Above Average*
3. *Slightly Below Average*	7. *Very Much Above Average*
4. *About Average*	

L. *Typewriting*		✓ If Done Now	Time Spent Current Job
1. Make carbon copies	(388)		
2. Make corrections on carbon copies	(389)		
3. Make typewriter corrections, correction fluid process	(390)		
4. Make typewriter corrections, eraser process	(391)		
5. Proofread typewritten copy	(392)		
6. Type acknowledgments	(393)		
7. Type addresses on envelopes and cards	(394)		
8. Type agendas	(395)		
9. Type and correct offset masters (mats or multilith)	(396)		
10. Type and correct spirit masters (ditto masters)	(397)		
11. Type and correct stencils (mimeograph process)	(398)		
12. Type balance sheets	(399)		
13. Type bank reconciliations	(400)		
14. Type bids and proposals	(401)		
15. Type bills of materials (bills of lading)	(402)		
16. Type budgets	(403)		
17. Type business letters	(404)		
18. Type cards such as index cards, file cards, or "address finder" cards	(405)		

*Used by permission of Vocational-Technical Education Consortium of States (V-TECS).

FIGURE 5–4. Background information sheet for an occupational inventory*

Please print information requested and check applicable boxes.

Date	THIS SPACE FOR OFFICE USE ONLY	Case Control No. 15-51
	O. E. No. 17.1007	D. O. T. No.

Name (Last, Middle Initial, First)

Address (Street, City, State, Zip Code)

Social Security Account Number ⬜⬜⬜ ⬜⬜ ⬜⬜⬜⬜

Work Telephone Number ⬜⬜⬜ ⬜⬜⬜⬜

Total Months in Present Job ⬜⬜⬜

Total Months in Career Field ⬜⬜⬜

Total Months at Present Location ⬜⬜⬜

Number of People Supervised ⬜⬜

Name of Firm or Employer

Employer's Address (Street, City, State)

Your Present Position (or Job Title)

Circle the Highest Education Level (or GED Equivalent) You Have Completed

	Elementary			High School				College				Graduate		Date of Completion
Grade 05	06	07	08	09	10	11	12	13	14	15	16	17	18	_____

---

*Used by permission of Vocational-Technical Education Consortium of States (V-TECS).

Selecting a worker sample

While, in some instances, information may be gathered from an entire population of workers, this procedure is usually not followed. Workers in a particular occupational area may number several thousand or even hundred thousand; thus data must be gathered from an appropriate sample of that population. Sampling not only cuts costs in terms of printing and mailing, it also reduces the magnitude of data to be analyzed. Numerous references are available that describe procedures for determining the appropriate sample size (e.g., National Education Association, 1960; Sudman, 1976). Regardless of the sampling procedure used, any sample selected must be truly representative of the population. An appropriate sampling technique will ensure that results from the worker sample can be generalized to the population.

Administering the inventory

Once the inventory has been developed and the sample selected, data can be gathered from incumbent workers. Perhaps the most expeditious approach is to mail the inventory out and rely on workers to complete and return it. Unfortunately, this is not always successful, since inventories usually contain twenty to thirty pages and hundreds of tasks. When care is not taken to follow up on those who fail to return forms, the result may be a low return rate. If fewer than 60 percent of the selected sample complete and return inventories, the generalizability of results to a population of workers may be seriously questioned. Therefore a high return rate should be secured whenever the inventory is mailed to workers. An alternative approach is to sample employers and make contact with persons at the managerial level to solicit the cooperation of their employees. By dealing directly with employers, the curriculum developer is able to obtain support "from the top" and thus encourage a good return rate. Workers whose employers support the inventory process may feel a strong personal obligation to complete and return the inventory promptly. A third alternative would be to interview workers at the job location. While this is often an expensive proposition, it may be the only effective way to gather data from workers in certain occupational areas.

Analyzing the collected information

After the data have been collected from workers, responses are typically placed on data cards or tape and processed via computer. This is certainly the most expeditious route to take, since each inventory contains so many different tasks and items of equipment. If, for example, 200 workers each completed an inventory with 300 tasks and 75 equipment items, 75,000 bits of data would be produced!

In the determination of what actually constitutes a meaningful task, the recommendation is made to establish some appropriate cutoff point. This might, for example, be "80 percent of the workers perform the task." Whatever standard is eventually established, it must be remembered that the vocational curriculum typically prepares students for entry level employment. Tasks should not be arbitrarily eliminated just because they are not performed by seasoned veterans, since these same tasks may be performed by a high percentage of novice workers. By taking information from the workers' background information sheets such as time spent on a job, a determination may be made of which tasks are performed by more experienced and less experienced workers.

Other meaningful content determination strategies

The aforementioned strategies are quite commonly associated with education in general and vocational education in particular. They are more often utilized when technical content decisions are to be made. However, two other strategies that have the potential to identify content of a less technical nature should be of equal interest to the contemporary curriculum developer. These are the critical incident technique and the Delphi technique. Each of these strategies is a variant on a research and development tool that may be quite useful in the applied curriculum area as well as in fundamental research.

The critical incident technique

Even though the critical incident technique has been available for many years, its use in deriving curriculum content has been quite limited. This technique is comprised of "procedures for collecting direct observations of human behavior in such a way as to facilitate their potential usefulness in solving practical problems" (Flanagan, 1954).

An incident is any observable human activity that enables "inferences and predictions to be made about the person performing the act" (Flanagan, 1954). Incidents are classified as critical when the observer sees their purpose and consequences as being clear. A major contribution that the critical incident technique can make to curriculum content identification is its potential to deal more directly with isolating important values and attitudes. While task analysis and similar approaches are useful in the identification of content, they tend to focus more exclusively on technical content and less directly on affective concerns. With the critical incident technique, one can select those behaviors which are attitude or value-laden and thus provide a firmer foundation for affective content in the curriculum (Kirchner and Dunnette, 1957).

The technique may be illustrated by using an example of a concern that many curriculum developers have. Assume that a certain curriculum has a poor record of graduates holding jobs. While placement has been high and no difficulties have been identified with workers' technical competence, persons who have been placed on jobs tend to be dismissed at a much higher rate than those in other curricula. When approaching this problem, one would first want to identify those nontechnical essentials that make the difference between job success and failure. To accomplish this, supervisors are asked to record in the form of anecdotes or stories those job behaviors which contributed to worker dismissal. The data gathered are then used to build a composite picture of job behavior.

In order to obtain the necessary information, a critical incident form is devised that allows supervisors who have day-to-day contact with workers to record specific instances of workers' inappropriate affective behavior. The form provided in Figure 5-5 may be used for this purpose. Each supervisor completes a form for each critical incident that he or she can remember. In addition to a description of the incident, information may be requested about the amount of time the worker has been employed. This assists in isolating incidents associated with entry level type workers. Examples of some incidents gathered from supervisors are presented below in summary form.

1. A worker was consistently "sick" on Mondays, using up sick time as soon as it was awarded.

2. Worker activity consisted of only that which was specifically assigned. The worker showed no initiative to find work to do.

3. Over a three-week period, the worker was late to work ten times. For each instance of being late, the worker had a questionable excuse.

The above incidents are merely illustrative and must be combined with many others to arrive at any meaningful inferences. Typically, from 100 to 200 incidents are gathered, with the actual useable number being somewhat less. The reported incidents are then conceptually grouped into categories with general headings. Categories associated with the area of nontechnical failures might consist of the following:

1. Punctuality

2. Interpersonal Relations

3. Interpretation of Company Policy

4. Personal Initiative

Other categories could, of course, be added, with the exact number being determined by the incidents that have been gathered.

The utility of this information is quite evident. Categories and their associated incidents serve as a foundation for curriculum content that focuses on developing appropriate attitudes and values. Curriculum developers must recognize that instruction based upon this type of content is not provided on a lesson, project, or similar basis. Affective education must be infused into the curric-

---

FIGURE 5-5.   Critical incident record form

Directions: Think of the workers you dismissed over the past six months. Focus your attention on any one nontechnical thing that one of your workers may have done that
contributed to his or her dismissal. In other words, think of a *critical incident*
related to nontechnical failures of your workers. Please do not place any person's name on this form.

WHAT LED UP TO THE INCIDENT?

EXACTLY WHAT DID YOUR WORKER DO THAT WAS CLASSIFIED AS A NONTECH-
NICAL FAILURE?

HOW DID THIS INCIDENT CONTRIBUTE TO HIS OR HER DISMISSAL?

WHEN DID THE INCIDENT HAPPEN?

---

ulum such that students develop appropriate values and attitudes across their
entire school experience instead of just during formal classroom or laboratory
sessions.

The Delphi technique

A more recently developed research tool, the Delphi technique, has much applicability when curriculum content is being determined. As its oracular name
implies, the Delphi technique focuses more directly on the future of a particular
area. Originally developed by the Rand Corporation for predicting alternate
defense futures, it has seen widespread use in many areas of education
(Weaver, 1971). The Delphi technique has been found to be a most useful tool in

setting priorities, establishing goals, and forecasting the future. Obviously, this technique would be of much value when persons desire to reach consensus regarding the content of a particular curriculum. All too often there is more content available than time in which to teach the material. The curriculum developer must provide a means of ensuring that the most relevant content is included and the least relevant content is excluded. A second use of the Delphi technique is related to emerging occupations. When curriculum development is conducted for a new occupation that has few workers or teachers, the opportunity to come up with valid curriculum information by regular means is quite remote. As an alternative to the approaches mentioned earlier in this chapter, the Delphi technique enables experts to speculate individually and then reach consensus collectively regarding the content necessary to prepare workers, even in areas where no workers exist at the present time.

Basically, the Delphi technique consists of a series of interrogations of samples of individuals (experts) by means of mailed questionnaires. The focus is on some curricular content area in which each individual is knowledgeable. Since respondents never meet face to face, the group is not biased by one individual's outlook. Anonymity enables each respondent to be more thoughtful and creative. Several rounds of questionnaires are typically used. The initial questionnaire requests a list of content that each participant feels should be included in the curriculum. This is followed by a second round, with each participant receiving a list of all opinions. The listing is reviewed and then each item is rated in terms of its importance to the curriculum. During the third round, participants are asked to review consensus ratings of items and, based upon the results, possibly revise their opinions. The fourth round provides participants with a chance to review updated consensus ratings and make final revisions (if any) to their individual ratings.

While the Delphi technique can provide much meaningful information, the entire process consumes a considerable amount of time and relies on participants who have much stamina. However, even with its obvious disadvantages, the Delphi technique may be the only route to take for certain curricular areas. It is best thought of as a first step in the content determination process, one that may perhaps be used because no other data source exists.

SUMMARY

This chapter has focused directly on the business of determining curriculum content. Efforts made to determine content must take into account the various factors that can affect the entire process. The actual time and dollars available to determine what content should be included in a curriculum constitute potential constraints for the developer. Likewise, internal and external pressures and concerns must be examined to determine which types of content are valid and justifiable. Requirements already established at federal, state, and local levels must be identified and taken into account as the curriculum is being established. The level at which content is provided needs to be examined in relation to the students served so that their needs may be fully met.

Other areas of concern to the curriculum developer include the educational setting, the occupational setting, and the various content determination strategies available. The unique aspects of an educational or occupational setting might result in choosing one strategy over another. Strategies range from the more subjective philosophical basis and introspection to the more objective function approach and task analysis. The critical incident technique has greatest utility in the values and attitudes area, while the Delphi technique is most useful for determining content in emerging occupational areas. Since the curriculum developer may not be able to gather complete information when one strategy is used, several strategies should be utilized to identify meaningful content. This will enable the developer to better meet all student needs.

REFERENCES

Adams, R. E. *DACUM Approach to Curriculum, Learning and Evaluation in Occupational Training.* Yarmouth, Nova Scotia: Department of Regional Economic Expansion, 1975.

Allen, David. "Instruction," in Melvin L. Barlow, ed., *The Philosophy for Quality Vocational Education Programs.* Washington, D.C.: American Vocational Association, 1974.

Berkey, Arthur L. *The Importance of Activities Performed and Functions of Farm Machinery Industry as a Basis for Training Programs,* Unpublished doctoral dissertation. East Lansing: Michigan State University, 1967.

Berkey, Arthur L.; Drake, William F.; and Legacy, James W. *A Model for Task Analysis in Agribusiness.* Ithaca, N.Y.: Cornell University, 1972.

Clark, Raymond M. *Vocational Competencies Needed for Employment in the Feed Industry,* Educational Research Service No. 22. East Lansing: Michigan State University, 1965.

Clark, Raymond M., and Meaders, O. Donald. *Function Approach to Identifying Curricular Content Appropriate to Vocational-Technical Programs.* East Lansing: Michigan State University, Department of Secondary Education and Curriculum, 1968.

Finch, Curtis R., and Sheppard, N. Alan. "Career Education Is Not Vocational Education," *Journal of Career Education* 2, No. 1 (Summer, 1975), pp. 37–46.

Flanagan, John C. "The Critical Incident Technique," *Psychological Bulletin* 51, No. 4 (July, 1954), pp. 327–358.

Fryklund, Verne C. *Occupational Analysis Techniques and Procedures.* New York: Bruce Publishing Company, 1970.

Gleason, William. *Functions of Industry Approach to Curriculum for Vocational Education,* unpublished doctoral dissertation. East Lansing: Michigan State University, 1967.

Kirchner, Wayne K., and Dunnette, Marvin D. "Identifying the Critical Factors in Successful Salesmanship," *Personnel* **34**, No. 2 (March-April, 1957), pp. 54–59.

Lee, Connie W. *Third Progress and Information Report of the Vocational-Technical Education Consortium of States.* Atlanta: Southern Association of Colleges and Schools, July, 1976.

Mager, Robert F., and Beach, Kenneth M., Jr. *Developing Vocational Instruction.* Belmont, Calif.: Fearon Publishers, 1967.

Melching, William H., and Borcher, Sidney D. *Procedures for Constructing and Using Task Inventories.* Columbus: Center for Vocational and Technical Education, Ohio State University, March, 1973.

Miller, Robert. "Organization of Vocational Education in the Educational Systems," in Melvin L. Barlow, ed., *The Philosophy for Quality Vocational Education Programs.* Washington, D.C.: American Vocational Association, 1974.

Morsh, Joseph E., and Archer, Wayne B. *Procedural Guide for Conducting Occupational Surveys in the United States Air Force.* Lackland Air Force Base, Texas: Personnel Research Laboratory, September, 1967.

Moss, Jerome, and Smith, Brandon B. "Some Steps in the Curriculum Development Process," in Gordon Law, ed., *Contemporary Concepts in Vocational Education.* Washington, D.C.: American Vocational Association, 1971.

National Education Association. "Small-Sample Technique," *National Education Association Research Bulletin* **38**, No. 4 (December, 1960), pp. 99-104.

Olivo, C. Thomas. "Philosophical Bases for Curriculum Development," in Gordon Law, ed., *Contemporary Concepts in Vocational Education.* Washington, D.C.: American Vocational Association, 1971.

Sudman, Seymour. *Applied Sampling.* New York: Academic Press, 1976.

United States Department of Labor. *Dictionary of Occupational Titles,* 3rd Ed. Washington, D.C.: U.S. Government Printing Office, 1965.

Weaver, W. T. "The Delphi Forecasting Method," *Phi Delta Kappan* **52** (January, 1971), pp. 267–272.

6

Making Curriculum Content Decisions

Introduction

Decision making is perhaps one of the highest level skills that a person can develop. It is a skill that permeates our society and is recognized as a part of virtually all professional, vocational, and technical occupations. Naturally, decision making is an integral part of the curriculum development process. Decisions must be made regarding numerous areas including whether or not to offer a curriculum, how curriculum content may be identified, and what the substance of a curriculum should be. Chapter 2 provided an overview of the decision-making process and showed how decision making applies to curriculum planning. This chapter applies the process in an equally important area: curriculum content. Initial consideration is given to the purpose and scope of the content decision-making process. This is followed by a description of how constraints are identified that may affect content decisions. Next are described the ways that potential content may be related to identified constraints. Finally, the curriculum framework is described and the ways it may be utilized are detailed. In sum, this chapter serves to emphasize further the role of decision making in the curriculum development process and to point out how it may be applied to curriculum content decisions.

The content decision-making process

Curriculum content decisions can be made as often as there is a need to determine what the curriculum's actual parameters will be. However, decisions of this type must not be taken lightly. When content is simply thrown together and arranged into a sketchy syllabus, the result is creation of problems rather than an effective curriculum. Basically, sound content decisions serve to bridge the gap between the identification of potential content (as detailed in Chapter 5) and the development of objectives (as explained in Chapter 7). Obviously, it is impossible to teach all the content that is identified as part of a task analysis or similar content determination strategy. The curriculum developer must, therefore, make some key determinations regarding which content is more beneficial to students and which content is less beneficial.

The content decision-making process may be expressed according to the following formula:

Potential Curriculum Content — Constraints = Usable Curriculum Content

Potential curriculum content consists of that which has been determined potentially relevant to students through one or more of the strategies described in Chapter 5. *Constraints,* on the other hand, are those factors which might place serious limitations on the teaching of certain content. *Usable content* is that which best contributes to the students' welfare and (given existing constraints) can be taught. While this formula may tend to oversimplify the process, it reflects how the curriculum developer can delineate content to the point where it is most meaningful and manageable for use in designing instruction.

Identifying constraints related to curriculum content

In order that constraints may be clarified, it is necessary to focus on limitations present in the teaching/learning process. These logically take the form of statements related to either given or anticipated curricular outcomes. For example, it might be that there are only twelve months available to prepare certain student groups for employment. Twelve months then becomes one constraint that serves as a focal point when decisions are made regarding curriculum content. If, however, two years preparation time were available, time would still be a constraint but one of lesser importance, since greater flexibility is available in the selection of content. While constraints may be associated with virtually every aspect of the curriculum, it is perhaps more productive to give consideration to four areas. These are the student, the teachers and support staff, the curricular arrangement, and the employment setting. The four areas tend to overlap each other; however, they will be discussed individually in the pages that follow.

The student

Vocational and technical students represent a major force in the shaping of curriculum content. Student characteristics can have great impact on curriculum content and should, therefore, receive close scrutiny as the content selection process takes place (Resnick, 1975). Initial consideration must be given to students' entering characteristics. What are the students' basic and applied skills? Are they interested and motivated? What are their maturity levels? These and other related questions are of particular relevance, since they greatly affect the amount and type of content that can actually be covered. While recognizing that it is not always beneficial to use group data when a curriculum focuses on meeting the needs of individual students, the curriculum developer may need to obtain some group information during the decision-making process. Assume that content is being determined for a printing program. Data from prospective students indicate that 50 percent read at or above the sixth grade level while the remainder read below this level. If it has been established that printing content mastery requires a sixth grade reading level or better, a number of content implications can be raised regarding the students who are poorer readers. These might include remedial reading instruction, tutorial help, or making provision for a printing instructor who is also skilled in teaching reading. All of the above have implications for the amount of printing content selected, since time would need to be spent providing some students with basic reading instruction.

Teachers and support staff

Several relevant questions may be posed about teachers and support staff as potential constraints in the content decision-making process. These include: What content are the vocational teachers qualified to teach? Are a sufficient number of teachers available to provide needed course work in support areas (e.g., mathematics, science, English)? Are qualified personnel available to provide adequate support services such as guidance, placement, and counseling? Since other questions will certainly come to mind, it is crucial to consider each in light of how teachers and support staff may ultimately affect the curriculum content. If, for example, a vocational teacher has sole responsibility for student placement as a part of his or her regular teaching load, content coverage may suffer while placement activities are being carried out. On the other hand, when placement is a responsibility shared by the teacher and the placement staff, more time is available to the teacher for dealing with important curriculum content areas.

The curricular arrangement

This category of constraints represents perhaps the broadest range of concerns about curriculum content decisions. It goes beyond the basic scope of vocational and technical education content and into the total set of requirements and standards associated with a curriculum. Questions posed by the curriculum developer in relation to this area would include (but not necessarily be limited to): What time is or can be made available to teach the students? What basic content coverage, if any, is required for certification or licensure of graduates?

Which general education content coverage is required? What dollars are available for equipment, resources, and supplies in support of certain content? Time becomes a basic limiting factor in relation to the amount of content that can be included in a curriculum and serves to act as a framework for the content that can be chosen. Required content coverage likewise limits the developer in his or her selection of content. It may be found in some instances that very little latitude is given to local personnel in content selection. This is particularly true in the health occupations areas, where state requirements tend to dictate what should be included in a curriculum.

While dollars have been a general concern during the curriculum-planning process, it is sometimes easier to pinpoint what costs are associated with specific content after the potential content is identified. If, for example, certain data-processing content must be supported by a computer and related hardware, this situation may well affect whether or not the content is included in a particular curriculum. It is important to examine each item of potential content and determine whether or not dollars are available to deal with the area in a professional manner. Content that is "too expensive" to teach may well suffer at this juncture; however, a decision needs to be made regarding which content is most important in relation to available dollars. Decisions in this area are often tentative and subject to reexamination after a year or so when hard cost data are available.

The employment setting

A final set of constraints may be drawn from the work environment that graduates are entering. In this regard, several important questions may be raised, which include: What minimum employability level is expected of graduates? What occupational areas will the graduates be prepared for? Which experiences (if any) may be best obtained in the work setting? These three questions are essentially related to the transition from school to work. If content essential to meet entry level employment is not included, graduates will be at a tremendous disadvantage. Content with too narrow a focus can, likewise, adversely affect the opportunities available to graduates. Consideration must be given to content breadth but not at the expense of depth. This requires a great deal of insight and creativity on the part of the curriculum developer, since both breadth and depth are important; however, sometimes other constraints (e.g., available time) will not allow both to be dealt with adequately.

Examining content as it relates to constraints

Once various constraints have been identified, the curriculum developer is then in a position to examine each constraint as it impacts on the potential curriculum content. It should be noted that this is a highly subjective process and one that attempts to arrive at the best fit of content and constraints from more of a logic base than a data base. This means the developer must place considerable reliance on available information sources, logic, and intuition (Kenneke et al., 1973). An additional problem associated with content is the fact that constraints may cut across the various content elements. One constraint area such as state-mandated content coverage may have tremendous impact on a variety of content. Given the difficulty of relating constraints to content, it is often best to utilize a group of knowledgeable persons in the examination process. While this could be an advisory committee, a group of experienced teachers, or some combination thereof, it is useful to have a number of people review both content and constraints and give their personal ideas about congruence of the two. Input from persons such as these greatly aids the curriculum developer in making the most meaningful decisions.

Content versus constraints

Examining content in relation to constraints can be a very difficult proposition, especially when a great deal of potential content must be eliminated from the curriculum. However, given the alternative of selecting content for a meaningful curriculum or not establishing any curriculum at all, the process is most useful. It sometimes becomes a problem to point out exactly where one should begin looking for the congruence between content and constraints. Certain individuals may prefer to start with the employment setting, since it constitutes a basic focal point for content. Others may see the student as a key starting point, since students represent the fundamental input to any curriculum. Regardless of the constraints chosen to be examined first or last, it is essential to remember that each must be reviewed and considered in relation to all others.

In order to illustrate the examination process, assume that a curriculum developer wants to consider content in relation to constraints for a curriculum associated with supply technology (a fictitious area). Initially, the decision is made to look at content as it relates to the curricular arrangement. This is followed by examining the employment setting, the student, and lastly, the teacher and support staff. Scrutiny of potential constraints associated with the curricular arrangement reveals the following:

No certification or licensure of graduates is required.

Content must align with state requirements for a two-year Associate of Applied Science degree.

Total productive instructional time in supply technology may not exceed 500 hours.

Dollars are available to provide student transportation to school-owned work sites and to enable the teacher to coordinate students' cooperative work experiences with employers in the immediate area.

These items serve to indicate limitations a curricular arrangement can impose on content. Certainly the instructional time limitation has much impact on the amount of content that can be covered. The associate degree requirement has numerous implications for general education content coverage. This means the curriculum must include post-high school level content in areas such as English, mathematics, and science, all of which would be specified in state requirements. The availability of dollars for transportation and travel allows greater flexibility in content coverage outside a school's facilities. For example, opportunities to establish cooperative work experience arrangements and offer laboratory experiences away from the school give the instructional staff a great deal of latitude in the ways content may be delivered.

Moving into the employment area, the following are found to exist:

> Graduates may be employed as entry level workers in the occupational area.
>
> Different physical requirements exist with regard to employment in businesses and industries.
>
> Persons in the occupational area have the opportunitiy to advance to supervisory positions if they become qualified.

These three statements provide useful input for content decisions because they help to point out the direction the curriculum should take. Since it is noted that graduates may be employed as entry level workers, content coverage should prepare persons to attain at least this minimum level. Assuming that entry level skills were detailed when potential content was identified, the curriculum developer may use these skills as a basis for content selection. At this point, however, some conflicts may arise between content coverage needed and time available to teach the content. Problems related to content coverage are not easily resolved and, in most instances, end up in a compromise between what is needed and what can actually be done. The indication that physical requirements exist in different occupational settings has major implications. While it would be possible to prepare persons for a variety of occupations with businesses and industries, this must be considered in light of student characteristics. Variations in employment requirements might serve to limit the enrollment of certain groups (e.g., handicapped) if these requirements are not taken into account as content is selected. Thus the employment settings prepared for can seriously affect the types of students to be enrolled in a curriculum.

With regard to students involved in the curriculum, the following information was identified:

> Entering students' ages range from eighteen to forty-one years.
>
> All entering students are sincerely interested in the curriculum.
>
> 30 percent of the entering students have deficiencies in the mathematics area.
>
> 20 percent of the entering students have deficiencies in the reading area.

The variation in students' ages gives some indication of heterogeneity among learners. How content relates to this factor depends upon the time available and the resources that may be used to individualize instruction. If both time and resources are available, more content may be taught to this diverse group. Student interest and motivation do not become as much of a problem at the postsecondary level as they do at the secondary level. In this case, student interest is apparently good and the instructors can, therefore, focus on productive educational pursuits. When students are not motivated and lack interest, particularly because of a lack of maturity, instructors who are not creative may spend much time on nonproductive activities such as maintaining discipline and order. This can have a marked effect on the content that is covered, sometimes resulting in a large reduction in productive teaching time. In terms of students' basic skill deficiencies, a decision must be made about the extent to which remedial instruction will be provided. If this is an integral part of the curriculum, time must be taken away from other content areas. The result could be a curriculum that does not fully prepare students for employment. An alternative would be to have remedial instruction and demonstrated mastery of that instruction serve as a prerequisite to enrollment in the curriculum. This arrangement serves to maintain the curriculum's integrity and, at the same time, not restrict enrollment. The data reported about students' basic skills make it obvious that some remediation is required. A basic question that remains is how can this be taken care of without seriously reducing the amount of curriculum content.

Information regarding a final area, teachers and support staff, is as follows:

> Teachers are available who qualify to instruct in the range of possible content areas.
>
> Support personnel are not available to assist with placement of graduates.
>
> Ratio of students to guidance counselors is 500 to 1.

It is clear that instructor qualifications should align with content to be taught. Otherwise, it might be necessary to eliminate certain content that would be beneficial to students. While this example poses no particular problem, the curriculum developer should be aware of potential difficulties with teacher qualifications. Careful consideration should be given to instructor qualifications *before* individuals are hired rather than after they have taught for a year or so. Since it appears that teachers are to be responsible for the placement of graduates, time must be allocated to this activity. The time commitment to placement entails a corresponding reduction in content coverage. While it is recognized that instructors can be responsible for a number of supplementary activities, placement is too important to be a "catch-as-catch-can" responsibility. Whoever is designated to work in the placement area must have adequate time provided to do an acceptable job. This, of course, means that time may well be taken from teaching. Since implications could be made that guidance counselors have little time for each student, the teacher may, either formally or informally, assume some of this responsibility. While a teacher may often counsel his or her students, excessive amounts of time spent counseling may detract from curriculum content coverage. It is, therefore, important to determine how much support is actually provided by the teaching staff, since this area has direct impact on curriculum content.

Implications of content and constraints

The foregoing has served to point out ways in which various factors can affect the content included in a curriculum. While it would be impossible to spell out all the constraints related to content, the curriculum example has provided a point of reference for those making curriculum content decisions. In terms of implications for the curriculum developer, there are several items that may be of value. First, recognize that examining content in relation to constraints is an inexact process. Curriculum development has not advanced to the point where we can base content decisions solely on conclusive evidence. Thus the curriculum developer must use sound professional judgement based upon input from other qualified professionals.

A second implication concerns the aspects of certain locales. Each educational setting, whether a community college, high school, or manpower center, has its own unique characteristics. Corresponding with these characteristics are staff, students, facilities, administration, supervision, and a host of other factors that tend to make each setting somewhat different from others. While the constraints and examples discussed on these pages provide a framework for the determination of meaningful curriculum content, individual educational settings may be unique in the ways that content relates to constraints. The curriculum developer needs to be aware of this situation and should examine each curriculum as a set of offerings and experiences having unique qualities, content, and constraints.

A final implication has to do with the creativity of a curriculum developer. The adequacy of content coverage is often a function of one's creative efforts in arranging, modifying, and sequencing curriculum content. Much can be gained by applying creative talents to the task of establishing content. The creative curriculum developer does not always approach problems with traditional solutions. He or she keeps in mind that instruction need not take place within the confines of an educational institution. When applied to content decisions, creativity has the potential to build curricula that better meet student, teacher, and community needs.

The curriculum framework

Educators often express concern about the ways curriculum content and associated areas may be documented. This concern has evolved from a perceived gap between curriculum as defined in its broader sense and instruction as defined in its narrower sense. While the curriculum encompasses all those experiences provided under the direction or auspices of the school, it is apparent that documentation of content often does not extend beyond the course level. Of particular note is the course syllabus, which serves as a formalized course outline. This type of document does little more than provide students and visitors with some idea about content scope and sequence. While it is recognized that the syllabus is important to instruction, this sort of documentation covers but a small part of the total curriculum.

Another form of instructional communication is the course of study. As indicated by Pautler (1971), the course of study is "a comprehensive guideline, which, when properly constructed and followed, will aid the teacher and the students in meeting the specific objectives of the course." The importance of a comprehensive course of study cannot be underestimated. It is certainly useful for a teacher to have program or course units and plans delineated so that instruction may be conducted most efficiently. However, the vocational course of study typically fails to include any information about nonvocational content as well as numerous other items such as teacher and support staff capabilities. Thus while the course of study serves a most useful function from an individual vocational or technical teacher's vantage point, it does not clarify the total scope of the curriculum.

Vocational and technical curriculum guides represent an additional form of documentation and communication. The curriculum guide is typically developed by a committee or group at a state or regional level and is used by vocational and technical teachers in their particular instructional areas. Representative titles include Horticulture, Welding, Quantity Food Preparation, and Secretarial Science. Curriculum guides often serve as guidelines for instruction in vocational areas and provide the instructor with meaningful information about suggested content coverage including time allocations. These guides are particularly useful for beginning teachers who, unlike their seasoned counterparts, do not have the experience upon which to base content decisions. Since their applicability is quite general, curriculum guides may be utilized "only after they are adjusted to the specific teaching situation" (Silvius and Bohn, 1976). While development at a higher level ensures wider applicability of the guide, local constraints may sometimes negate the use of certain elements contained in it.

The foregoing concerns point to the need for a comprehensive curriculum document, *one that takes a host of factors into account at the local level and serves as a foundation for the total curriculum.* This document is termed the *curriculum framework.* The preparation of a curriculum framework document makes the course of study, curriculum guide, and syllabus of no less importance. It merely serves to complement and enhance each by providing an overall frame of reference for curriculum substance and structure.

Nature of the curriculum framework

While some may look at the development of a curriculum framework document as just some more busy work, it must be recognized that this is certainly not the case. Complaints have been leveled at vocational educators for many years regarding the lack of articulation with academic areas and most conventional curriculum documents have tended to perpetuate this separation. The curriculum framework document serves to involve a variety of teachers, since it considers the range of learning experiences encountered within the curriculum. Whether it be vocational, technical, mathematics, or science content, information is clearly documented for use by all persons associated with the curriculum. The document provides a much needed means of communication for all who are involved in the curriculum development process. This includes not only vocational and academic faculty but support personnel and administrators as well. Basic to the establishment of such a document is a recognition that professionals view and understand the role each person has in the total curriculum.

The curriculum framework serves to display meaningful curriculum experiences and activities as well as identified constraints. It is extremely important to clarify exactly what will be provided in the curriculum and the reasons why. Spelling out the content and constraints associated with a curriculum enables everyone to see just what limitations are imposed on the content. An additional benefit has to do with accountability. When content and constraints are detailed, it is easy to understand why certain areas are emphasized in a curriculum. Without this information, one may only speculate about the various reasons for certain content selections. This particular condition is frequently evident in curriculum guides and courses of study where content is present but the logic behind its selection is not included.

Additionally, the curriculum framework serves as a basis for developing specific objectives. Some persons may feel that the most logical approach to curriculum development consists of identifying objectives and then selecting content that aligns with them. While this strategy can work, it reflects content being built on conjecture rather than on a comprehensive data base. If objectives are to be most meaningful, they must flow from the identified content for a curriculum. This helps to ensure content coverage that is of greatest value to vocational and technical students (and ultimately, graduates).

Developing the framework

The establishment of a curriculum framework document is a simple and straightforward task. In reality, much of the work has already been accomplished if proper planning has been done. In order to illustrate the use of available information in preparing a framework, an example of a table of contents is provided in Figure 6–1. As may be noted by the various headings, much of the needed information would have been identified as determinations were made about the content to be included in the curriculum. Initially, the institution's philosophy and goals are stated. These serve to tie the curriculum to a broader perspective, that of the total institution. Next are documented the various items that have impact on curriculum content. These include the students served, instructional and support staff, the curricular arrangement, and the employment

---

FIGURE 6–1.   Table of contents from a curriculum framework document

---

I.	Philosophy and Goals of the Institution	1
II.	Students Served	2
III.	Instructional and Support Staff	4
IV.	Curricular Arrangement	6
V.	Employment Setting	10
VI.	Content Coverage	12
	A. Vocational and Technical	12
	B. General Education	17
	C. Cocurricular Activities	20

---

setting. It is important that each be detailed enough so any professional will understand the curricular focus. Content is then detailed to include vocational, technical, and general coverage. Information regarding cocurricular activities (e.g., student vocational organizations and athletics) is also provided, since large portions of time may be allocated to these areas. Tentative time allocations for content coverage may also be included in the framework; or, in the case of a competency-based, individualized curriculum, average estimated completion time can be used. Developing the curriculum framework document is essentially a process of bringing information together that has already been developed and ensuring that it is fully documented. While this process is going on, it is most beneficial to involve all those who will eventually use the curriculum. Included would be vocational and academic teachers, support personnel, administrators, and students. Widespread involvement assists in the identification of potential problems and enables a variety of persons to give their personal reactions to the document. This is most important, since the curriculum framework document serves as a basis for instructional planning activities.

SUMMARY

Making sound curriculum content decisions has been pointed out as an essential element of the curriculum development process. The content decision-making process involves an examination of potential content and constraints to determine what content will actually be used in the curriculum. Constraints associated with the curriculum appear in relation to four distinct areas: the student, the teachers and support staff, the curricular arrangement, and the employment setting. It must be recognized that these factors tend to limit the content that can logically be taught. Thus the curriculum developer must select the best content for a given educational setting. The curriculum framework document provides an overall structure for planning instruction. It is comprehensive in scope, including vocational, academic, and related content. Since this document serves as a basis for the development of specific curricular objectives, it is important that content be identified which is of greatest value to students.

REFERENCES

Kenneke, Larry J.; Nystrom, Dennis C.; and Stadt, Ronald W. *Planning and Organizing Career Curricula: Articulated Education.* Indianapolis: Howard W. Sams and Company, 1973.

Pautler, Albert J. *Teaching Shop and Laboratory Subjects.* Columbus: Charles E. Merrill Publishing Company, 1971.

Resnick, Lauren B. "The Science and Art of Curriculum Design," in Jon Schaffar-zick and David H. Hampson, eds., *Strategies for Curriculum Development.* Berkeley, Calif.: McCutchan Publishing Corporation, 1975.

Silvius, G. Harold, and Bohn, Ralph C. *Planning and Organizing Instruction.* Bloomington, Ill.: McKnight Publishing Company, 1976.

7

Setting Curriculum Goals and Objectives

Introduction

The establishment of sound goals and objectives represents one of the most crucial steps in curriculum development. Without quality objectives, a curriculum might wander from topic to topic and result in students being unprepared for employment. One can often find references in the literature to goals, general objectives, specific objectives, terminal objectives, enabling objectives, performance objectives, as well as others. Realistically, a clear understanding of each is needed if the curriculum developer intends to comprehend and deal with their basic similarities and differences.

This chapter deals with the different types of curricular outcomes as well as how goals and objectives may be prepared for use in vocational and technical education. Specific examples have been included to help clarify differences between goals and objectives and to better indicate how they may be prepared.

Curriculum outcomes

The development of meaningful outcomes for the curriculum can be one of the most frustrating and time-consuming tasks facing an educator. This is especially true if the individual preparing them is unfamiliar with the various types of goals and objectives. Before dealing directly with objectives, it must be realized that in vocational education outcomes are of prime importance. Outcomes can represent program graduates or the extent to which students demonstrate competence after specific curriculum content has been taught. Furthermore, curriculum developers must recognize that some outcomes are more measurable than others and, in fact, some may be unmeasurable.

Measurable outcomes

Measurable outcomes in vocational and technical education can take many forms; for example, a student identifying twenty carpentry tools, baking a cake according to the directions in the recipe, or completing a job application form. In reality, measurable outcomes represent those results which can be assessed with quantifiable data or in an objective manner.

Unmeasurable outcomes

The other extreme represents outcomes that tend to be unmeasurable. Examples of these outcomes might be that a student develops an appreciation of the value of work in society, develops the ability to use leisure time wisely, or forms an attitude conducive to working in a group setting. As can be seen, measuring student performance associated with these outcomes would be most difficult. This is not to say unmeasurable outcomes are undesirable in vocational education. The three examples just cited, as well as other similar types of outcomes, represent important aspects of vocational education.

Any vocational curriculum will have both measurable and unmeasurable outcomes, thus objectives that are developed should speak to both types. A basic rule to be followed by the developer is that a sufficient number of measurable outcomes be identified in order to assure student competence as measured by objective student performance measures in critical vocational or technical areas. This enables vocational programs to be evaluated more accurately in terms of graduates' competence and assists in making vocational education more accountable when the curriculum is being evaluated.

Types of goals and objectives

The establishment of sound, realistic goals and objectives requires the developer to be familiar with their similarities and differences. A discussion of goals and objectives follows with examples provided to help clarify the unique aspects of each.

Goals

Goals are broad (unmeasurable) aims or purposes of a total educational curriculum or even, in some cases, the broad outcomes expected within a specific program. The purpose of each goal is to give direction and provide a basis for the development of more detailed general and specific objectives. Since numerous goals have been developed at the national, state, and local levels, it is often quite easy to find statements that align closely with a particular school or curriculum.

A review of goal statements for a typical local school serves to illustrate how goals are usually stated. These goals tend to be broad and unmeasurable and attempt to reflect the philosophy of the community. Examples of goal statements for a local high school might include the following:

Students will:

Become competent in the fundamental academic skills;

Become qualified for further education and/or development;

Participate as responsible citizens;

Develop positive and realistic self-images;

Exhibit a responsibility for the enhancement of beauty in their daily lives;

Practice sound habits of personal health.

Broad goals are often established for specific curricular areas. As an example, the following selected goals might be appropriate for consumer and homemaking education:

The Consumer and Homemaking Education Department at Washington High School will:

Provide preparation for the vocation of homemaking for youth and adults of both sexes;

Contribute to homemaking abilities and the employability of youth and adults in the dual role of homemaker and wage earner;

Encourage interest in home economics-related occupations and home economics careers;

Develop competencies in intelligent consumer practices in the marketplace.

By closely scrutinizing these examples, one can visualize the difficulties that might arise if measurable outcomes were to be sought from these goals. Goals can and do serve a useful purpose in giving further direction for the development of specific objectives; however, they never serve as substitutes. Broad goals can also provide a basis for discussion in determining the direction that an educational program should be taking.

General objectives

General objectives are similar to goals in that they tend to be broad statements and are usually unmeasurable. The major difference seems to occur in the use of general objectives. General objectives are more apt to be used for a vocational or technical education course or to appear as general objectives in a specific course syllabus. In reality, goals and general objectives are sometimes interchanged to the point where a clear distinction between the two is impossible. Examples of general objectives might include:

> The general objectives for Accounting I at Coolidge Community College are to develop:
>
> Specific skills associated with entry level employment as an accountant;
>
> Relevant related knowledge associated with the accounting occupation;
>
> Appropriate human relations attitudes associated with the accounting occupation.

While these three general objectives may appear at first glance to focus on specific preparation for a certain occupation, it soon becomes evident that they defy measurement. Skills, knowledges, and attitudes have not been specified; thus a teacher would have difficulty determining when a student has fulfilled the objectives. Using these objectives to answer a question such as, "What will these students be able to do when you are through teaching them?" (Broadwell, 1969) can become extremely difficult and perhaps even embarrassing!

Specific objectives

Specific objectives—or performance objectives, as many prefer to call them—are precise, measurable statements of particular behaviors to be exhibited by a learner under specified conditions. The performance objective is different from a general objective in clarity and specificity in that the activity to be performed is described as well as the level of acceptable performance, and the condition under which the performance must take place (Mager, 1962).

For each general objective developed, at least one performance objective must be established to indicate precisely what is expected of the student. In fact, several specific or performance objectives usually need to be developed for each general objective in order to assure that students develop the competence associated with the general objective. Examples of specific objectives include:

> Given a 6' folding rule, a 2' length of 3/8" diameter copper tubing, holding device, hacksaw, and reamer, measure and cut 6" from a length of copper tubing. A tolerance of $\pm 1/8$" will be allowed for the cut piece. All burrs must be removed from cut ends.
>
> Given sample specimens of grass, the student will be able to identify the blade, sheath, collar, and ligule with 100-percent accuracy.

The establishment of performance objectives permits the student to know precisely what performance is expected and to what degree it must be demonstrated. Performance objectives give clearer direction for the teacher in the selection of technical information and curriculum materials. Furthermore, each performance objective serves as a contributor to the achievement of general objectives and ultimately to the fulfillment of curriculum goals.

Foundations of educational goal formation

Goal statements may be found at all levels of education. Virtually all of these statements tend to be quite broad and stated in unmeasurable terms. Before the development of a goal statement begins, one should become familiar with goals that have been already established at various educational levels and that may have a direct influence on the development process. The development of goals is certainly related to philosophy; however, further discussion will not be devoted to the impact of philosophy on educational goals and programs, since this topic was discussed in Chapter 5.

National goals for education

The preparation of national goals for education dates back to the early efforts in providing quality education for our youth. One of the first and most influential efforts dealing with goal development that still has much impact today consists of the *Seven Cardinal Principles* (The Reform of Secondary Education, 1973). These principles were:

> To secure a command of the fundamental processes;
>
> To develop good habits of citizenship;
>
> To maintain good health and habits of safety;
>
> To develop ideals for worthy home membership;
>
> To develop a sense of ethical character;
>
> To furnish a background for vocational efficiency;
>
> To develop socially desirable leisure-time activities.

Although these goals were developed to meet the needs of society in 1918, the substance of each can still be found today in many goal statements.

Several other major national efforts were conducted after 1918 to revise the original Seven Cardinal Principles. In 1938, four broad goals were outlined in the *Purposes of Education in American Democracy*. The White House Conference on Education in 1955 developed fourteen basic goals of education, and in 1961, the National Education Association stressed the common thread of education as the "ability to think."

A more recent effort to develop broad goals of education took place in 1973, when eighteen statements were developed by Phi Delta Kappa based upon a survey of randomly selected members (Phi Delta Kappa, 1973). These eighteen goals are presented here, since they have much relevance for anyone who is developing educational goals.

1. Develop skills in reading, writing, speaking, and listening.
   A. Develop ability to communicate ideas and feelings effectively.
   B. Develop skills in oral and written English.

2. Develop pride in work and a feeling of self-worth.
   A. Develop a feeling of student pride in his or her achievements and progress.
   B. Develop self-understanding and self-awareness.
   C. Develop the student's feeling of positive self-worth, security, and self-assurance.

3. Develop good character and self-respect.
   A. Develop moral responsibility and a sound ethical and moral behavior.
   B. Develop the student's capacity to discipline himself or herself to work, study, and play constructively.
   C. Develop a moral and ethical sense of values, goals, and processes of free society.
   D. Develop standards of personal character and ideas.

4. Develop a desire for learning now and in the future.
   A. Develop intellectual curiosity and eagerness for lifelong learning.
   B. Develop a positive attitude toward learning.
   C. Develop a positive attitude toward continuing independent education.

5. Learn to respect and get along with people with whom we work and live.
   A. Develop appreciation and respect for the worth and dignity of individuals.
   B. Develop respect for individual worth and understanding of minority opinions and acceptance of majority decisions.
   C. Develop a cooperative attitude toward living and working with others.

6. Learn how to examine and use information.
   A. Develop ability to examine constructively and creatively.
   B. Develop ability to use scientific methods.
   C. Develop reasoning abilities.
   D. Develop skills to think and proceed logically.

7. Gain a general education.
   A. Develop background and skills in the use of numbers, natural sciences, mathematics, and social sciences.
   B. Develop a fund of information and concepts.
   C. Develop special interests and abilities.

8. Learn how to be a good citizen.
   A. Develop an awareness of civic rights and responsibilities.
   B. Develop attitudes for productive citizenship in a democracy.
   C. Develop an attitude of respect for personal and public property.
   D. Develop an understanding of the obligations and responsibilities of citizenship.

9. Learn about and try to understand the changes that take place in the world.
   A. Develop ability to adjust to the changing demands of society.
   B. Develop an awareness and the ability to adjust to a changing world and its problems.
   C. Develop understanding of the past, identity with the present, and ability to meet the future.

10. Understand and practice democratic ideas and ideals.
    A. Develop loyalty to American democratic ideals.
    B. Develop patriotism and loyalty to ideas of democracy.
    C. Develop knowledge and appreciation of the rights and privileges in our democracy.
    D. Develop an understanding of our American heritage.

11. Learn how to respect and get along with people who think, dress, and act differently.
    A. Develop an appreciation for and an understanding of other people and other cultures.
    B. Develop an understanding of political, economic, and social patterns of the rest of the world.
    C. Develop awareness of the interdependence of races, creeds, nations, and cultures.
    D. Develop an awareness of the processes of group relationships.

12. Understand and practice the skills of family living.
    A. Develop understanding and appreciation of the principles of living in the family group.
    B. Develop attitudes leading to acceptance of responsibilities as family members.
    C. Develop an awareness of future family responsibilities and achievement of skills in preparing to accept them.

13. Gain information needed to make job selections.
    A. Promote self-understanding and self-direction in relation to students' occupational interests.
    B. Develop the ability to use information and counseling services related to the selection of a job.
    C. Develop a knowledge of specific information about a particular vocation.

14. Learn how to be a good manager of money, property, and resources.
    A. Develop an understanding of economic principles and responsibilities.
    B. Develop ability and understanding in personal buying, selling, and investment.

C. Develop skills in management of natural and human resources and man's environment.

15. Practice and understand the ideas of health and safety.
A. Establish an effective individual physical fitness program.
B. Develop an understanding of good physical health and well-being.
C. Establish sound personal health habits and information.
D. Develop a concern for public health and safety.

16. Develop skills to enter a specific field of work.
A. Develop abilities and skills needed for immediate employment.
B. Develop an awareness of opportunities and requirements related to a specific field of work.
C. Develop an appreciation of good workmanship.

17. Learn how to use leisure time.
A. Develop ability to use leisure time productively.
B. Develop a positive attitude toward participation in a range of leisure-time activities—physical, intellectual, and creative.
C. Develop appreciation and interests that will lead to wise and enjoyable use of leisure time.

18. Appreciate culture and beauty in the world.
A. Develop abilities for effective expression of ideas and cultural appreciation (fine arts).
B. Cultivate appreciation for beauty in various forms.
C. Develop creative self-expression through various media (art, music, writing, etc.).
D. Develop special talents in music, art, literature, and foreign languages.*

National goals for vocational education

Nationwide efforts to formulate broad goals for all of vocational education were not fully evident until the early 1960s. However, individual vocational service areas did develop goal statements prior to 1960, many of which provided direction for local programs. The main impetus to develop goals for vocational education was the Panel of Consultants on Vocational Education appointed by President John F. Kennedy in 1961. Emerging from the efforts of the Panel were five general recommendations; these have served as a basis for the development of goals at the national, state, and local level. The recommendations were that in a changing world of work, vocational education must:

> Offer training opportunities to the twenty million noncollege graduates
> who would enter the labor market in the 1960s;

---

*Reprinted with permission of *Phi Delta Kappan* (September, 1973), pp. 31–32, and Harold Spears, author.

Provide training or retraining for the millions of workers whose skills and technical knowledge must be updated as well as those whose jobs will disappear due to increasing efficiency, automation, or economic change;

Meet the critical need for highly skilled craftsmen and technicians through education during and after the high school years;

Expand the vocational and technical programs consistent with employment possibilities and national economic needs;

Make educational opportunities equally available to all regardless of race, sex, scholastic aptitude, or place of residence (*Education for a Changing World of Work*, 1963).

These recommendations were instrumental in the wording of the Vocational Education Act of 1963, which focused upon all vocational education service areas in a changing world of work. Thus the primary goal of vocational education as reflected in these recommendations is to prepare learners for entry into and advancement in their chosen careers.

Since the Vocational Education Act of 1963 was initiated, each of the vocational service areas has updated its national goals for the purpose of bringing these goals in line with the new emphasis on the world of work, and eventually to stimulate states and localities in the development of new goals and objectives. Representative of the efforts put forth by various vocational service areas, was a committee convened in 1966 by the Agricultural Division of the American Vocational Association for the purpose of formulating objectives relevant to the agricultural needs of society. While these were developed and referred to as objectives, they represent goal statements for all agricultural education programs. The statements recommended by this committee included abilities required to develop:

Agricultural competencies needed by individuals engaged in or preparing to engage in agricultural production;

Agricultural competencies needed by individuals engaged in or preparing to engage in agricultural occupations other than farming;

An understanding of and preparation for career opportunities in agriculture and the preparation needed to enter and progress in agricultural occupations;

The ability to secure satisfactory placement and to advance in an agricultural occupation through a program of continuing education;

Those abilities in human relations that are essential in agricultural occupations;

The abilities needed to exercise and follow effective leadership in fulfilling occupational, social, and civic responsibilities (*Objectives for Vocational and Technical Education in Agriculture*, 1965).

Goals for vocational education at the state level

Consistent with the new thrust put forth by vocational education at the national level in relation to the world of work, many states have redefined their goal statements. While goals from many different states could have been used as examples, the goal statements for Virginia have been included here. Virginia, in stating its broad goals, first developed what it called a "mission statement." To enable the reader to form an idea of a statement of goals for vocational education at the state level, the following goals were taken from the *Virginia State Plan for Vocational Education, 1976–77* (1976):

MISSION STATEMENT

> The mission of the Division of Vocational Education, is through joint effort with local school divisions and other agencies, to seek to ensure that the vocational education needs of all youths and adults are met and that through the school foods program good eating habits are developed.

GOALS

Consistent with their abilities, interests, and educational needs:

1. Youths and adults will acquire the skills and knowledge needed for initial and continuing employment or self-employment in occupations of their choice and for which there are employment opportunities.

2. Youths and adults will acquire the competencies needed as consumers of goods and services, for home and family living, and for personal use.

3. Youths and adults will become aware of employment, self-employment opportunities, and requirements for use in making career choices and in determining their educational programs.

4. Youths and adults will exhibit pride in work well done; confidence in ability to perform in the world of work; and will develop leadership abilities, responsible citizenship, and a realistic self-image in relation to work in their chosen vocation.

5. Youths and adults will benefit from programs improved and expanded through ancillary activities.

Goals for vocational education at the local level

Evans (1971) has identified three basic areas that any public school vocational education curriculum should address. Each of these can be related directly to the development of goal statements. The areas include meeting the manpower needs of society, increasing the options available to each student, and serving as a motivation force to enhance all types of learning.* Goals for vocational education at the local level may be stated separately or they may be included in the broad goal statements for all of education. Broad goals such as those which follow are not uncommon for public education at the local level.

> The primary goals of public education in Knox County are twofold: to help pupils realize their greatest personal potential for happiness and success, and to educate them in order that they may become worthwhile citizens of the home, school, and community.

> The faculty of Butler Community College believe that the basic mission of education is to provide all persons, regardless of economic status or locality, the opportunity to develop to the highest capacity of their own ability, and thus strengthen our system of self-government and freedom as a people.

Other schools may choose to list several goals in statement form and thus end up with five, ten, or even more separate goals.

For the most part, goals for vocational education at the local level should be closely aligned with goals at the state level. However, an exact duplication of state goals is not recommended, since each school and community should develop goals consistent with its unique local needs. For example, goals for vocational and technical education at Butler Community College that were referred to earlier might include the following points:

> Vocational and technical education at Butler Community College strives to:

> Provide vocational and technical education of excellence that relates to the specific needs and interests of the students and the community;

> Develop the marketable skills of students who do not plan to continue their formal education after they have left the community college;

> Encourage each student to be a worthy citizen;

> Develop among students a spirit of tolerance and understanding through supervised work experience so that all students may become active participants in a democratic society;

> Cultivate an atmosphere in which students can develop self-discipline, intellectual curiosity, and moral worth.

This entire discussion of goals from the national level to the local level has been designed to provide a foundation from which goals may be developed.

---

*From *Foundations of Vocational Education* by Rupert N. Evans (Columbus, Ohio: Charles E. Merrill Publishing Co., 1971), p. 2.

A broad review and understanding of goals already developed at various levels and for a particular curriculum should assist in the development of more relevant and realistic goals.

Preparing goals

Although it has been indicated that their preparation can be frustrating, the actual development of goals is relatively easy. The frustrating aspect of goal preparation occurs when a group of individuals attempts to reach agreement that a set of goals reflects the true purposes of the organization. The development of broad goals for a vocational education curriculum must take three factors into consideration. These include ensuring that 1) individuals who will be affected by the goals are involved in their development, 2) the goals being developed are consistent with goals established at other educational levels, and 3) careful consideration is given to each goal developed. This is important, since each goal must be supported by relevant objectives. Each of these factors will be discussed in the sections that follow.

Individual involvement

The involvement of various individuals in the development of goal statements has been emphasized and stressed in vocational education for many years. Vocational education curricula must be designed for students and it is philosophically sound that these persons assume active roles in their education. This implies that regardless of the level for which goals are being developed—students, parents, educators, citizens, and others—the people concerned should be involved as the goals are being established. This involvement can occur via advisory councils, review by concerned individuals, or by other appropriate means. Persons are more apt to accept and use established goals if they have actively participated in the preparation of them.

Consistency of curriculum goals with other goals

Goals that are established at the state, local, or vocational service area level should be consistent with those goals established at the national level. Specifically, any set of goals in vocational education should speak to the preparation of individuals for entry level employment and their preparation for full participation in a democratic society. Furthermore, goals at the vocational service area level in a local school should align with those goals developed for the total vocational education program at the local level, the local goals for education, the goals at the state level, and so forth. Goal formation throughout our educational system has been illustrated in Figure 7–1 to display graphically the ways that goals relate to each other.

As indicated in Figure 7–1, the influence of goal formation tends to move from upper left to lower right. For example, national goals for education influence the state level goals for education, which in turn influence local goals for education. National goals for education likewise influence national goals for vocational education and ultimately local goals for vocational education service areas. While the influence of goal formation moves from the national to the local level, a reverse influence may also occur. Persons who establish goals at the local level for vocational service areas may use these goals to influence the way state goals for vocational education service areas are expressed and, ultimately, national goals for education may be affected. There are a variety of factors that tend to influence goal formation, regardless of the level for which goals are being developed. Thus the developer must be aware of goals that have already been established at other levels and determine how they can give direction to goal formation at the local level.

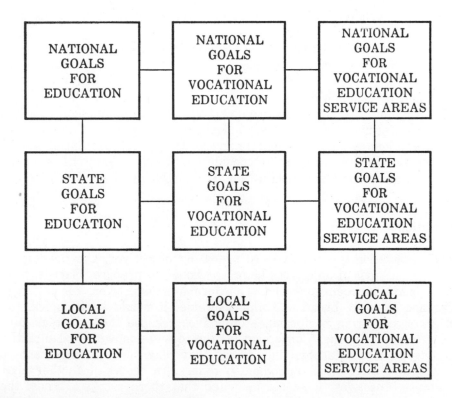

FIGURE 7–1. Structure of goal formation

Goals and objectives

While development of objectives typically follows the establishment of goals, it is most useful to give some thought to possible related objectives for each goal statement as it is being devised. Since each objective developed should correlate with a goal statement and each goal statement should relate to one or more performance objectives, the developer may find it beneficial to consider which objectives might be classified with certain goals. If this is carried out it should make the accomplishment of broadly stated goals a much easier task, since related objectives will help define what these goals actually are.

Preparing objectives

It is widely acknowledged that objectives serve as facilitators of a sound curriculum and that, without them, instruction may be irrelevant and ineffective. However, once the question is raised about how generally or specifically an objective should be stated, controversy seems close behind. Teachers, administrators, and even students often cannot agree on what constitutes a "good" objective.

As was mentioned earlier, some curriculum outcomes may be unmeasurable while others are readily measurable. Even though the difficulty of preparing meaningful objectives is fully recognized, it is firmly believed that every effort should be made to develop relevant, measurable objectives for key areas in the curriculum. If key measurable objectives are not developed, it will be impossible to determine when students have attained whatever they are supposed to attain or even to measure their progress. In the preparation of measurable objectives, several factors must be considered. These include the identification, selection, classification, and specification of objectives (Kibler et al., 1974).

Identification

When consideration is first given to preparing objectives, the developer must identify which kinds of objectives he or she hopes to prepare. Earlier, a distinction was made between general and performance objectives. Since general objectives are typically broad and unmeasurable, it would seem logical to focus attention on preparing performance objectives because they most closely align with the learner's needs. Consequently, this discussion will deal directly with developing performance objectives, since they play such an important role in communicating curriculum outcomes to others. In terms of further clarifying performance objectives, it should be noted that there are two types: the terminal objective and the enabling objective. These two types are both used in the curriculum, with each having a distinct purpose.

Terminal objective.   The terminal objective represents performance in the worker role or a close approximation of that role. It focuses on the way a student should perform when in the intended work situation. The terminal objective should, therefore, be valued in and of itself and be stated at the level required for meaningful use in life (Tyler, 1964). For example, a terminal objective might specify that the student close a sale. In order for this to be classified as a terminal objective, performance must take into account that an actual sale has been closed with a customer in a sales setting. A terminal objective that focuses on straightening a damaged fender should specify that a customer's car is repaired and that repair time is within the limits specified in the manufacturer's flat rate manual. When it is not feasible to assess performance in an actual employment setting, every effort should be made to simulate this condition as closely as possible. Appropriate terminal objectives that focus on key aspects of the occupation can often be developed and used in the school laboratory or, in certain cases, within the classroom. This allows the teacher to utilize realistic objectives even when work stations or settings outside the school are not readily available.

Enabling objective.   The enabling objective focuses on what the student must learn if he or she is to attain the terminal objective. The enabling objective serves to "bridge the gap between where the student is at the beginning of instruction and where he (or she) should be upon completion of instruction" (Ammerman and Melching, 1966). It may focus on basic factual knowledge, awareness, fundamental skills, or attitudes. Basic to any enabling objective is the contribution it makes to achieving one or more terminal objectives. If this supportive relationship does not exist, one may question the value of having the enabling objective in the first place. As an example of how enabling objectives might relate, let us consider a terminal objective that focuses on completing a successful job interview. Enabling objectives that might conceivably contribute to this terminal objective include exhibiting proper dress and grooming, understanding questions that should and should not be asked, and demonstrating skill in answering questions posed by prospective employers.

Selection

Once the appropriate types of objectives have been identified, it is necessary to select those which will actually be used in the curriculum. During the selection process, a number of relevant factors must be considered. These include the content, the students, and the available resources.

Content.   At this point in the curriculum development process, it must be assumed that relevant content has already been identified. Chapter 5 has pointed out the ways that curriculum content may be identified, while Chapter 6 has focused on making content decisions. The next logical step in this process is selecting and developing those objectives which align with the chosen content.

By using meaningful content as a basis for establishing objectives, the curriculum developer may be assured that each terminal objective will focus on an important aspect of the occupation. Using relevant content as a base for developing enabling objectives is of equal importance. Enabling objectives should be selected that are logically related to performance in the worker role. While there is nothing wrong with developing objectives that focus on areas such as knowledge, understanding, and appreciation, it is important for the developer to ensure that these objectives contribute to the achievement of terminal objectives, and ultimately, to meaningful performance in the world of work.

Students.   While a close examination of students' concerns may have already been accomplished as curriculum content decisions are being made, it is important that consideration be given to the ways objectives can be aligned with students' needs. For example, enabling objectives in a power sewing machine operator program might well be different for handicapped students than they would be for nonhandicapped students. In this case, the difference in objectives is a function of identified disabilities that do not allow the student to progress through a program in the same manner. While the end may remain the same, the means to this end varies in relation to student needs. The selection of appropriate objectives is not limited to handicapped students. Similar concerns may exist with disadvantaged and adult learners. Regardless of the student group to be served, the curriculum developer has an obligation to identify those objectives which will enable each student to achieve his or her optimum potential.

Resources.   Resources have likewise been discussed in the context of curriculum content decisions. While basic resources may be available to operate the curriculum, specific resources needed to aid students in achieving certain objectives may not be on hand. It might be that while a great deal of standard equipment is available for students enrolled in an appliance repair program, this equipment is not appropriate to assist them with an enabling objective focusing on troubleshooting strategy development. In this case, a need exists for different equipment or some sort of equipment simulator. If resources cannot be made available, consideration must then be given to selecting different objectives for the curriculum.

Classification

As objectives are being prepared, it is most beneficial to classify them according to their basic behavior. Classifying objectives is necessary in order "1) to avoid concentrating on one or two categories to the exclusion of others, 2) to make sure that instruction is provided for prerequisite objectives before attempting to teach more complex ones, and 3) to assure that appropriate instruments are employed to evaluate desired outcomes" (Kibler et al., 1974). Numerous classification schemes have evolved over the last two decades, each of which has attempted to assist educators in organizing objectives logically and systematically. Several of the more useful classification schemes are described briefly in the paragraphs that follow.

Classification of objectives in the cognitive domain is most thoroughly detailed in a document by Bloom (1956). A taxonomy is presented for objectives "which deal with the recall or recognition of knowledge and the development of intellectual abilities and skills" (Bloom, 1956). Six major classes included in the taxonomy consist of knowledge, comprehension, application, analysis, synthesis, and evaluation. These classes represent the hierarchical order of different cognitive objectives. Curriculum developers may find this classification scheme quite useful when cognitive objectives are being prepared, since levels of the taxonomy can correspond with the way objectives are sequenced and taught.

A companion publication focuses on classifying affective objectives (Krathwohl et al., 1964). The authors establish a taxonomy for objectives "which emphasize a feeling tone, an emotion or a degree of acceptance or rejection" (Krathwohl et al., 1964). The affective domain consists of five major classes: receiving (attending), responding, valuing, organizing, and characterizing. This taxonomy also distinguishes among levels, with "receiving" representing the lowest level and "characterizing" the highest. By using this taxonomy, affective objectives may be distinguished from each other and more effectively incorporated into the curriculum.

Classification of objectives in the psychomotor domain is dealt with most comprehensively in a report by Simpson (1966). Psychomotor objectives "emphasize some muscular or motor control, some manipulation of material or objects, or some act which requires a neuromuscular coordination" (Krathwohl et al., 1964). Given that specialized psychomotor skill development is an integral part of most vocational and technical education curricula, it is certainly important to examine objectives in this area. Simpson has tentatively established the following five classes of psychomotor objectives: perception, set, guided response, mechanism, and complex overt response. While it may be difficult to distinguish between some of these classes, the taxonomy provides a much needed framework for curriculum developers.

Interestingly enough, authors of the aforementioned classification schemes all note that questions may be raised about the rigid distinctions among the cognitive, affective, and psychomotor domains. Simpson comments that exploration needs to be made of broad objectives that encompass all three domains. This possibility has been explored and documented by Harmon (1969). Harmon's classification scheme, which has proved useful in establishing job training programs, includes three classes of objectives: verbal performance, physical performance, and attitudinal performance. As noted in Figure 7–2, subclasses under each class assist in distinguishing among the various types of performance objectives that may be used in vocational curricula. As Harmon indicates, some performance objectives deal with two or more numbers. The strength of Harmon's classification scheme lies in its flexibility. Since most terminal objectives in vocational education curricula deal with more than one class of behavior, it is often difficult (if not impossible) to consider a single class or domain. By using the classification shown in Figure 7–2, objectives may be arranged more logically and systematically, giving full consideration to the complexities of vocational and technical education. If it were desired to classify an objective dealing with finding a malfunction in a tractor engine, several numbers could be used to describe collectively what is entailed; e.g., 2.5 (perform an appropriate skilled action in a problem-solving situation) and 3.3 (respond with limited or controlled responses in given social situations). Physical performance would be directly related to locating the malfunction, while attitudinal performance would be associated with safe practices followed during the troubleshooting process. While only a brief introduction has been given to this as well as other classification schemes, there can be no doubt that each has the potential to assist in systematically classifying curriculum objectives.

Specification

In order for performance objectives to be useful, they must be clearly delineated. Just as it becomes quite difficult to hit a target when one does not know what the target is, the vocational educator must first have clear objectives if he or she expects to develop relevant instructional strategies. While numerous references are available that describe how performance objectives may be specified, they typically include the three elements espoused by Mager (1962). These elements are the activity, the conditions, and the standard.

Activity.   This element of the performance objective is used to indicate what the student should actually do. It is important to state exactly what activity is to be performed so that the student and the teacher will both be able to communicate clearly with each other. Since each performance objective is designed to be measurable, provision must be made to ensure that it is readily observable. It is not enough to state simply that the student should "understand the binary system." A clear indication should be made of what a student must do to show that he or she understands it. This might include the following: "Translates any decimal number into its binary equivalent" or, "Translates any binary number into its decimal equivalent" (Smith, 1964). In the specification of activities it is important to keep away from ambiguous terms such as know, understand, enjoy, appreciate, have faith in, and believe. Instead, terms such as list, construct, solve, write, recite, define, state, recall, select, measure, etc., should be utilized. Using more precise terms aids greatly in the communication process and in the meaningful measurement of objectives.

Conditions.   The second element of any performance objective is the conditions under which the performance is to be observed. Several kinds of conditions may be considered as the objective is being developed. These include the range of problems a student must learn to solve, tools and equipment that may be used, auxiliary materials such as books and manuals, environmental conditions, and special physical demands (Smith, 1964). If a student were asked to "formulate

---

FIGURE 7-2. A classification of performance objective behaviors*

1.0   Verbal Performance Objectives

    1.1   Recall a name; list a set of names; state a simple rule or fact.
    1.2   Explain an ordered set of actions (how to do a task).
    1.3   Respond to a series of statements or questions.
    1.4   Solve a specific symbolic problem.
    1.5   Solve a general type of symbolic problem.

2.0   Physical Performance Objectives

    2.1   Make physical identifications (point to things).
    2.2   Perform simple physical acts.
    2.3   Perform complex actions (with instructions or by rote).
    2.4   Perform physically skilled actions.
    2.5   Perform an appropriate skilled action in a problem-solving situation (determine what is to be done and then do it).
    2.6   Determine acceptable quality in physical products.

3.0   Attitudinal Performance Objectives

    3.1   State or list probable consequences of a given action.
    3.2   Evidence memory of correct social responses over an extended period of time.
    3.3   Respond with limited or controlled responses in given social situations.

    Some objectives do not fall into any of these categories. Some objectives involve two or more types of behaviors. For example, often personal/social objectives involve both attitudinal and physical behaviors. In these cases, it is easy to classify a performance objective using two numbers.

---

*From Paul Harmon, "A Classification of Performance Objective Behaviors in Job Training," *Educational Technology* (January, 1969), pp. 5–12.

---

and prepare a growing medium for a common plant," conditions might include provisions for soil, sand, peat moss, and artificial soil amendments such as perlite, calcified clay, and vermiculite. If it is important that a student be able to multiply numbers without any aids, this should be indicated; however, if a calculator may be used, this needs to be specified. Conditions are most useful in further clarifying student performance, especially when they serve to point out any differences in performance created by these conditions.

Standard.   A final element included in each performance objective is the standard of acceptable performance. This element serves to establish the student performance level or levels used in a curriculum. Standards can focus on several areas of performance such as speed, accuracy, frequency, or some form of production. For most complex skills in vocational education, multiple standards are specified. An objective dealing with keypunching computer data cards might use standards such as: "200 cards punched," "100-percent accuracy in punching," and "within a half-hour time limit." While any one of these standards would be important in itself, collectively they focus on realistic student performance.

In the establishment of standards, it is important to keep in mind that variations may exist across a particular curriculum. Standards at the first-year level may require less of the student than would those used in the final phases of instruction. Minimum standards in first-year typing might be, "Fifty words per minute with no more than three errors," whereas standards set for program graduates might be, "Seventy words per minute with no errors." While these standards are merely illustrative of the possibilities that might exist, it must be realized that work entry level performance is not usually required of students just beginning a program. It is essential to develop meaningful standards that align with student development within the curriculum and to ensure that standards associated with terminal performance correspond with what is expected in the worker role.

Sequencing objectives within the curriculum

While much has been discussed in the literature about the ways objectives may be sequenced within the curriculum, little empirical evidence exists to support one approach over any other. The lack of concrete information in this area makes one wonder if students learn in spite of sequencing rather than because of it. Even though problems exist in pinpointing a basis for correct sequencing of objectives, it is nonetheless important that this activity take place. Perhaps the best way to think of sequencing is as "common sense logical ordering" (Gagné and Briggs, 1974). When the time comes to arrange objectives in the best possible manner, it is the professional educator's responsibility to establish this sequence. This reliance on professional judgement tends to make sequencing more of an art than a science.

As the sequencing activity gets underway, it is important to consider factors that can impact on the sequencing as well as ways objectives might be sequenced. While sequencing is not an exact process, the curriculum developer must be aware of how objectives can be arranged if he or she expects to make reasonable decisions about sequencing.

Sequencing factors

Several factors can have impact on the way that objectives are sequenced. These are essentially practical considerations that relate to the entire curriculum; however, each must receive due consideration when the sequencing process takes place.

Logistics. Sequencing plans must be examined in light of logistical considerations within the school. Since sequencing is often contingent upon what may be available and when, the logistics of providing instruction become extremely important. Consideration needs to be given to facility needs, instructional staff availability, seasonal variations, equipment availability, and travel arrangements needed. These as well as other areas have to be closely examined, since they can affect an otherwise perfect sequencing of objectives.

Preparation for work. Regardless of the particular approach taken to sequencing, it is important to provide each student with some salable skills early in the curriculum. While this may be a narrow range of skills and only a small part of the curriculum, it is essential to do so, since some students may choose to drop out prior to completion of the course. By providing for development of some marketable skills toward the beginning of a curriculum, students who leave should be in a better position to compete on the job market.

Face validity. No matter how logically objectives may seem to be sequenced, the arrangement is only successful to the extent that it is accepted by teachers. In this situation, face validity encompasses the extent to which teachers accept sequencing as being logical and meaningful. While face validity may have nothing to do with the actual quality of sequencing, it is certainly of no less importance. The way objectives are sequenced must be accepted by instructional staff if they will eventually be expected to use this sequence in their respective classes.

Approaches to sequencing

Numerous approaches to sequencing objectives have been suggested in the literature. Some are drawn from a theoretical base while others are quite pragmatic, but most have not been validated to any great extent. Thus the curriculum developer is often faced with a trial (and hopefully no error) situation. The approaches that will be discussed are representative of those found to be useful by certain teachers in certain instructional settings. The ultimate test of any approach to sequencing lies in its acceptability and utility within the curriculum.

Sequencing may be viewed as being of at least five major types. As Posner and Strike (1976) reveal in their comprehensive paper on sequencing content, these include world-related, concept-related, inquiry-related, learning-related, and utilization-related. Within these five types of sequencing principles are a host of subtypes, each of which may be useful to persons who are responsible for sequencing objectives.

World-related. World-related sequencing can be utilized when the content structure has an empirical alignment with events, people, or things. This might include spatial relations, time relations, and physical attributes (Posner and Strike, 1976). Examples of world-related sequencing would be closest-to-farthest, top-to-bottom, north-to-south (space); cause and effect, earliest to most recent (time); size, age, shape, complexity (physical).

Concept-related. Concept-related sequencing may be most clearly associated with the content's logical structure. It includes four subtypes: class relations, propositional relations, sophistication level, and logical prerequisite (Posner and Strike, 1976). Examples of concept-related sequencing would be whole to part, part to whole (class); theory to application, rule to example (propositional); concrete to abstract (sophistication); sequence of operation, sequence of repair (logical prerequisite).

Inquiry-related. Inquiry-related sequencing deals with "the process of generating, discovering or verifying knowledge" (Posner and Strike, 1976). Two subtypes of inquiry-related sequencing are logic of inquiry and empirics of inquiry. Examples from this type of sequencing would be generalization from a number of instances (logic of inquiry) and providing empirical bases before dealing with practical problems (empirics of inquiry).

Learning-related. Learning-related sequencing draws heavily on research in the psychology of learning. It includes six subtypes: empirical prerequisite, familiarity, difficulty, interest, development, and internalization (Posner and Strike, 1976). Examples of learning-related sequencing would be: teaching a basic manipulative skill before teaching the application of that skill (empirical prerequisite), most familiar to most remote (familiarity), less difficult to most difficult (difficulty), more interesting to less interesting (interest), providing content that parallels student maturity (development), ordering content to reflect increasing degrees of internalization (internalization).

Utilization-related. A fifth type of sequencing deals with utilization of content in social, personal, and career contexts (Posner and Strike, 1976). It involves sequencing by procedure and anticipated frequency of utilization. Examples associated with utilization-related sequencing would be teaching steps of a task in the order they are performed (procedure) and teaching content based upon anticipated number of future encounters (utilization).

While these various approaches to utilization may seem rather abstract, it is because they have not been attached to specific vocational or technical content. This task is essentially one that the curriculum developer and his or her colleagues must perform. Unique content often dictates unique content arrangements and the five types of sequencing provide a sound base for sequencing efforts.

SUMMARY

This chapter has focused on goals and objectives as two essential elements in the vocational education curriculum. A strong distinction has been made between measurable and unmeasurable curricular outcomes and it was recognized that one cannot assess all outcomes associated with the curriculum. Goals that are broad, unmeasurable outcomes serve as a foundation for further curriculum building. Objectives represent the measurable outcomes in a curriculum. Their development requires detailed and systematic effort if objectives are to communicate exactly what is expected of the learner. Basic elements included in each performance objective include the activity to be performed, the conditions under which it should be performed, and the standards of acceptable performance. Finally, five types of sequencing arrangements have been presented, each of which has the potential to aid curriculum developers in arranging objectives to best meet students' needs.

REFERENCES

Ammerman, Harry L., and Melching, William H. *The Derivation, Analysis, and Classification of Instructional Objectives.* Alexandria, Va.: George Washington University Human Resources Research Office, 1966.

Bloom, Benjamin S., ed. *Taxonomy of Educational Objectives, Handbook I: Cognitive Domain.* New York: David McKay Company, Inc., 1956.

Broadwell, Martin M. "Questions Trainers Ask," *Training in Business and Industry* (October, 1969), p. 43.

Education for a Changing World of Work. Panel of Consultants on Vocational Education. Washington, D.C.: Office of Education, U.S. Department of Health, Education, and Welfare, 1963.

Evans, Rupert N. *Foundations of Vocational Education.* Columbus: Charles E. Merrill Publishing Company, 1971.

Gagné, Robert M., and Briggs, Leslie J. *Principles of Instructional Design.* New York: Holt, Rinehart and Winston, Inc., 1974.

Harmon, Paul. "A Classification of Performance Objective Behaviors in Job Training Programs," *Educational Technology* 9, No. 1 (January, 1969), pp. 5–12.

Kibler, Robert J.; Cegala, Donald J.; Miles, David T.; and Barker, Larry L. *Objectives for Instruction and Evaluation.* Boston: Allyn and Bacon, Inc., 1974.

Krathwohl, David R.; Bloom, Benjamin S.; and Masia, Bertram B. *Taxonomy of Educational Objectives, Handbook II: Affective Domain.* New York: David McKay Company, Inc., 1964.

Mager, Robert F. *Preparing Instructional Objectives.* Palo Alto, Calif.: Fearon Publishers, 1962.

Objectives for Vocational and Technical Education in Agriculture. Washington, D.C.: U.S. Government Printing Office, Bulletin 1966, No. 4, 1965.

Posner, George J., and Strike, Kenneth A. "A Categorization Scheme for Principles of Sequencing Content," *Review of Educational Research* **46**, No. 4 (Fall, 1976), pp. 665–690.

The Reform of Secondary Education. A Report to the Public and the Profession. New York: McGraw-Hill Book Company; The National Commission on the Reform of Secondary Education, 1973.

Simpson, Elizabeth J. *The Classification of Objectives, Psychomotor Domain.* Urbana, Ill.: University of Illinois, 1966.

Smith, Robert G., Jr. *The Development of Training Objectives.* Alexandria, Va.: George Washington University Human Resources Research Office, 1964.

Spears, Harold. "Kappans Ponder the Goals of Education," *Phi Delta Kappan* **LV**, No. 1 (September, 1973).

Tyler, Ralph W. "Some Persistent Questions on the Defining of Objectives," in C. M. Lindvall, ed., *Defining Educational Objectives.* Pittsburgh: University of Pittsburgh Press, 1964.

Implementing
the
Curriculum

The final section of this book builds directly upon planning and content determination. The preceding sections have dealt with planning the curriculum and establishing curriculum content; however, they have not focused directly on the ways a curriculum may be implemented in a school setting. This section provides meaningful information for curriculum developers responsible for the implementation of relevant vocational curricula.

Once curriculum content has been established, quality materials must be obtained to aid in planning and conducting meaningful student learning experiences. These materials may already be available from various sources. Thus the task of the vocational educator is to identify and select materials that can aid students in reaching predetermined objectives. Chapter 8 treats this area in a comprehensive manner and is designed to aid vocational educators in the selection of quality curriculum materials. If materials are not available and must be developed, Chapter 9 provides information that is useful in guiding the materials development process. Approaches to learning can vary widely and the implementation of curriculum content in the future will take on more of an individualized concept. Chapter 10 is designed to provide the curriculum developer with a broad understanding of individualized instruction through the development and use of competency-based packages.

Evaluation must be a continuous process in order to assure that the curriculum is relevant for today's needs and for future needs of society. Chapter 11 emphasizes the comprehensive nature of evaluation and provides direction for evaluating both programs and materials. While treated as a separate chapter, it must be recognized that evaluation is an integral part of curriculum development, all the way from planning through content determination and implementation.

Identifying and Selecting Curriculum Materials

Introduction

Many different resources are employed to achieve an effective teaching-learning environment. One important resource consists of curriculum materials, which are often synonomous with instructional materials. These materials play a key role in establishing, implementing, and evaluating the vocational education curriculum (Walsh, 1976). Some individuals even go so far as to say that curriculum materials determine whether an individual learner succeeds, not the teacher.

While arguments could be made against such a statement, educators must not underestimate the role that quality curriculum materials can have in an effective teaching-learning environment. Chapter 8 deals specifically with identifying and selecting the best curriculum materials available.

Curriculum materials

Curriculum materials may be of many different types and forms. One of the first areas to clarify when discussing them is a definition, and the following paragraphs will serve as a basis for future comments on these materials.

A definition of curriculum materials

Curriculum materials are resources that, if used properly, can assist a teacher in bringing about intended desirable behavior change in individual students.

These materials must not be confused with teaching techniques or methods. One way to consider the difference between the two is that curriculum materials are tangible resources used by the teacher and/or students, whereas teaching techniques are mainly approaches to teaching where success depends heavily upon the professional skill of the teacher. For example, in role playing, student success in the teaching-learning environment depends upon the skillful direction of a teacher; whereas the effective use of workbooks depends not only upon the skillful use of the workbook by a teacher, but also upon the quality of the workbook itself.

Types of curriculum materials

In general, curriculum materials may be classified into three categories: printed matter; audiovisual materials; and manipulative aids. Materials classified in these categories may be used separately or in combination with each other when applied in a teaching-learning situation.

Printed matter.   Curriculum materials classified as printed matter are those which rely mainly upon reading for comprehension and are currently printed on paper. Types of printed material include:

1. Manuals
2. Workbooks
3. Pamphlets
4. Study guides
5. Reference books
6. Standard textbooks
7. Magazines
8. Newspapers
9. Modules

Audiovisual materials.   Audiovisual materials may involve seeing and hearing at the same time, although not in all cases. Furthermore, audiovisual materials require some type of equipment for their use. For example, slides require a slide projector. These materials include (but are not limited to):

1. Pictures
2. Graphics
3. Posters
4. Audiotapes
5. Records
6. Films
7. Transparencies
8. Filmstrips
9. Film loops
10. Slide series
11. Videotapes

Manipulative aids. Instructional materials classified as manipulative aids are those which must be physically handled. Examples include:

1. Puzzles
2. Games
3. Models
4. Specimens
5. Puppets/figures
6. Learning kits
7. Experiments
8. Trainers
9. Simulators

Need for securing curriculum materials

A master teacher must make wise use of all potential resources when planning for and conducting instruction. This implies that innovative teachers rely upon a variety of curriculum materials to supplement and complement their professional expertise in teaching situations. This is not to be construed that instructional materials are the sole basis upon which an effective teaching-learning situation rests. The point is that curriculum materials can make teaching more effective for a teacher and more efficient for a learner.

A second reason for securing curriculum materials is the lack of time a teacher usually has to develop his or her own materials. Time may be the critical factor as to whether a teacher develops certain materials or purchases the completed product from a publisher or other source. Many teachers do not have ample time to devote to curriculum material development. Thus if any such development is undertaken, it is usually restricted to the transparency, slide, or model.

Costs constitute a third factor determining whether materials should be purchased or developed. If a teacher fully accounts for his or her time required to develop quality materials in addition to needed monetary inputs, the savings experienced, if any, in materials development may not be sufficient to warrant the effort.

Quality control is another concern in the development of curriculum materials. Some teachers may have the time to develop certain materials; however, sufficient time and resources may not be available to field test, revise, and retest them in order to assure a quality product. Materials available through commercial sources may not always be of superior quality; however, the materials may have been tested and used to determine their effectiveness prior to marketing. Thus the purchase of curriculum materials that have already been developed may result in a higher quality product than those which could be developed using resources available to the vocational teacher.

In some cases, a teacher may not find desired instructional materials from commercial sources and thus must rely upon developmental efforts to provide them. While this chapter is concerned with the identification and selection of materials already available, Chapter 9 deals specifically with the process involved in developing such materials.

Selecting curriculum materials

The selection of quality curriculum materials must take several factors into consideration. All of these factors are important and the failure to examine materials in relation to each of these factors may result in the purchase of items that cannot be used to achieve the desired learning outcomes.

The assessment of curriculum materials must be carried out in a logical and planned order. Factors that the developer should consider when selecting materials include: 1) general description of the materials, 2) readability grade level, 3) bias, 4) accuracy, 5) appropriateness, 6) verbal and visual fluency, 7) usefulness and versatility, 8) filing and storage ease, and 9) cost (Bennett and Muncrief, 1975). Each of these factors is discussed on the following pages, while a complete Materials Assessment Form is included in Appendix C. In addition, sample exercises are provided to illustrate how materials can be assessed and selected.

General description of materials

The first step in the selection process is to obtain an overall understanding of the material. Section I of the Materials Assessment Form may be used as a guide in this process (see Figure 8-1). Completing Section I enables an individual to develop an overall understanding of the materials. Space is provided to indicate the title, author, publisher, and supplier of the publication. In addition, the year and place published, cost, and form of packaging can be indicated. The items can be categorized according to printed matter, audiovisual materials, and/or manipulative aids. As mentioned earlier, curriculum materials may constitute only one of these categories or may involve any two or a combination of the three categories and subcategories used to describe them.

Many materials are developed for a particular vocational service area and provision is made to indicate for which area they are meant. Since materials related to trade and industrial education may focus on any one of many different specialized areas, space is provided to indicate the area, such as auto mechanics, cosmetology, or air conditioning. However, a situation may arise where materials have been developed for a specific vocational service area, but application can be made to other areas. For example, a publication focusing on interviewing for a job in the distributive education area would also have implications for other service areas. The target population (the group for which the material

---

FIGURE 8–1.   Curriculum materials assessment form*

SECTION I | GENERAL DESCRIPTION

TITLE_____

AUTHOR_____PUBLISHER/SUPPLIER_____

YEAR PUBLISHED_____PLACE_____COST_____

PACKAGING (check one)

_____ 1. Single piece (item)   _____ 3. Set of ____ items, available separately

_____ 2. Set of ____ items, packaged   _____ 4. Other _____
             together   (specify)

TYPE OF MATERIAL (check all appropriate items)

1. *Printed Matter*   2. *Audiovisual Materials*   3. *Manipulative Aids*
    (pages   )

____ A. Manuals   ____ A. Graphics   ____ A. Puzzles
____ B. Workbooks   ____ B. Pictures   ____ B. Games
____ C. Pamphlets   ____ C. Posters   ____ C. Models
____ D. Study guides   ____ D. Audiotapes   ____ D. Specimens
____ E. Reference books   ____ E. Transparencies   ____ E. Puppets/figures
____ F. Textbooks   ____ F. Filmstrips   ____ F. Learning kits
____ G. Magazines   ____ G. Slide series   ____ G. Experiments
____ H. Newspapers   ____ H. Records   ____ H. Other_____
____ I. Other_____   ____ I. Films
                             ____ J. Film loops
                             ____ K. Videotapes
                             ____ L. Other_____

VOCATIONAL AREA

____ 1. Agricultural Education   ____ 6. Home Economics Education
____ 2. Business Education   ____ 7. Trade & Industrial Education
____ 3. Career Education   (specify subject area_____)
____ 4. Distributive Education   ____ 8. Other _____
____ 5. Health Education

TARGET POPULATION

____ 1. Grades K–1   ____ 4. Grades 7–8   ____ 7. Special Needs
____ 2. Grades 2–3   ____ 5. Grades 9–12   _____
____ 3. Grades 4–6   ____ 6. Postsecondary/Adult   _____

BRIEF DESCRIPTION OF MATERIAL _____

_____

_____

_____

---

*Adapted from Instructional Materials Assessment Form in *Instructional Materials for Occupational Education*, Martha C. Muncrief and James G. Bennett, authors. (Project funded by Grants Administration Unit, New York State Education Department, under the Education Professions Development Act, Section 554.)

was developed) is another important area to note, and a separate category is provided to indicate for which target group the material could best be used.

The final area in the general description section is a space provided for the reviewer to record any personal observations concerning the material. These observations might include special descriptive comments about the material not treated on the form.

Readability grade level

Section II of the Materials Assessment Form concerns the determination of the material's reading level. The importance of determining the reading level can easily be appreciated, especially if a teacher attempts to use materials designed for tenth-to-twelfth-grade level students with students who read at the eighth-grade level. If this occurs, students will have difficulty reading the material and the information may not be understood. Figure 8–2 contains Section II of the Materials Assessment Form.

If a readability score is desired, the *Simplified Flesch Formula* is one type of procedure that can be used (Farr, Jenkins, and Paterson, 1951). The procedure is as follows:

1. Selecting Samples
   a. Select enough samples from the materials so that the test will not be biased. Do not purposely select good or bad samples, but use a random approach for identification of pages from which to select them.
   b. Each sample should start at the beginning of a paragraph. For example, in a 250-page book and through a random selection of pages, a reviewer might come up with pages 12, 37, 42, 69, 81, and so forth.

FIGURE 8–2.   Readability grade level*

SECTION II | READABILITY GRADE LEVEL

___ 1. Not Applicable ___ 2. Readability Check Performed _____ Grade Level Is

Readability Formula Used _____

COMMENTS _____

---

*Adapted from Instructional Materials Assessment Form in *Instructional Materials for Occupational Education*, Martha C. Muncrief and James G. Bennett, authors. (Project funded by Grants Administration Unit, New York State Education Department, under the Education Professions Development Act, Section 554.)

2. Counting Words
   a. Starting at the beginning of a paragraph, count the words until 100 has been reached.
   b. Count contractions, hyphenated words, numbers, and letters as one word. For example, *can't, in-service, 1977*, and *USDA* would each count as one word.

3. Counting Sentences
   a. Using each 100-word sample, count the number of complete sentences or complete units of thought.
   b. Sentences joined by conjunctions, such as *and* or *but*, should be counted as one sentence.

4. Calculating Average Sentence Length
   Add the number of words in all samples (seven samples would have 700 words) and divide by the number of sentences and complete units of thought.

5. Calculating Average Number of One-syllable Words
   In each 100-word sample, count the number of one-syllable words, total these for all samples, and divide by the number of samples.

6. Determining the "Reading Ease" Score
   Taking the average sentence length in words calculated in Step 4 and the average number of one-syllable words calculated in Step 5, apply these to the "Flesch Reading Ease Index Table." This will give the reading ease index number.

Application of the Flesch Formula.   The following paragraphs taken from *Understanding Electricity and Electrical Terms* (American Association of Vocational Instructional Materials, Athens, Ga., 1970) illustrate how a readability score can be obtained. First, a person selects a page to begin the test. Starting at the beginning of a paragraph, count the words until 100 have been reached. Then, count the one-syllable words; in the sample that follows, these have been noted by underlining.

No one knows exactly what electricity is. To this all scientists agree. But this need not bother you. Electricity has been used so much and its actions observed so closely that scientists understand it quite well. Most people accept the widely held beliefs about it.

For many years scientists tried to find the smallest particle in nature. At one point their search led them to believe that the atom was the smallest particle. Later they found that the atom is made up of still smaller units called protons and electrons (Figure 2). These are electrical in nature. Although much more

With this sample test, sixty-five one-syllable words were identified. The average sentence length was 11.1 words, since there were nine sentences within this 100-word sample. Referring to Figure 8–3, a reading ease score of 59 is ascertained. In the Flesch Conversion Table (Figure 8–4), a reading ease score of 59 indicates that the sample material is at the tenth-to-twelfth-grade reading level.

FIGURE 8-3. Determining reading ease score

		Average Sentence Length							65 One-syllable words ↓					

Number of One-syllable Words per 100 Words

9 sentences—to find average sentence length:
$$\frac{100}{9} = 11.1$$

	84	82	80	78	76	74	72	70	68	66	64	62	60	58
9	94	90	87	84	81	78	74	72	68	65	61	58	56	52
10	93	89	86	83	80	77	73	71	67	64	60	57	55	51
11	92	88	85	82	79	76	72	70	66	63	59	56	54	50
12	91	87	84	81	78	75	71	69	65	62	58	55	53	49
13	90	86	83	80	77	74	70	68	64	61	57	54	52	48
14	89	85	82	79	76	72	69	67	63	60	56	53	50	47
15	88	84	81	78	75	71	68	66	62	59	55	52	49	46
16	87	83	80	77	74	70	67	65	61	58	54	51	48	45
17	86	82	79	76	73	69	66	64	60	57	53	50	47	44
18	85	81	78	75	72	68	65	63	59	56	52	49	46	43
19	83	80	77	74	71	67	64	61	58	55	51	48	45	42

FIGURE 8-4. Flesch conversion table*

	Reading Ease Score	
	90 to 100	5th Grade
	80 to 90	6th Grade
	70 to 80	7th Grade
	60 to 70	8th-9th Grade
59 ——	50 to 60 ——	10th-12th Grade
	30 to 50	13th-16th Grade (College)
	0 to 30	College Graduate

*From p. 177 in *The Art of Readable Writing*, Revised and Enlarged Edition, by Rudolf Flesch. Copyright ©1949, 1974 by Rudolf Flesch. By permission of Harper & Row, Publishers, Inc.

Bias

Public concern with bias today has strong implications for vocational educators as materials are selected for use. Developers of materials in the past gave little consideration to whether photographs or words were biased. Thus highly biased

TABLE 8-1. Flesch reading ease index table*

	Number of One-syllable Words Per 100 Words																									
	84	82	80	78	76	74	72	70	68	66	64	62	60	58	56	54	52	50	48	46	44	42	40	38	36	34
9	94	90	87	84	81	78	74	72	68	65	61	58	56	52	49	45	42	40	36	33	29	27	23	20	17	13
10	93	89	86	83	80	77	73	71	67	64	60	57	55	51	48	44	41	39	35	32	28	26	22	19	16	12
11	92	88	85	82	79	76	72	70	66	63	59	56	54	50	47	43	40	38	34	31	27	25	21	18	15	11
12	91	87	84	81	78	75	71	69	65	62	58	55	53	49	46	42	39	37	33	30	26	24	20	17	14	10
13	90	86	83	80	77	74	70	68	64	61	57	54	52	48	45	41	38	35	32	29	25	23	19	16	13	9
14	89	85	82	79	76	72	69	67	63	60	56	53	50	47	44	40	37	34	31	28	24	22	18	15	12	8
15	88	84	81	78	75	71	68	66	62	59	55	52	49	46	43	39	36	33	30	27	23	21	17	14	11	7
16	87	83	80	77	74	70	67	65	61	58	54	51	48	45	42	38	35	32	29	26	22	20	16	13	10	6
17	86	82	79	76	73	69	66	64	60	57	53	50	47	44	41	37	34	31	28	25	21	19	15	12	9	5
18	85	81	78	75	72	68	65	63	59	56	52	49	46	43	40	36	33	30	27	24	20	18	14	11	8	4
19	83	80	77	74	71	67	64	61	58	55	51	48	45	42	39	35	32	29	26	23	19	17	13	10	7	3
20	82	79	76	73	70	66	63	60	57	54	50	47	44	41	38	34	31	28	25	22	18	16	12	9	6	2
21	81	78	75	72	69	65	62	59	56	53	49	46	43	40	37	33	30	27	24	21	17	15	11	8	5	1
22	80	77	74	71	68	64	61	58	55	52	48	45	42	39	36	32	29	26	23	20	16	14	10	7	4	
23	79	76	73	70	67	63	60	57	54	51	47	44	41	38	35	31	28	25	22	19	15	13	9	6	2	
24	78	75	72	69	66	62	59	56	53	50	46	43	40	37	34	30	27	24	21	18	14	12	8	5	1	
25	77	74	71	68	65	61	58	55	52	49	45	42	39	36	33	29	26	23	20	17	13	11	7	4		
26	76	73	70	67	64	60	57	54	51	48	44	41	38	35	32	28	25	22	19	16	12	10	6	3		
27	75	72	69	66	63	59	56	53	50	47	43	40	37	34	31	27	24	21	18	15	11	9	5	2		
28	74	71	68	65	62	58	55	52	49	46	42	39	36	33	30	26	23	20	17	13	10	8	4	1		
29	73	70	67	64	61	57	54	51	48	45	41	38	35	32	29	25	22	19	16	12	9	7	3			
30	72	69	66	63	60	56	53	50	47	44	40	37	34	31	27	24	21	18	15	11	8	6	2			
31	71	68	65	62	59	55	52	49	46	43	39	36	33	30	26	23	20	17	14	10	7	5	1			
32	70	67	64	61	58	54	51	48	45	42	38	35	32	29	25	22	19	16	13	9	6	4				
33	69	66	63	60	57	53	50	47	44	41	37	34	31	28	24	21	18	15	12	8	5	2				
34	68	65	61	59	56	52	49	46	43	40	36	33	30	27	23	20	17	14	11	7	4	1				
35	67	64	60	58	55	51	48	45	42	38	35	32	29	26	22	19	16	13	10	6	3					
36	66	63	59	57	54	50	47	44	41	37	34	31	28	25	21	18	15	12	9	5	2					
37	65	62	58	56	53	49	46	43	40	36	33	30	27	24	20	17	14	11	8	4	1					
38	64	61	57	55	52	48	45	42	39	35	32	29	26	23	19	16	13	10	7	3						

Average Sentence Length (row labels at left)

*J. N. Farr, J. J. Jenkins, and D. G. Paterson. "Simplification of Flesch Reading Ease Formula," *Journal of Applied Psychology* **35** (1951), p. 333.

materials were unintentionally developed that ultimately had effect on students' attitudes and opinions. Bias may occur as any of the following:

Job denigration	Age discrimination
Sex-role stereotyping	Racial bias
Ethnic bias	Religious bias

Figure 8-5, containing Section III of the Materials Assessment Form, provides the opportunity to analyze materials for bias.

In addition to bias, materials such as magazines containing advertising must be analyzed to determine if any content is objectionable. For example, an ad may use language offensive to a minority group or a photograph may depict one race as superior to another.

Pratt (1972) has developed an extensive procedure to determine bias in publications through content analysis. This procedure is referred to as ECO Analysis (Evaluation Coefficient Analysis). Briefly, this procedure involves 1) the identification of the subject (idea, individual, or concept) to be studied, 2) listing all value terms (either positive or negative) about the subject, and 3) calculating an ECO analysis by totaling the number of positive terms multiplied by 100 and divided by the combined total number of positive and negative terms. A coefficient of 0.0–50.0 represents material containing unfavorable content toward a subject, while a coefficient 50.0–100 indicates material with favorable content.

Accuracy

Section IV of the Assessment Form provides the opportunity to evaluate the accuracy of curriculum materials. Considerations in this area are content accu-

---

FIGURE 8–5.   Bias*

| SECTION III | BIAS

Materials that stereotype sex roles, show bias toward age, race, ethnic or religious groups, and/or impose artificial hierarchies of social values on occupational categories (job denigration) should be avoided. Bias may also be evident in advertising that detracts from the educational value of the material.

1.   Is bias present in the material? (check all appropriate bias and indicate Evaluation Coefficient Analysis—ECO)

		ECO			*ECO*
_____	Job denigration	_____	_____	Ethnic bias	_____
_____	Sex-role stereotyping	_____	_____	Religious bias	_____
_____	Age discrimination	_____	_____	Other (explain)_____	_____
_____	Racial bias	_____	_____	Objectionable advertising	_____

2.   Is the material sufficiently free of bias to justify its use? (check one)

_____Yes   _____No

COMMENTS _____

_____

_____

_____

---

*Adapted from Instructional Materials Assessment Form in *Instructional Materials for Occupational Education*, Martha C. Muncrief and James G. Bennett, authors. (Project funded by Grants Administration Unit, New York State Education Department, under the Education Professions Development Act, Section 554.)

racy, currentness of the content, and whether the content is clear and complete. The assessment is subjective and can be rated on a scale from 1 to 5, with 5 representing the highest positive rating. Figure 8-6 contains information related to the assessment of material accuracy.

Calculation of a total score for this section is done by adding the numerical values of the boxes checked. This value will later be used to develop an overall assessment of the instructional material.

FIGURE 8-6. Accuracy*

SECTION IV   ACCURACY

Materials that provide inaccurate or misleading information have little utility in the total teaching-learning process.

1. To what extent is the content accurate?

_____1   _____2   _____3   _____4   _____5

Unrealistic or incorrect   Realistic and correct

2. To what extent is the content timely and up-to-date?

_____1   _____2   _____3   _____4   _____5

Outdated in information, ideas, and/or   Current in information, ideas,
illustrations   and/or illustrations

3. To what extent is the content clear and complete?

_____1   _____2   _____3   _____4   _____5

Vague and inconclusive   Sufficiently detailed to prevent
                                                misinterpretation

_____ TOTAL SCORE FOR SECTION IV
(add numerical values checked)

COMMENTS _____

_____

_____

_____

---

*Adapted from Instructional Materials Assessment Form in *Instructional Materials for Occupational Education*, Martha C. Muncrief and James G. Bennett, authors. (Project funded by Grants Administration Unit, New York State Education Department, under the Education Professions Development Act, Section 554.)

Appropriateness

Appropriateness refers to whether the material is desirable for the group that will be using it. Desirability is interpreted as appropriateness of the language used, the visuals used, and the level of content in relation to the target population. Also of concern is the relevance of content to the total subject matter area. Scales ranging from 1 to 5 have been incorporated into the form so that a numerical assessment can be made. Figure 8-7 includes Section V of the Assessment Form, which treats the appropriateness evaluation.

FIGURE 8-7.   Appropriateness*

| SECTION V | APPROPRIATENESS

Appropriateness of materials should be judged in relation to the target population and the total subject matter area.

1. To what extent are the language and/or visuals appropriate to the target population?

    _____1   _____2   _____3   _____4   _____5

    Stilted; antiquated language used; trite or   Fluent and easy to understand;
    too complex   appropriate to maturity level of
                                                      learner

2. To what extent is the content appropriate to the target population?

    _____1   _____2   _____3   _____4   _____5

    Lacking in challenge or too difficult to   Challenging but not beyond the
    comprehend   ability of the learner

3. To what extent is the content relevant to the total subject matter area?

    _____1   _____2   _____3   _____4   _____5

    Unnecessary; emphasizes an unimportant   Important and necessary to
    aspect of the subject   the subject matter area

                              _____ TOTAL SCORE FOR SECTION V
                                       (add numerical values checked)

COMMENTS _____

_____

_____

_____

---

*Adapted from Instructional Materials Assessment Form in *Instructional Materials for Occupational Education*, Martha C. Muncrief and James G. Bennett, authors. (Project funded by Grants Administration Unit, New York State Education Department, under the Education Professions Development Act, Section 554.)

Verbal and visual fluency

Section VI of the Assessment Form provides curriculum planners the opportunity to determine if the materials have been developed in a simple and attractive way. On a 1-to-5 scale, subjective evaluations can be made as to the appeal and organization of the material, including the extent to which it will stimulate students. Figure 8–8 contains Section VI of the Assessment Form.

FIGURE 8–8.   Verbal and visual fluency*

SECTION VI │ VERBAL AND VISUAL FLUENCY

Instructional materials should make learning easier by presenting the subject matter in a simple and attractive way.

1. To what extent is the material appealing to the learner?

   _____1   _____2   _____3   _____4   _____5

   Unattractive; cluttered; poor in design   Attractive; simple; effective in design

2. To what extent is the organization of the material easy to follow?

   _____1   _____2   _____3   _____4   _____5

   Too many ideas treated inadequately; distracting or extraneous parts   Ideas developed adequately in a logical manner; clear general theme

3. To what extent is the material interesting and stimulating?

   _____1   _____2   _____3   _____4   _____5

   Treats too few ideas in a redundant manner; dull and boring   Contributes to the development of critical thought and creativity

   _____ TOTAL SCORE FOR SECTION VI
   (add numerical values checked)

COMMENTS _____

_____

_____

_____

---

*Adapted from Instructional Materials Assessment Form in *Instructional Materials for Occupational Education*, Martha C. Muncrief and James G. Bennett, authors. (Project funded by Grants Administration Unit, New York State Education Department, under the Education Professions Development Act, Section 554.)

Usefulness and versatility

Curriculum materials that have versatility will be used in a wide variety of settings. Section VII of the Assessment Form deals with the following three evaluative concerns: 1) use of materials with learners of varying needs, 2) use of materials in varying learning environments, and 3) the relationship of cost to degree of usability. Figure 8–9 illustrates assessment of the material's usefulness and versatility.

FIGURE 8–9.   Usefulness and versatility*

| SECTION VII | USEFULNESS AND VERSATILITY

Instructional materials should be useful in a variety of situations and adaptable to varied needs of students.

1.   To what extent can the material be used with learners having varying needs?

　　———1　　　———2　　———3　　　———4　　———5

Suitable for a limited group of learners

Appropriate to target group with varying level of maturity, economic backgrounds, and learning styles

2.   To what extent can the material be used in a variety of learning environments?

　　———1　　　———2　　———3　　　———4　　———5

No provisions for adaptability; useful in only one type of situation

High level of adaptability; suitable for varying learning environments

3.   To what extent are cost and packaging of the material consistent with the degree of usability?

　　———1　　　———2　　———3　　　———4　　———5

Poorly constructed or packaged; more costly than is justified by probable use

Durably packaged; easy to handle and store; available at a cost commensurate with value

———— TOTAL SCORE FOR SECTION VII
(add numerical values checked)

COMMENTS _____

_____

_____

_____

---

*Adapted from Instructional Materials Assessment Form in *Instructional Materials for Occupational Education*, Martha C. Muncrief and James G. Bennett, authors. (Project funded by Grants Administration Unit, New York State Education Department, under the Education Professions Development Act, Section 554.)

Summary profile

Section VIII of the Assessment Form provides an opportunity for the material's reviewer to summarize the numerical ratings given in Sections IV-VII. Referring to Figure 8–10, the numerical ratings for each section can be placed in this one profile chart and then summed to arrive at a total numerical rating for these four assessment sections. Since a 1-to-5 scale is used and 5 represents a positive reaction on the part of the reviewer, ratings of 3 or above reflect material that would be desirable to use. Thus the numerical value of these four sections should total 36 points or higher for the material to be considered for purchase. Any material receiving less then 36 points would be considered deficient and should not be purchased unless a second review reveals that the ratings are not reflective of the material's quality.

Learning environment use

Section IX of the Assessment Form provides the opportunity to consider the environment in which the material might be used to the best advantage. Figure

---

FIGURE 8–10. Summary profile*

SECTION VIII | SUMMARY PROFILE

SECTIONS	MAXIMUM POINTS POSSIBLE	SCORE OF TASK
IV	15	_____
V	15	_____
VI	15	_____
VII	15	_____
TOTAL	60	

1. Overall assessment of material (check one)

_____ Unacceptable; below 36 points
_____ Useful; 36 to 48 points
_____ Excellent; 49 to 60 points

2. Does the rating above accurately reflect your general assessment of the material?

_____ Yes   _____ No (explain)

COMMENTS _____

_____

---

*Adapted from Instructional Materials Assessment Form in *Instructional Materials for Occupational Education*, Martha C. Muncrief and James G. Bennett, authors. (Project funded by Grants Administration Unit, New York State Education Department, under the Education Professions Development Act, Section 554.)

8-11 illustrates this section of the Assessment Form. Not only can the reviewer indicate the use that could be made of the material in the classroom and/or laboratory, but he or she can also indicate if any special in-service training should be provided to teachers before the materials can be used effectively.

FIGURE 8-11. Learning environment use*

| SECTION IX | LEARNING ENVIRONMENT USE

1. Have you used this material in your classroom?

　　＿＿＿Yes　　＿＿＿No

2. Have you used this material in your laboratory?

　　＿＿＿Yes　　＿＿＿No

3. Does this material require in-service training for effective use?

　　＿＿＿Yes　　＿＿＿No

4. Are consultant services available to provide in-service training for use?

　　＿＿＿Yes (explain)　　＿＿＿No

Where?＿＿＿＿＿＿＿＿＿＿＿＿＿＿＿＿＿＿＿＿＿＿＿＿＿＿＿＿＿＿＿＿＿＿＿

＿＿＿＿＿＿＿＿＿＿＿＿＿＿＿＿＿＿＿＿＿＿＿＿＿＿＿＿＿＿＿＿＿＿＿＿＿

＿＿＿＿＿＿＿＿＿＿＿＿＿＿＿＿＿＿＿＿＿＿＿＿＿＿＿＿＿＿＿＿＿＿＿＿＿

5. Do you know of any type of validation that has been done on this material; i.e., learner verification, pre/posttests, ratings, etc.?

　　＿＿＿ Yes (explain)　　＿＿＿ No

＿＿＿＿＿＿＿＿＿＿＿＿＿＿＿＿＿＿＿＿＿＿＿＿＿＿＿＿＿＿＿＿＿＿＿＿＿

＿＿＿＿＿＿＿＿＿＿＿＿＿＿＿＿＿＿＿＿＿＿＿＿＿＿＿＿＿＿＿＿＿＿＿＿＿

＿＿＿＿＿＿＿＿＿＿＿＿＿＿＿＿＿＿＿＿＿＿＿＿＿＿＿＿＿＿＿＿＿＿＿＿＿

6. Are there other discipline areas or target populations for whom this material might be appropriate? (list)

＿＿＿＿＿＿＿＿＿＿＿＿＿＿＿＿＿＿＿＿＿＿＿＿＿＿＿＿＿＿＿＿＿＿＿＿＿

＿＿＿＿＿＿＿＿＿＿＿＿＿＿＿＿＿＿＿＿＿＿＿＿＿＿＿＿＿＿＿＿＿＿＿＿＿

＿＿＿＿＿＿＿＿＿＿＿＿＿＿＿＿＿＿＿＿＿＿＿＿＿＿＿＿＿＿＿＿＿＿＿＿＿

Sign-off by Material Assessor

Name＿＿＿＿＿＿＿＿＿＿＿＿＿＿＿＿＿＿＿＿＿

Date＿＿＿＿＿＿＿＿＿＿＿＿＿＿＿＿＿＿＿＿＿

---

*Adapted from Instructional Materials Assessment Form in *Instructional Materials for Occupational Education*, Martha C. Muncrief and James G. Bennett, authors. (Project funded by Grants Administration Unit, New York State Education Department, under the Education Professions Development Act, Section 554.)

Overall summary of ratings

An overall summary of ratings can be made in Section X of the Assessment Form. This one page provides a concise summary of the ratings made on the material in Sections II-IX. Use of the Material Assessment Form does not guarantee that materials purchased will result in quality learning. However, the probability of eliminating those materials of questionable quality and/or use can more easily be accomplished through the use of such a device.

Sources of curriculum materials

The number of sources from which curriculum materials can be obtained is only limited by ingenuity and innovative thinking. Many sources may be identified in any one community. However, curriculum developers and teachers must look beyond their own communities to assess what is available. To help reduce the amount of time spent identifying such sources, there are specific people and firms that should be contacted first. These include commercial publishers, journals and magazines, and curriculum centers, to name just a few.

Commercial publishers

Commercial publishers can be divided into those who print materials containing technical information for teacher or student use and those who basically print books for the professional development of educators. In addition, some publishers may print both types of materials. The publisher to be contacted first in the search for materials may depend upon the vocational area under consideration. For example, over the years one publisher has been a source of technical information in textbook form for the area of agricultural education, while others have focused upon business education. Even though textbooks may tend to lag technical advancements in certain areas because of lead time needed for printing, commercial publishers are, nonetheless, an important source of instructional materials.

Journals and magazines

Periodicals serve a useful purpose in keeping the teacher up to date in specific vocational areas. They are a rich source of information about curriculum materials, since they have the advantage of being able to reflect the latest information. All vocational service areas have periodicals that focus specifically upon their areas and, in some cases, cut across several areas.

Curriculum centers

Curriculum centers are ususally located at major universities and have as one of their major functions the development of curriculum materials. Similar to journals developed for a specific vocational area, some centers are noted for their efforts in a specific area. Another type of curriculum materials development effort that has implications for locating current materials available or under development is the National Network of Curriculum Coordination. One of the major purposes of this Network, comprised of six regions in the United States, is to share information on materials available and under development.

ERIC system

One of the most extensive listings of vocational instructional materials may be found in the ERIC system. Initially, these listings were produced in AIM/ARM publications, but now are published bimonthly as *Resources in Vocational Education*. Specifically, these publications contain abstracts of materials related to vocational education. Other information is also included regarding where the material can be obtained and the cost. Any educator desiring to locate materials for a specific area should investigate this source.

State educational agencies

Each state has an agency for coordinating efforts within that state regarding curriculum materials. While the most common material might be printed matter, film libraries should also be checked for appropriate material. Most states devote their efforts to collecting materials and providing teachers with sources to contact outside of the state. However, some states also develop a variety of useful materials.

United States Government Printing Office

Materials can be obtained from the U. S. Government Printing Office for virtually any area related to vocational education. Anyone securing materials from this source must realize that the materials were not developed for student use and thus must be aware of the reading level involved. A catalogue of publications can be secured by writing to: U. S. Government Printing Office, Washington, D.C. 20402.

Military service

The military service has provided technical training for many years and has developed extensive materials that can be adapted to public vocational education. These materials are of particular value to trade and industrial and technical education curricula. Vocational educators should not overlook the possibilities of this vital source. However, accessibility to certain military materials may not be possible due to restrictions placed on distribution.

Companies

Major companies are often overlooked as sources of instructional materials. John Deere and Company has developed an extensive list of materials in the area of equipment and tractors. Organizations such as Briggs and Stratton, Lincoln Welders, and local banks have developed materials. Purebreed livestock and pet associations have also developed materials. The user of these materials must keep in mind that they have been based upon the companies' own products or services. Thus time may need to be spent familiarizing the student with other brands of equipment or situations that he or she may face on the job.

Additional sources of materials

While some materials must be purchased, many of them may be secured free of charge. Local newspapers, catalogues, road maps, charts, animals, and wrecked automobiles are just a few examples of resource materials. The list is endless and is limited only by a teacher's imagination in relation to the topic being discussed in class.

Planning to secure curriculum materials

The tendency to overlook the purchase of much-needed curriculum materials in vocational education is a serious mistake. For example, if vocational teachers are allotted $1,000 to spend for their department, they will usually spend most, if not all, of the money for equipment, supplies, and tools needed for laboratory instruction. While these resources may be critical to the effectiveness of the program, continual expenditures in the laboratory area may develop into a critical shortage of materials needed for both the classroom and the laboratory. Thus special attention should be given to the development of short- and long-range plans for securing curriculum materials.

Short-range planning

Short-range planning for curriculum materials consists of determining which materials are essential for the coming year. Criteria for determining essential materials would be those items which include information desired to be taught during the year. Another factor might be those materials which could be used in a variety of situations or learning environments. For example, basic texts or visuals that contain pertinent information might represent a higher priority the first year than workbooks that could not be used again. Another consideration would be the amount of money available. As an illustration, assume that sufficient money were available to buy printed resource materials. It might be better to by these materials the first year and schedule the purchase of transparencies for the second year, since some transparencies could be made by the teacher during the year.

Long-range planning

The value of giving consideration to long-range planning in purchasing curriculum materials becomes evident when one starts to look at the prices of such materials. Very few budgets will permit any teacher to select and order all the materials desired for a given year. Thus it is vital that a long-range plan be developed for securing them. Materials that might be included in long-range plans would be those which treat the more advanced subject matter. Another way to approach this decision would be to consider those materials which build upon prior student knowledge or learning sessions. As was commented in the preceding section, limited budgets must be considered. Materials that entail a high cost or require special hardware equipment might be included in the long-range plans if current situations would prevent their being used effectively.

Developing a plan for securing materials

The establishment of priorities for securing commercially produced curriculum materials usually evolves from a subjective thought process. While this may be sufficient in certain cases, development of a logical, systematic procedure may serve as a more objective basis upon which decisions can be made regarding their purchase. For this reason, a Materials Priority Form has been developed to assist teachers, curriculum planners, or administrators either as individuals or as groups in arriving at priorities for the purchase of materials. This form is provided in Figure 8–12 with illustrative data.

Curriculum materials identified as a lesser priority for the short-range needs and not purchased would need to be considered later as the long-range plans are implemented. Again referring to Figure 8–12, if the fourth-priority materials in the short-range plan (Auto Electrical Systems) were not purchased, these materials might later become a first priority as the time draws near for the purchase of materials identified in the long-range plan.

FIGURE 8-12. Materials priority form

Course: Auto Mechanics

Number of Students: 10

Year: 19 × 1

Material	19 × 2 Short-range Needs			19 × 3 Long-range Need by Year		
	Cost Each	Total Cost	Priority	Cost Each	Total Cost	Priority
1. ABC of Auto Mechanics	$ 5.00	$ 50.00	3	$	$	
2. ABC of Auto Mechanics Transparencies					100.00	2
3. Beginning Auto Mechanics	12.50	125.00	1			
4. Intermediate Auto Mechanics				12.50	125.00	1
5. Advanced Auto Mechanics				15.00	150.00	4
6. Auto Electrical Systems	7.50	75.00	4			
7. Acme Transmissions				10.00	150.00	3
8. Troubleshooting Auto Engines	5.00	50.00	2			
Total Cost		$300.00			$525.00	

SUMMARY

The impact of curriculum materials on the effectiveness of the teaching-learning environment cannot be underestimated. For this reason, educators must develop and use some type of logical procedure in identifying and selecting curriculum materials.

First, one must consider exactly what curriculum materials are. Basically, they are resources that assist a teacher in bringing about a desirable change of behavior in students. Curriculum materials may consist of printed matter, audiovisual materials, and/or manipulative aids. While teachers can and should develop some of the materials needed, eventually the situation will exist where materials need to be purchased.

Educators must consider several important factors before a decision is made to purchase or not to purchase a specific item. Factors to consider in selection of materials include: an overall general description of the material; readability grade level; bias; accuracy; appropriateness; verbal and visual fluency; usefulness and versatility; and learning environment use.

Sources of curriculum materials are only limited by one's ingenuity and creativity. General areas of sources are commercial publishers, journals and magazines, curriculum centers, ERIC: AIM-ARM, state educational agencies, the United States Government Printing Office, military service, and private companies.

Securing curriculum materials should follow a logical and systematic plan. Short-range planning is used to identify those materials which are basic for the units of instruction to be taught in the near future. Long-range planning serves to identify materials that represent advanced units of instruction occurring at a later date. But following a systematic process, teachers, either individually or as a group, will be more likely to secure materials that are appropriate for the instructional units planned and eliminate others.

REFERENCES

Baker, E. L., and Schutz, R. E., eds. "Rules for the Development of Instructional Products," *Instructional Product Development*, W. J. Popham and E. L. Baker, 1971, pp. 129–168.

Bennett, James G., and Muncrief, Martha C. *Instructional Materials for Occupational Education*, Misc. Pub. 75-3. Albany: Bureau of Inservice Education, New York State Education Department, June, 1975.

Dale, Edgar. *Audiovisual Methods in Teaching*. Hinsdale, Ill.: The Dryden Press, Inc., 1969.

Erickson, Carlton W. H., and Curl, David H. *Fundamentals of Teaching with Audiovisual Technology*. New York: The Macmillan Company, 1972.

Farr, J. N.; Jenkins, J. J.; and Paterson, D. G. "Simplification of Flesch Reading Ease Formula," *Journal of Applied Psychology* 35 (October, 1951), p. 335.

Flesch, Rudolf. *The Art of Readable Writing.* New York: Harper & Row, Publishers, 1974.

Logan, Edwin. "A Model for Making Military Curriculum Materials Available," *American Vocational Journal* (April, 1977), pp. 30–32.

Mager, Robert F., and Beach, Kenneth M., Jr. *Developing Vocational Instruction.* Belmont, Calif.: Fearon Publishers, 1967.

Popham, W. James. "Product Research: A New Curriculum Specialty," *Educational Leadership*, No. 6 (March, 1966), pp. 507–513.

Pratt, David. *How to Find and Measure Bias in Textbooks.* Englewood Cliffs, N.J.: Educational Technology Publications, Inc., 1972.

Schaffarzick, Jon, and Hampson, David H., ed. *Strategies for Curriculum Development.* Berkeley, Calif.: McCutchan Publishing Corporation, 1975.

Understanding Electricity and Electricity Terms. Athens, Ga.: American Association of Vocational Instructional Materials, 1970.

Walsh, Lawrence A. "The Role of the Textbook in Vocational Education," *School Shop* XXXVI, No. 4 (December, 1976).

Developing Curriculum Materials

Introduction

Even with the variety of vocational and technical curriculum materials available today, the curriculum developer is often faced with the need to produce new materials. This need becomes evident when materials are required for a certain instructional situation and are not available. Furthermore, a need may be established when available materials are not appropriate for the intended audience or their use is limited by other factors that might prohibit a teacher from using them with established instructional objectives.

This chapter deals directly with factors associated with the development and the dissemination of curriculum materials. During the development process, consideration must be given to factors such as the time and dollars available, the audience, and the development alternatives. In addition, the actual development process must take on a logical and orderly process to assure that usable materials are produced.

Determining the need for curriculum materials

Ultimately the need for curriculum materials must be determined in relation to content. Once the content has been established, plans must be made to secure meaningful materials that align with established instructional objectives. Two different situations could exist at this time.

After an exhaustive search has been conducted, the conclusion may be reached that curriculum materials are not currently available from either commercial or private sources. Thus a most logical alternative is to develop the needed materials. On the other hand, a search may produce several items that are related to the instructional content, but for some reason, the materials appear to be deficient in certain areas. Thus educators are faced with the task of developing or adapting the curriculum materials.

Factors to consider in curriculum materials development

The development of quality curriculum materials depends upon several factors, with any one of them having great impact on product quality. Thus individuals who assume leadership for any development effort must carefully consider all areas that might affect the quality of the final product. Furthermore, management of the development process must be such that materials can be produced at a smooth and steady pace, thus helping to assure that quality materials are developed. Factors that must be considered when developing curriculum materials include the time available, the dollars available, and the audience for which the materials are intended. Each of these factors will be discussed in the following paragraphs.

Time available and needed

One of the most critical factors to consider when the development of curriculum materials is undertaken is the time available to devote to a development project in relation to the time needed. The development of quality materials can be very time-consuming when the total effort is considered. When time is a concern, one must not only think about the time needed to develop the product, but also the time needed for testing, revising, printing, and disseminating the finished item. This time may be as short as a few weeks or more than a year in duration, depending upon the quantity of materials to be produced.

While the time needed to develop quality materials is crucial, consideration must also be given to the time available from those individuals who are to be involved in the development. Persons who have little time available can only be expected to contribute minimally to a developmental effort, and thus the quantity of materials produced would be smaller or the length of time required to develop the materials would need to be extended.

Expertise available

Regardless of the experience and knowledge possessed by those individuals involved in curriculum materials development, there will often be instances where outside assistance should be sought. Special assistance might be needed with regard to technical information, editing, media, and duplication.

Technical information.   Accuracy of the technical information is a basic concern of those who develop curriculum materials. While materials are, for the most part, developed by those who are knowledgeable in a particular technical area, there are some instances when outside technical assistance may be desirable. For example, if materials are being developed that include some federal or state laws or interpretation of statutes, then the review of the materials by a lawyer might be appropriate. Another example where technical assistance might be desirable is when materials will be disseminated over a large audience, say a state or region. Securing input from others in this situation may avoid materials being developed that might not be applicable to all of the geographic areas intended.

Editorial assistance.   Curriculum materials writers often do not have the necessary expertise in grammatical matters to handle all problems that arise during the development process. Thus persons who are competent in the editorial area need to be contacted for assistance prior to the time materials are utilized by student groups. After materials have been prepared in draft form, they should be reviewed for correct grammar, punctuation, and spelling.

Media.   Curriculum materials are seldom used alone in a teaching situation. Typically, they are utilized in conjunction with overhead transparencies, slides, audiotapes, or a variety of other media. For this reason, the curriculum materials developer would be advised to contact a media specialist as the development process begins and to obtain help in the selection and use of media. Helpful suggestions can be obtained in areas such as how to arrange material attractively and how much media will cost.

Duplication.   After materials have been developed, they need to be duplicated in quantity and distributed if any use is expected. Thus individuals developing materials need to secure estimated costs of duplication, turnaround time (time from submission to delivery), and the style and format that would be best suited for the material being developed and the intended audience.

Although printing curriculum materials on paper still appears to be a most popular approach, the need to explore alternative methods of duplication may become more critical, especially as wood becomes scarce and the cost of paper rises. The use of microfilm, microfiche, and other methods of reproducing information will need to be considered in the future.

Dollars available

One of the most important factors to consider when developing curriculum materials is the monetary resources available. Obviously, the amount of money available can have great impact on the quality of materials developed. The relationship between dollars available and curriculum materials development can be pointed out in several ways. First, compensation may need to be made to outside experts who are asked to provide assistance. For example, seeking input from a lawyer regarding legal concerns may result in a substantial expense. A second set of expenses is associated with the actual development of materials. This might include, but not be limited to, pencils, paper, resource materials, typing, and general supplies. Third, costs will occur when the materials are duplicated. This cost, which involves the printing of materials and associated media, is often quite expensive, and therefore must receive close attention. A fourth cost relates to the dissemination of materials, which might include workshop expenses, travel costs for the developer and teacher, or postage charges. And fifth, the time required of those individuals actually developing the material represents a monetary investment. Thus when one considers all the expenses associated with curriculum materials development, some thought must be given to the current budget as it relates to the development effort and whether an additional source of funds needs to be identified.

If materials are being developed over a lengthy time period, some provision must be made for inflation. For example, if materials that are now being developed will not be duplicated until a year from now, the current printing prices may not be appropriate figures to use when preparing operational budgets for next year. Failing to allow for inflation may later result in reducing the quantity of items printed.

Decisions to make regarding materials development

As educators begin the task of curriculum materials development, there are several crucial decisions to be made. These decisions could be thought of as the what, why, who, when, and where of materials development.

What materials should be developed and why?   The answer to this question is quite obvious. If the material needed to complete an instructional unit successfully is not available, then the typical response is to develop it. However, a more complex situation arises when individuals with different philosophical beliefs attempt to decide exactly what information to include in the material and what to delete.

Who should develop the materials?   This type of decision is critical, since individuals developing the materials must be knowledgeable in the technical area for which the items are to be used. These individuals must be up-to-date as to the latest developments in the area of concern. Furthermore, they must have the ability to put their thoughts down on paper in a clear, logical, and concise manner. Other considerations include the time available to devote to a project of this magnitude as well as who is actually willing to undertake the task.

When should the materials be developed?   The decision associated with this question depends to some degree on the individuals involved. If the material developers are responsible for teaching, time that can be devoted to materials development will probably be somewhat restricted. Of course, more time could be devoted to materials development during the summer or if an individual were released from some or all of his or her teaching load. Regardless of when the materials are developed, blocks of time—at least two to three hours per work session—are needed in order for developers to be productive and efficient.

Where should the materials be developed? While this may seem to be a minor consideration, functional space is important for those who develop materials. The space must be adequate such that materials can be laid out and readily used while the development process is underway, and that the developer is not cramped for writing space. Furthermore, a location is needed where the developer is free from unnecessary distractions or interruptions.

Target population

The target population represents the audience for which the materials are being developed. There are basically two factors to consider with regard to target population as the development process begins. First, consideration must be given to the grade level(s) of the group(s) who will be using the materials. This will not only influence the reading level at which the material is written, but also the depth to which technical information will be covered. A second consideration deals with the use of materials on a local, state, regional, or national basis. Curriculum materials developers want to be sure that the materials being developed will be applicable to the entire audience and not be limited due to differences in geographical locations.

Dissemination

Dissemination involves the process of distributing materials produced to those who have a need. A planned dissemination scheme is important to help assure that materials are adopted and used. To overlook this step may result in quality materials being shelved, which would represent a waste of money and human effort. The dissemination of curriculum materials is treated in greater depth later in this chapter.

Support needed

In addition to adequate physical facilities needed in support of preparation efforts, there are several other types of support needed. Reference materials are needed as materials are being developed. In fact, multiple copies of certain references may be needed if a team approach to development is used. If overhead transparencies are to be developed to supplement written materials, overhead projectors, screens, thermofax machines, and other types of equipment will be needed.

In addition to the above support items, moral support needs to be provided by those who are giving leadership to the project. The development of quality curriculum materials in vocational and technical education is an essential part of curriculum development and this process should be encouraged and supported by vocational administrators and supervisors when the need arises.

Development alternatives

One factor that must be considered is the way materials will actually be developed. Basically there are two approaches to development: individual or team. While either approach can be used, there are distinct advantages to each and these will be discussed in the following paragraphs.

Individual development. The individual approach to development places total responsibility upon one person. While input may be obtained from others, such as superiors, colleagues, and subject matter experts, responsibility for the actual writing, testing, revision, and completion of materials falls upon one individual. The advantages of such an approach are management-related. With only one person involved, problems experienced when working with a group of professionals are not present.

Several distinct limitations are associated with the individual approach. The most obvious limitation concerns the limited amount of materials that can be developed by one individual compared with a group of developers. Another limitation is the reluctance of others to adopt materials developed by one individual. For a variety of reasons, teachers tend to prefer materials developed through the combined efforts of several knowledgeable individuals. In addition, the amount of time needed to develop materials is longer with the individual approach, thus more time needs to be allotted for the development process. Concern can also be raised as to the product quality. With one individual responsible for carrying out all the development steps, several steps may be slighted or eliminated completely if the project falls behind anticipated completion dates.

Team development. The team approach offers some unique opportunities for curriculum materials development. This approach basically relies upon a group of individuals who all have one ultimate objective in mind, the development of quality materials. Several different team arrangements may be used. One such arrangement consists of the total team being divided into small groups who each have responsibility for the development of a different set of materials. When the materials produced by each group are combined, they constitute a complete set of curriculum materials. Another arrangement utilizes one group to develop the materials and another to assume responsibility for reviewing and testing. This arrangement enables the reviewing and testing to be conducted by persons who are not intimately involved with the development and thus ensures a less biased estimate of the materials quality. Ideally, a team approach provides for an equitable division of responsibility with activities being assigned on the basis of each individual team member's expertise.

Many limitations associated with the individual approach to materials development can be minimized through a team approach. For example, a greater volume of materials may be developed and in a shorter period of time. Furthermore, concerns that individuals might have with the materials quality would be fewer, since input is secured from several people during the development process.

While each of the factors to consider in curriculum materials development is certainly important, to say that one factor is more important than another cannot be justified. Any one of these factors can seriously affect materials quality or the projected outcome of the development effort. Thus all factors must be considered and a determination made as to how each might limit their quality.

The curriculum materials development process

Curriculum materials development must follow a systematic and logical process from beginning to end. Whether an individual or team approach is used, it is important to keep in mind that development consists of several stages, each of which contributes to the overall materials quality. When each stage in the development process is followed, materials produced will be of higher quality and well worth the effort involved.

Stages in the development of curriculum materials

The various stages included in the curriculum materials development process are important contributors to materials quality. These stages, listed below, are presented in the order one should follow when carrying out development activities.

1. Prepare a preliminary development plan

2. Determine curriculum content to be investigated

3. Determine terminal and enabling objectives

4. Identify special curriculum materials needed

5. Review literature to determine what materials are available

6. Identify materials lacking in the content area

7. Establish priorities for needed materials

8. Finalize the development plan

9. Conduct an intensive literature review

10. Obtain relevant references and resources

11. Prepare a first draft of the materials

12. Edit the first draft

13. Prepare a second draft

14. Pilot test the second draft

15. Prepare a third draft

16. Field test the third draft

17. Prepare the final draft

18. Duplicate the materials

Prepare a preliminary development plan. The preliminary plan serves to establish general guidelines to follow during the materials development process. The individuals who are involved in developing this plan include those responsible for providing leadership to the overall project as well as teachers or other persons who will be actively involved in the preparation of materials. Representatives from those who will be teaching the curriculum content and using the materials should also be included when the preliminary planning is taking place. Specific concerns that may be brought up during this preliminary planning include the curriculum content to be focused upon, who will assume responsibility for stages 2 through 7, and the projected timetable for the first seven stages. While the preliminary plan is not usually a formal document, it serves to provide direction for activities to follow and establishes a tangible frame of reference for those who will develop and use the materials.

Determine curriculum content to be investigated. The actual process that should be followed in making curriculum content decisions was detailed in Chapter 6. At this stage in the materials development process, a decision needs to be made as to which part(s) of the curriculum supporting curriculum materials should be developed. Let us assume that a two-year distributive education program has just been established at a local school. The distributive education coordinators realize that materials are available for one part of the curriculum, but they are not sure if materials are available for another segment of the content. Thus the most logical decision at this time would be to focus upon that part of the curriculum where supporting materials may not be available.

Determine terminal and enabling objectives. The identification of curriculum content will not, by itself, clearly indicate what students are to accomplish as a result of content taught. Thus before a determination can be made of the materials needed to teach a specific segment of the curriculum, terminal and enabling performance objectives must be established. Detailed information about developing these objectives is provided in Chapter 7. These objectives provide specific direction as to what technical information must be included in the materials. Once technical content has been clarified through objectives, development of relevant curriculum materials may then proceed.

Identify special curriculum materials needed. This stage provides the opportunity to identify special curriculum materials known to be needed while teaching the technical content. An example might well serve to point up the necessity of this stage. Assume that a curriculum has been established for deaf students. In this particular curriculum, any materials involving audio communication would be of limited usefulness in the classroom or laboratory. Time could be better spent identifying materials that rely upon visual communication to transfer knowledge. In summary, this stage provides the opportunity to reflect upon the characteristics of the audience for which the curriculum is designed and identify materials that can best be utilized by them.

Review literature to determine what materials are available. The ultimate goal of this stage is to determine what materials are already available pertaining to the curriculum content under consideration. Special efforts should be focused upon contacting those sources of curriculum materials identified in Chapter 8. Failure to review the literature extensively may ultimately result in materials being developed that are already available. Individuals who are assigned the task of reviewing the literature must not be too narrow in their thinking and they should exhaust all possible sources in their search for appropriate materials. In fact, some materials may be found that could be appropriate if subjected to an extensive revision.

Identify materials lacking in the content area. The identification of materials lacking in the content area should become evident during the preceding stage and now need to be listed for further discussion. Furthermore, curriculum materials developers may want to hold a brainstorming session to identify some creative approaches or materials needed to present information in a different or more interesting manner.

Establish priorities for needed materials. The situation may arise where several different materials have been identified as being needed, but available resources will not permit the development of every item. When this occurs, priorities need to be established as to which materials are more important than others. While it is difficult to provide precise guidelines to use in establishing priorities, there are several factors to be considered. These include competencies of the teachers who will be using the materials, the type and level of other available materials related to the content, and the projected length of time needed to develop each identified item.

Finalize the development plan. At this stage in the development, those persons who first met during the preliminary planning stage should reconvene to discuss what has occurred during each of the first seven stages. In fact, one of the actions taken during this stage is to decide whether the materials development plan should continue through the completion of a final product or whether it is most logical to cease at this point. Special factors to be considered tie in with ones discussed earlier in this chapter; namely, time available and needed, expertise available, and dollars available.

If the decision is made to develop materials identified as high priority items, assignments must be given to those who will carry out the work. At this time it is also appropriate to involve other individuals who may need to be involved with other aspects of the development. For example, if five different areas of curriculum materials were identified for development, additional people may need to be brought in to develop materials in each area. Other decisions to be made include target completion dates for various stages, estimated costs, and other details regarding the operational framework of the entire materials development process. Another consideration at this point would be whether a team approach or individual approach might be used. For example, if a group of teachers could be assembled during the summer, the team approach might permit a greater quantity of material to be developed in a relatively short period of time. A team approach also provides more flexibility for testing in the latter stages of the development process.

Discussion at this time must also focus upon the desired format the materials are to take. While philosophical differences will tend to alter the format between different individuals and situations, several major headings can serve to give direction for the format. These headings include:

Cover Page

Table of Contents

Directions for Use

Technical Content

Bibliography

Conduct an intensive literature review. This stage becomes most important when any great length of time passes between the initial review of literature and the actual development of curriculum materials. New materials are becoming available each day and those responsible for the actual preparation of materials certainly need to review the latest ones available. Another activity that might prove beneficial at this time would be to contact individuals or organizations who are currently developing materials. The situation could develop where materials that closely align with established high priority items are being developed by individuals or curriculum centers in other locations.

Obtain relevant references and resources. All references and resources that may be of assistance in the preparation of materials should be secured and made available to persons who will be responsible for developing them. These items should be available before an initial draft of the materials is prepared.

Prepare a first draft of the materials. Preparation of the initial draft may be the most time-consuming activity in the development of curriculum materials. Based upon the performance objectives and identified content, individuals charged with the responsibility of actually preparing the materials can now begin the task of merging technical content with sound educational principles.

Edit the first draft.   Once the first draft of materials has been completed, a thorough editing should be conducted before proceeding further. Materials should be subjected to three types of editing, which include technical accuracy, composition, and applicability (Butler, 1972). Furthermore, possible ideas for needed improvement can be identified if the materials being developed are evaluated with the Curriculum Materials Assessment Form, which was discussed in Chapter 8.

Technical accuracy.   The purpose of this type of editing is to determine the accuracy of the materials prepared. Editing for technical accuracy may be best conducted by team members who were not involved in the preparation process or by persons external to the curriculum development group. Once the materials have been verified for technical accuracy, any subsequent revisions will need to be reexamined to be sure that the intent of the original content has not been changed.

Composition.   Editing for composition focuses upon several areas. These are:

> Do the materials appear to be capable of communicating with the intended audience?
>
> Is the language used suitable for the intended audience?
>
> Are the materials free of ambiguous, unnecessary words?
>
> Are explanations, illustrations, and examples clear and concise?
>
> Are the materials grammatically correct?

While editing for composition serves to eliminate words, phrases, or sections that may lead to difficulty in understanding the technical information, the true value of the materials will be determined during the testing stage.

Applicability.   Editing for applicability becomes more subjective, since materials are reviewed in terms of the degree to which applications may be made to learning situations. For example, how well do materials conform to an approved format, if one exists? Several questions related to applicability include:

> Do the materials present information that will aid in meeting the established objectives?
>
> Are the materials structured according to the approved format?
>
> Do the materials either incorporate sound learning strategies or provide for the inclusion of such learning strategies?

Similar to the editing discussed earlier on composition, the true applicability of materials will not be determined until the materials have been field tested.

Prepare a second draft.   After the materials have been edited for technical accuracy, composition, and applicability, revisions must be made. These revisions are typically based on the suggestions provided by reviewers and are to be made by the same individuals who prepared the first draft. This will help to avoid the possibility of changing the writing style throughout the materials.

Pilot test the second draft. The materials should now be ready to try out with a small group from the intended audience (e.g., teachers and students). Details about the pilot testing process are provided in Chapter 11. Generally, the group who pilot tests the materials need not be large. Most important is the criterion that persons using the materials have sufficient opportunity to try them out in realistic settings and that they can provide meaningful feedback to the developer. Students need to be informed that the purpose of the exercise is to assist in evaluating the materials and not student performance.

Prepare a third draft. A third draft of the materials is prepared so that any suggestions or recommendations resulting from the pilot testing can be taken into account. The revision at this point occurs only after all student data as well as teachers' comments from the pilot testing have been gathered and analyzed.

Field test the third draft. As detailed in Chapter 11, field testing should be carried out with several groups in settings representative of those where the materials are to be used. The purpose of this field testing is to assess materials quality with a larger number of students and teachers.

Prepare the final draft. Although few major revisions are likely to be needed at this point, the field testing results should be carefully examined to determine if any steps must be taken to make appropriate changes in the materials so that they can be ready for dissemination.

Duplicate the materials. The last stage involves duplication of sufficient numbers of copies needed for those who are to receive the materials. In addition, ample copies need to be on hand for meeting future needs and maintaining a supply until a revision of the materials occurs.*

Managing the curriculum materials development process

One has only to review the many stages involved in the development of curriculum materials to realize that this process is quite complex. However, if quality materials are to be developed, all stages must receive due consideration. Thus it

*Adapted from *Instructional Systems Development for Vocational and Technical Training*, by F. Coit Butler. Englewood Cliffs, N.J.: Educational Technology Publications, 1972, pp. 143–144.

is essential for those who provide leadership in the development of materials to incorporate sound management techniques with the development stages identified earlier.

Accountability

If resources such as money and time are to be associated with the development of materials, then some form of accountability must be employed to ensure that these resources are used wisely. Accountability is necessary regardless of who is providing the resources. For example, if a special proposal has been written and approved for the development of materials with funds from some outside agency (e.g., state department of education), then the sponsoring organization will be expecting quality materials to be developed within the time frame specified in the original proposal.

Another example of accountability deals with materials produced using resources provided at the local level. As mentioned earlier, time is money and where the development of materials is concerned, the time devoted by teachers to their development should not be wasted.

Quality control

Another important consideration in the management of curriculum materials development is quality control. The quality of materials must be considered continuously during the entire development process, with every effort made to help ensure that the final product is of the highest possible quality. The development of quality materials takes two key areas into consideration: standards of quality and management of quality.

The first quality area concerns factors associated with materials quality. These factors can be the sections comprising the Curriculum Materials Assessment Form (see Chapter 8). Such factors include grade level readability, appropriateness, biases, accuracy, verbal and visual fluency, usefulness and versatility, and learning environment use (Bennett and Muncrief, 1975). These and perhaps others must be considered during the development process if the materials produced are to be of high quality. Detailed discussions of each of these factors are provided in Chapter 8 and, therefore, will not be discussed here.

A second key area of quality control that was briefly mentioned earlier concerns the systematic approach to materials development. It is imperative that management techniques be developed and followed to assure quality control. While a number of management schemes may be used, two will be discussed here. These are a checksheet approach and the Program Evaluation and Review Technique (PERT).

Checksheet approach to quality control. One way of ensuring quality throughout the curriculum materials development process is to use a comprehensive checksheet. An example of a checksheet is provided in Figure 9–1. Through the

FIGURE 9–1. Checksheet for the development of interviewing for a job

Com-pleted	Development Stage	Person[s] Responsible	Completion Dates*		Comments
			Proposed	Actual	
✓	A. Preliminary Development Plan	S. Long	S	S	
✓	1. Determine curriculum content to be investigated	C. Brown	S+15 days	S+13 days	
✓	2. Determine terminal and enabling objectives	C. Brown	S+1 mo.	S+1 mo.	
✓	3. Identify special materials needed	C. Brown J. Smith	S+2 mos.	S+2 mos.	
✓	4. Review literature to determine what materials are available	C. Brown J. Smith	S+2 mos.	S+2½ mos.	
✓	5. Identify materials lacking in the content area	C. Brown J. Smith	S+3 mos.	S+3 mos.	
✓	6. Establish priorities for needed materials	C. Brown J. Smith	S+4 mos.	S+4 mos.	
✓	B. Finalize Development Plan	S. Long	S+5 mos.	S+5½ mos.	
✓	1. Conduct an intensive literature review	Brown, Smith, Bailey, Jackson	S+5½ mos.	S+5½ mos.	

*S denotes starting date.

FIGURE 9-1. [continued]

Com-pleted	Development Stage	Person[s] Responsible	Completion Dates*		Comments
			Proposed	Actual	
✓	2. Obtain relevant references and re-sources	Brown, Smith, Bailey, Jackson	S+6 mos.	S+6 mos.	
	3. Prepare a first draft of the materials	Brown, Smith, Bailey, Jackson	S+7 mos.		
	4. Edit the first draft	Black, Griner, Jones	S+7½ mos.		
	5. Prepare a second draft	Brown, Smith, Bailey, Jackson	S+8 mos.		
	6. Pilot test the second draft	Combs, James	S+9 mos.		
	7. Prepare a third draft	Brown, Smith, Bailey, Jackson	S+9½ mos.		
	8. Field test the third draft	Roller, Coffey, Richards, Bass	S+10 mos.		
	9. Prepare the final draft	Brown, Smith, Bailey, Jackson	S+10½ mos.		
	10. Duplicate the materials	S. Long	S+12 mos.		

use of a form such as this, each stage in the materials development process can be easily identified. Furthermore, individuals associated with the various stages can be identified and their responsibilities delineated. Provision is made for noting the actual completion date for each stage, which serves as a means of maintaining accountability and provides information that may be used when planning future materials development efforts. As each development stage is completed, it may be checked off and the completion date recorded. This serves to keep a record of the progress made to date.

The checksheet is divided into two major phases. The first phase constitutes the preliminary development plan, which serves to collect information leading up to the decision as to whether materials should be developed. If the decision is made to develop high priority materials, the second phase serves to list those stages that will lead to the completion of the materials.

Program evaluation and review technique [PERT]. Another management scheme that may be used to assist with quality control is the Program Evaluation and Review Technique (PERT). The PERT chart can be used to plot out the various stages in the materials development process. In addition, projected completion dates can be noted for each stage. A PERT chart using the example depicted in the previously discussed checksheet is provided in Figure 9-2. While Figure 9-2 does not indicate what individuals are responsible for which stages, a strategy sheet can be attached to the chart to indicate who these persons are.

These management schemes are but two examples of the many that can be used. The point is that some type of procedure must be formulated to help assure quality control during the development of materials. The scheme selected must be shared with all those involved in the development to help avoid duplication of effort and to graphically illustrate the importance of each stage in the successful completion of the materials.

Disseminating curriculum materials

The curriculum materials development cycle is not complete until materials have been disseminated to the intended users. The value of disseminating curriculum materials is quite clear, since valuable and useful material may end up on a shelf and never be used if teachers are not made aware of their worth. Failure to provide plans for dissemination would be a great loss to those who might have benefited from the materials and a great waste of human and monetary resources to those who developed the materials. When devising plans for the dissemination of materials, several factors need to be considered in order to assure that those who are to be reached during the dissemination are efficiently and effectively informed about how the materials may be used.

FIGURE 9-2.   PERT chart for the development of interviewing for a job

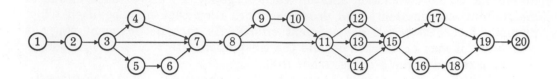

1. Preliminary Development Plan Prepared (S)*
2. Curriculum Content Determined (S+15 days)
3. Terminal and Enabling Objectives Determined (S+1 mo.)
4. Needs for Special Materials Identified (S+2 mos.)
5. Literature Reviewed (S+2 mos.)
6. Materials Lacking Identified (S+3 mos.)
7. Priorities Established (S+4 mos.)
8. Development Plan Finalized (S+5 mos.)
9. Intensive Review of Literature Conducted (S+5½ mos.)
10. References and Resources Obtained (S+6 mos.)
11. First Draft Prepared (S+7 mos.)
12. First Draft Edited–Technical Accuracy (S+7½ mos.)
13. First Draft Edited–Composition (S+7½ mos.)
14. First Draft Edited–Applicability (S+7½ mos.)
15. Second Draft Prepared (S+8 mos.)
16. Pilot Tested (S+9 mos.)
17. Third Draft Prepared (S+9½ mos.)
18. Field Tested (S+10 mos.)
19. Final Draft Prepared (S+10½ mos.)
20. Materials Duplicated (S+12 mos.)

*S denotes starting date.

Potential audience

One of the first steps in dissemination is to determine the potential audience for the materials. Since primary consideration has been given to the development of materials in vocational education, the major audience will naturally be vocational educators. In addition to these people, consideration should also be given to applicability in other teaching areas.

Vocational educators.   Vocational educators who might be interested in curriculum materials could be classified into two groups. One group would be those teachers who are in the vocational specialty area for which the material was originally developed. If, for example, a group of health occupations instructors developed curriculum materials in the occupational nurses' aide area, other health occupations instructors may also have an interest in securing this material.

A second group of vocational educators would be those individuals who are not in the specific vocational area for which the materials were developed.

Assume that a group of home economics educators developed curriculum materials in the area of displaying various types and colors of fabrics. Distributive education coordinators might also be interested in the materials. In fact, sharing materials across vocational education speciality areas should be encouraged, since content is often found to be similar in a variety of curricula. Even if the curriculum materials must be adapted or revised in order to make specific application to a vocational area, they may be of help to teachers who are experiencing a void of curriculum materials in a content area being taught.

Academic teachers.   Academic teachers constitute another potential audience for vocational curriculum materials. Vocational educators have maintained for years that more contact and interdisciplinary planning is needed among academic and vocational teachers. Vocational curriculum materials can serve a useful purpose in this area, since many of them may be used by academic teachers, especially those materials designed for student use. As an illustration, assume that trade and industrial teachers develop curriculum materials for student use in the area of carpentry and each student must read the materials. Thus the materials could be used by reading or English teachers to develop the student's reading ability. Another example would be a set of materials developed in agribusiness management that includes numerous mathematical problems. Mathematics teachers could make use of these problems in their classes. Without a doubt, many of the materials developed for use in vocational education classes could be used by academic teachers in teaching students the skills, knowledges, and attitudes associated with their particular teaching areas.

Geographical considerations

The size of the potential audience for curriculum materials is difficult to assess. If materials are developed at the local level, local schools may not see the dissemination of materials to other parts of the state as a high priority. In this case, any dissemination that occurs may take place more by accident than through any planned effort. However, if the materials are developed by a university, state educational agency, or other similar group, the dissemination should be targeted to a larger audience. In fact, materials developed through these organizations should be disseminated widely, since this is typically one of their responsibilities. The dissemination might take on a statewide, regional, or even national flavor.

Dissemination in relation to cost

One decision that must be made before dissemination is carried out concerns the price of the materials in relation to the mode of distribution. Three modes of distribution are free distribution, cost recovery, and distribution for profit.

Free distribution.   The dissemination of materials without cost appeals to many individuals; however, several problems arise when this mode is used. If materials are to be distributed free of charge, the cost of developing and duplicating them must be supported by another source of income. If the materials are developed through special grants, their duplication may be included as a part of the project. However, this does not imply that all other costs incurred during their development are covered. It must also be kept in mind that the development of materials does not come entirely free. If personnel are assigned this task, then something else (e.g., teaching) must be given up. Some states support individuals to develop curriculum materials for teachers and do not charge teachers for them. Even though the materials may be provided free to teachers, costs do occur at the state level for their development.

Another concern associated with the free distribution of materials is the number of copies that are to be distributed per individual request. Again, if the materials are developed with special project funds or with state funds, the decision regarding the number of items to disseminate per individual request is usually decided when the development project is started. If materials are to be distributed free, many agencies limit distribution to one copy per individual.

Cost recovery.   The cost recovery approach is designed to recoup expenses incurred during the development of curriculum materials. This dissemination mode is used by many nonprofit organizations such as universities or other public educational agencies. When the cost recovery mode is used, accurate records must be maintained to ensure that the actual development costs are recovered. Postage for mailing the publications, secretarial assistance in filling orders, and other similar areas must not be overlooked. The major objective of this approach is to provide materials to others at the lowest possible cost with no cost incurred nor profit made by the developer. Materials disseminated through this mode are often highly competitive with similar materials produced through commercial companies.

Distribution for profit.   The dissemination of materials for profit is similar to the previously mentioned cost recovery, except that a profit margin is established and this amount is added to the development cost. One major concern with this alternative is whether the developing organization can legally sell materials at a profit. Many agencies have policies against selling curriculum materials for profit. Regardless of the mode selected, prior approval for the distribution of materials should be obtained before they are disseminated. Realistically, this decision should be made when development of the materials is initiated.

Adoption of curriculum materials

The dissemination and, hopefully, the eventual adoption of materials that are produced represent the true goals of any materials developer. The adoption of materials cannot be left to chance, but should be the culminating step in a well planned educational program designed to disseminate the materials produced. In planning for the dissemination of curriculum materials, developers need to consider how people adopt new ideas or innovations. Palda (1966), Rogers (1962), Rogers and Shoemaker (1971), and Robertson (1971) are just a few of many individuals who have identified various stages in the adoption process that have relevance to the adoption of curriculum materials. In reviewing these and other appropriate sources, five stages have been identified as a basis for dissemination of materials. The stages, which can guide the dissemination and eventual adoption of curriculum materials in education, include:

> *Awareness.* The point at which an educator first learns of the materials.
>
> *Interest.* The educator develops curiosity in the materials and seeks or desires to seek more information.
>
> *Evaluation.* Mental application of the materials is made to the educator's particular situation to assess the materials' potential.
>
> *Trial.* The materials are actually used by the educator to determine their value.
>
> *Adoption.* If the materials prove to be valuable, the educator adopts the materials.

Any dissemination program must include planned activities that will place an educator or prospective user of the materials in contact with them in such a way as to experience these five adoption stages in a positive manner. This dissemination applies to in-service programs as well as preservice programs.

In-service and preservice materials orientation programs

As was stressed earlier, the dissemination of materials must include a planned educational program for those who could utilize the materials. Dissemination typically focuses upon in-service programs for teachers; however, orientation for preservice students is also vital.

In-service level. The purpose of conducting an in-service program for the dissemination of curriculum materials is to maximize the use of the materials. Although in-service programs may take many different formats, several basic components should be incorporated into any in-service session.

 Provide hands-on, practical exercises. Teachers will be more likely to adopt new materials if they are provided with the opportunity for a hands-on exercise. This experience should closely parallel the situation the teachers will be facing with their students. In this way, they will be made aware of the necessary skills or procedures needed in order to use the materials effectively.

Provide for relating materials to teachers' speciality areas. Teaching situations differ, and thus teachers may need some assistance in adapting the materials to their own particular situations. Examples should be provided of the ways materials can be used in different situations. Involving teachers in the in-service program who have had experience using the materials is a real benefit to others in attendance, since they will be able to understand how the materials have been used by their colleagues.

Provide teachers with examples of the materials as they leave. An effective way to end an in-service program is to have something for the teachers to take with them. This could be a complete set of the materials or just a small section. For example, if only part of the materials are to be distributed, then providing the teachers with a form for students to fill out as part of the complete set of materials might encourage the teachers to use the form on a trial basis and eventually to secure and use the entire set of materials. Teachers are more apt to feel the in-service program was beneficial if they have something to carry home with them to use.

Provide for follow-up of teachers. A follow-up session with teachers (either individually or as a group) who have used the materials on a trial basis may help in their eventual adoption. Some teachers may have experienced difficulty using the materials and assistance at this point can aid greatly in finding solutions to problems encountered. Other teachers may actually improve the materials or change the suggested format and make them even more effective. Furthermore, follow-up activities by curriculum materials developers or their colleagues serve to encourage those who have not used the materials to do so.

Preservice program. The education provided to preservice teachers regarding the value and use of new curriculum materials should not be overlooked. The discussion relating to in-service education applies equally well to the preservice program. An appropriate time for this orientation is during student teaching. Preservice teachers will be able to see how the materials can assist them to become better teachers and how curriculum materials will better prepare their students for employment.

Updating curriculum materials

Once curriculum materials are developed, the curriculum developer must make a conscious effort to update materials as appropriate. This is most important, since technological changes occur so rapidly. For example, the recommendation to use a certain pesticide last year may not represent a safe or desirable recommendation for the current year. While teacher educators and curriculum specialists must share the responsibility for keeping teachers up-to-date, the major responsibility rests with the teacher to assure that the information being taught is accurate and represents the best knowledge students should be learning.

SUMMARY

Regardless of the materials available on the market today, curriculum specialists and teachers are often faced with the situation of needing certain types of curriculum materials and discovering that none exist in the content area where teaching is to be done. This situation leaves few alternatives for the educator, with the most logical one being to develop the materials needed.

Before the actual decision is made to develop these materials, several important factors must be considered to determine if such development is feasible. These factors include dollars and time available, time needed to develop the materials, and available expertise. Among the decisions that must be made concerning the development of materials are what materials are needed and why, who should develop them, and when and where they should be developed. Other factors to consider are the target population, dissemination planned, support needed, and development alternatives, either through a team or individual approach.

The curriculum materials development process consists of several stages. Once the needed materials are identified, the development stages include obtaining the references and resources needed, preparing the first draft, editing the first draft, pilot testing, revising, field testing, preparing the final copy, and duplicating. Management of the curriculum materials development process can be guided by use of a PERT chart, checksheet, or other similar management scheme.

The dissemination of materials is a critical and important step. Without teacher adoption and use, materials may be shelved and thus would be useless. For this reason, materials need to be disseminated in an orderly manner to vocational educators and others who may have an interest in them. Before the dissemination is conducted, decisions regarding cost must be made as well as how the materials will be introduced through in-service education to teachers and to preservice students.

Once materials are released and made available to teachers, continuous efforts must be made to keep them up-to-date. Otherwise, materials that have been developed will soon become obsolete.

REFERENCES

Baker, Robert L., and Schutz, Richard E. *Instructional Product Development*. New York: Van Nostrand Reinhold Company, 1971.

Bennett, James G., and Muncrief, Martha C. *Instructional Materials for Occupational Education*, Misc. Pub. 75–3. Albany, N. Y.: Bureau of In-Service Education, New York State Education Department, June, 1975.

Butler, F. Coit. *Instructional Systems Development for Vocational and Technical Training*. Englewood Cliffs, N. J.: Educational Technology Publications, Inc., 1972.

Dale, Edgar. *Audiovisual Methods in Teaching*, 3rd Ed. Hinsdale, Ill.: The Dryden Press, Inc., 1969.

Gerlach, Vernon S., and Ely, Donald P. *Teaching and Media, A Systematic Approach*. Englewood Cliffs, N. J.: Prentice-Hall, Inc., 1971.

Law, Gordon F., ed. *Contemporary Concepts in Vocational Education*, First Yearbook of the American Vocational Association. Washington, D.C.: American Vocational Association, 1971.

Morgan, Barton; Holmes, Glenn E.; and Bundy, Clarence E. *Methods in Adult Education*. Danville, Ill.: The Interstate Printers and Publishers, 1976.

Palda, Kristian S. "The Hypothesis of a Hierarchy of Effects: A Partial Evaluation," *Journal of Marketing Research* 3 (February, 1966).

Pucel, David J., and Knaak, William C. *Individualizing Vocational and Technical Instruction*. Columbus: Charles E. Merrill Publishing Co., 1975.

Robertson, Thomas S. *Innovative Behavior and Communications*. New York: Holt, Rinehart, and Winston, Inc., 1971.

Rogers, Everett M. *Diffusion of Innovations*. New York: The Free Press, 1962.

Rogers, Everett M., and Shoemaker, F. Floyd. *Communication of Innovations: A Cross-cultural Approach*, 2nd Ed. New York: The Free Press, 1971.

Silvius, G. Harold, and Bohn, Ralph C. *Planning and Organizing Instruction*, 2nd Ed. Bloomington, Ill.: McKnight Publishing Co., 1976.

10

Individualized, Competency-based Packages

Introduction

If the establishment of a quality curriculum is to take place, examination must be made of emerging as well as conventional approaches to education. One such approach that has gained much support from vocational and technical educators is the individualized competency-based package or module. Modules have been used most effectively as an alternative to conventional forms of education. This is particularly true when they have been utilized in conjunction with competency-based education (CBE).

The discussion that follows provides the reader with an opportunity to learn more about the character of CBE as well as examine the potential it has for improving vocational and technical education. Initially, a rationale for competency-based education is provided. This is followed by a description of how modules may be used within the framework of CBE. Discussions of module components and module development procedures provide detailed information and examples for those who may choose to develop individualized, competency-based packages.

Rationale for competency-based education

As one might expect, vocational teachers and administrators alike have expressed concern about why a competency-based instructional focus should be any different from that already being used. A vocational teacher may, for example, comment that all of his or her graduates are competent, so why should any changes be made in the curriculum. In a broad sense, any mode of instruction aims at, or should aim at, competence of students and graduates. However, as will be indicated, CBE does not differ from other modes of education in its goals. Instead, CBE is unique in terms of its underlying assumptions and the approaches that characterize it.

Assumptions underlying competency-based education

There are several aspects of CBE that distinguish it from traditional instruction. Although each of these aspects may be found in some conventional curricula, it is their collective use that constitutes a truly competency-based program. CBE has been variously described by authors (e.g., Elam, 1971; Finch and Hamilton, 1974; Clark, 1973) as focusing on several key areas. These areas include the nature of competencies, criteria used to assess the competencies, ways that student competence is assessed, student progress through the program, and the program's instructional intent.

Competencies. At the core of CBE is competency. It reflects the ability to do something in contrast with more traditional ability to demonstrate knowledge. Specifically, competencies for vocational and technical education are *those tasks, skills, attitudes, values, and appreciations that are deemed critical to successful employment*. Just because something is performed by a worker does not mean that it is automatically classed as a competency. The worker must, in fact, find this competency to be a critical aspect of employability in the occupation. Each competency, then, evolves from explicit statements of worker roles; and, since competencies align so closely with the occupation, student competence is ultimately assessed in much the same way as that of a worker. In order to ensure that assessment will be fair to the student, all competencies are detailed and made available for anyone to examine.

Criteria. In the assessment of student competence, it is not enough to merely call for a global exhibition of performance. The teacher must also have available those specific criteria which clarify each competency. For example, it might be that each student in a particular curriculum should be able to complete a job application form. In order to judge student competence in this area accurately, one must know what standards the completed form should meet as well as the conditions under which it should be filled out. Criteria associated with each competency have to reflect both the level of acceptable performance and the conditions associated with this performance. As with competencies, criteria are also made available to each student so there is no question as to what constitutes mastery.

Assessment of competence. When student competence is being assessed, primary consideration should be given to application. Although it may not be possible for all vocational students to be assessed as they perform in actual work settings, this is the ultimate evaluation environment one should strive for, since it is the most realistic. Even though it may not be possible to assess competency on the job, each student should be evaluated as objectively as possible using the most realistic applied standards available. Unlike some traditional instructional modes, student competence and not grading provides the primary evidence of achievement. Consequently, instructional staff are required to move beyond the traditional knowledge type measures such as multiple-choice and essay examinations and focus on assessment that aligns with worker competence in the real world.

Student progress.   A curriculum is typically divided into clearly identifiable time frames such as years, quarters, terms, semesters, and weeks. These serve as starting and ending points for various portions of the instruction and enable an instructor to say that students have completed a certain phase of the curriculum. In fact, students do not always achieve at the same rate. Abilities such as reading, mathematics, and verbal comprehension vary greatly among vocational students and a time-based curriculum cannot take this wide variance into account to the extent that any instructor would like. In contrast with a time-based mode, competency-based education uses demonstrated competence as a determiner of student progress toward program completion. This enables students to proceed through a program at their own particular rates, based upon their individual abilities, and thus master specified competencies in a shorter (or longer) time period.

Instructional intent.   The explicit intent of competency-based education is to facilitate student achievement of competencies specified in the program. Each instructor is obligated to provide a sufficient variety of learning experiences so that students will be afforded an opportunity to master a minimum set of competencies; and, in effect, the instructor may be held accountable for student achievement. If it is indicated that each student should be able to prepare a résumé which meets certain specific criteria, the instructor cannot just provide basic information on this area and assume that all the learners will be able to perform the task. The instructor is obligated to make available to students those experiences which facilitate the development of résumé writing skills. This might include the use of role playing and other simulation activities, outside resource persons, and other techniques that enhance and aid each student's attainment of competence.

Instructional focus of competency-based education

Several additional aspects of competency-based education may not be classified as mandatory elements but are quite often found in programs of this type and, in many respects, enhance the operation of a competency-based program. In fact, many operational programs utilize these elements as primary means of aiding students in achieving mastery of program competencies. Those elements most often found in CBE programs include individualization, instructional technology, and systematization. Although it must be recognized that there is considerable overlap across these three elements, the character of each element is distinctive enough to allow separate discussion.

Individualization.   Individualizing instruction has been a concern of educators for a number of years and one might say that its beginning was in the minds of early teacher-philosophers such as Plato and Aristotle. These scholars as well as Rousseau, Froebel, and others relate to a common theme in their writings, that of providing consideration to the needs of the individual within the instructional process.

However, current conceptions of individualized instruction take on a much more comprehensive focus (Impellitteri and Finch, 1971; Finch, 1974). Individualized instruction as provided in contemporary educational curricula is comprised of at least five basic components. As indicated in Figure 10–1, these components are the student, instructional environments, instructional content, instructional media, and instructional strategies. Of these five components, the student is central, with the others arranged in a manner designed to maximize learning. Obviously, different arrangements might be more appropriate for attaining different instructional objectives or for two students to achieve the same objective. For example, providing a nonreading option (the media component) might be most critical in aiding a poor reader to achieve mastery of a certain competency, whereas another student might be aided to a greater extent by the physical setting (the environments component).

If instruction is to be truly individualized, these components cannot be dealt with one at a time. Instead, they must be examined, organized, and used in concert. The teacher should assure that all factors which may contribute to student learning are taken into account. When instructional content, media, environments, and strategies are being selected for and used in individualized instruction, the student should always serve as the primary focal point.

Since CBE is inherently geared toward meeting students' needs, it comes as no surprise that most competency-based curricula are also individualized. This can be most readily evidenced by the instructor's basic commitment to aid each student in attaining mastery of specified competencies. However, it should be remembered that individualized and competency-based education are not synonymous. One could develop an excellent individualized program focusing on the development of drama appreciation that may not necessarily assist a student in building competence needed for employability in a particular occupation or occupational area. Individualization, then, is seen as a means of enhancing competency-based instruction so there may be greater assurance of meeting students' individual needs and providing learning experiences that align with personal capabilities. By making a commitment to individualizing instruction the teacher is saying that he or she will provide whatever arrangements necessary to ensure that each student may be constantly engaged in learning those things which are of greatest value to himself or herself. This is what makes individualization a most meaningful contributor to the goals of CBE.

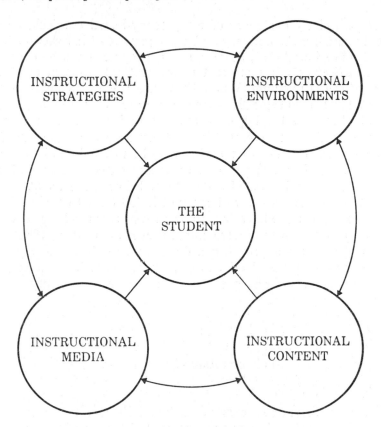

FIGURE 10–1. **Basic components of individualized instruction**

Instructional technology. Although CBE can be carried out using many of the same instructional materials and media one may already have on hand, many instructors employ various forms of technology designed to assist students in meeting specified objectives. These can be hardware (e.g., cassette tapes, computers, single-concept films), software (e.g., programmed instruction, booklets, modules), or some combination of these two that will help meet students' needs. If, for example, students are required to develop competence in the area of interpersonal relations, audio- or videotaped feedback to students who are role-playing various parts might provide the necessary link between theory and actual practice. As one might expect, technology can play a major role in the individualization of instruction. Students may go back and view a single-concept film several times, whereas a live demonstration of skill by the teacher cannot be repeated each time a student wants a review. It is imperative to remember that the use of instructional technology does not automatically lead to individualization or CBE. Technology must be employed to truly aid students in the development of competence. For if technology is used indiscriminately, the result will be far worse than not using it at all.

Systematization.   Many designers of competency-based curricula provide some means of systematizing the delivery and management of instruction. Persons involved in CBE have found that, in most cases, programs can be conducted more efficiently and effectively if some sort of instructional system is utilized as an integral part of the curriculum. What, then, are the key aspects of an instructional system? First, it is typically learner-centered. This goes beyond the traditional concept of merely helping each student to learn. The system is usually designed so that student involvement in the learning process is maximized. Additionally, each student knows exactly what is to be learned and how far he or she has progressed toward meeting specified learning outcomes. Second, evaluation and feedback are integral parts of the system. Information about the extent to which instructional objectives have been met is fed back to the student and the instructor. This allows modification to improve areas where deficiencies or shortcomings may exist in the instructional process (Banathy, 1968). Obviously, the instructional systems approach can do much to enhance any curriculum in general and competency-based education in particular. With a sound instructional system supporting CBE, greater control over the quality of instruction can be assured.

Modularization of instruction

Traditionally, administrators, curriculum specialists, and teachers have arranged instruction to take place over a designated period of time such as hours, days, weeks, or months. Although this sort of arrangement has proven to be very useful for scheduling purposes, it often leaves much to be desired as far as students are concerned. Distributing instruction over a specified time frame often forces the vocational and technical teacher to organize content and instruction so that the primary focus is on the average learning level of class members. The result of this arrangement is obvious. With a lack of opportunity to progress at their own rates, some students may be held back while others are not able to keep up with the pace of instruction.

Conventional instruction is also arranged in a somewhat arbitrary manner. A curriculum often takes the form of courses or semesters that relate more readily to grading periods than anything else. Since this arrangement is usually imposed upon teachers, they are required to fit varying amounts of instructional content into rigidly prescribed units of instruction. Consequently, some courses may be too short for the material to be covered while others are too long—the result being that course length and content coverage needed to meet specified objectives are seldom completely congruent.

In recent years, the modularization of instruction has been put forth by certain educators as a viable alternative to conventional instructional arrangements. This approach is based upon the premise that students are better able to learn if they do so at their own rates and study those areas which focus directly on mastery of a particular objective or set of objectives. Naturally, persons who are concerned with the establishment of individualized, competency-based curricula have recognized the potential of modularized instruction, since it appears to focus directly on meeting students' needs and development of those competencies which are critical for successful employment. For these reasons, instructional modules are often found in use where individualized, competency-based education has been implemented. Since the instructional module is quite different and distinct from its traditional counterpart, anyone who is contemplating use of the modular approach to instruction should be aware of its characteristics as well as certain advantages and limitations associated with it.

The instructional module

In contrast with conventional curriculum design, the modular approach utilizes the module as a basic instructional building block instead of arranging content around a subject, unit, or lesson. This is a fundamental difference that exists and it has many implications for anyone involved in curriculum development and implementation. What, then, is an instructional module? Briefly stated, it may be defined as *a self-contained package that includes a planned series of learning experiences designed to help the student master specified objectives* (Goldschmidt and Goldschmidt, 1972; Russell, 1974). Although modules are not always individualized, this appears to be the rule rather than the exception. Naturally, when one is designing an instructional package, it is fairly simple to incorporate various aspects of individualized instruction into the finished product. It would, therefore, be in order to include "individualized" in the above definition if a developer is intent on assisting all of his or her students to the maximum extent possible.

Module characteristics. A clearer understanding of the module may be obtained if its basic characteristics are described. These characteristics focus on the way a module is organized and packaged as well as how it relates to student needs.

First, the module is self-contained. This means the student does not have to go to the instructor and ask what to do next or what materials he or she should use. Instead, information and directions are provided within the module. Each module should provide explicit guidance with regard to what the student is to do, how he or she should proceed, and what resources and materials might be used. Instructional resource materials are usually either incorporated into the module or made available on a check-out basis.

Next, the module is typically individualized. Although development costs and time constraints may preclude the complete and absolute individualization of a module, the developer should attempt to include as many characteristics of individualized instruction as possible. As a minimum, each module should make provision for self-pacing, feedback, and mastery. Examples of these character-istics as they apply to modular instruction would be as follows:

> *Self-pacing:*   The student may progress through the module at his/her own rate. Each may set up a working-learning schedule based upon personal capabilities.

> *Feedback:*   The student receives an assessment of progress as he/she proceeds through each module learning experience. At the end of each learning experience, the student is provided with immediate re-sults of performance.

> *Mastery:*   The student focuses on attainment of specific, measurable ob-jectives within each module. By taking module learning experiences, attainment of these objectives is enhanced.

Third, the module is a complete package. This reflects a logical and sys-tematic flow of module content with a definite beginning and ending. In other words, the student knows when he or she has begun, progressed to a certain point, and completed a particular module. There is no question as to what must be done to achieve certain objectives and whether or not they have been achieved.

Fourth, the module includes learning experiences and objectives. Expe-riences are provided to assist each student in mastering specified objectives as efficiently as possible and may make provision for a broad range of student involvement from reading and listening to role playing, simulation, and coopera-tive work experience.

Fifth, included in each module is some mechanism for assessing the ex-tent to which a student has achieved module objectives. This aspect of the module is extremely important, since it relates quite closely to student feedback and mastery. Equally important, however, is the fact that assessment provides a means of formalizing the criteria or standards associated with module com-pletion.

The module and competency-based education.   Although the modular approach may serve as an excellent vehicle for implementing CBE, it should be recog-nized that just because instruction is modularized does *not* mean it is compe-tency-based. For example, a set of modules might be developed that focus on improving students' avocational pursuits. While these modules may be of great value in their own right, they do not necessarily focus directly on the develop-ment of vocational and technical competencies—tasks, skills, attitudes, values, and appreciations identified as being critical to successful employment. It is ex-tremely important to make this distinction, since time and effort devoted to module development may be wasted if the developer does not give initial consid-eration to what competencies the module will focus on. Just because certain as-pects of a curriculum focus on general education does not mean that they must be taught in a traditional mode. Modules can be developed that assist students in achieving a multitude of objectives. However, it must be recognized that not all modules are competency-based. Only those which focus directly on the development of actual competencies may be classed in this manner. The discussion that follows will, naturally, focus on developing individualized, competency-based modules, since these are of most value to the vocational and technical teacher. Many of the basic development procedures apply equally well to all individualized instructional packages. Developers should find these procedures of value no matter what sort of module is being contemplated.

Advantages of instructional modules

When serious consideration is being given to the use of modular instruction in a vocational and technical curriculum, decision makers may have a great deal of concern about the benefits derived from this instructional approach as contrasted with more traditional modes. Does the module tend to stimulate students or turn them off? How does this approach affect the instructor in terms of his or her role? What difficulties may arise with regard to grading? These and other questions may be asked by anyone who is considering the use of instructional modules.

There are several distinct advantages afforded by the modular approach to instruction. Although they apply to a greater or lesser degree in different educational settings, each can be considered a basic plus when the modular approach is implemented. These advantages take the form of more direct **focus** on the individual student, greater quality control, and increased relevance within the curriculum.

Focus on the individual student. As modules are incorporated into the instructional process, the instructor will begin to note a change in his or her role. Instead of lecturing to groups, the instructor becomes more involved in facilitating, managing, and evaluating module learning experiences and serving as a student resource. Time that might otherwise be spent speaking to groups of students can now be used to assist individual students where *they* need help. One student may move through a series of modules at a fairly rapid pace and need little assistance, while another might need help many times and proceed rather slowly. The fact is that, because students are able to work on their own and are more responsible for their actions, the instructor can be available more often to meet with each student, determine how he or she is progressing, and decide what assistance, if any, is needed.

Quality control. Although the need for extensive quality control in education is well recognized, incorporating this concept in a curriculum is quite difficult. All too often the instructor "feels" that students can demonstrate competence in a certain area but lacks the system necessary to be sure that this is true. Because the conventional instructional process may not allow each and every student to demonstrate how well he or she can perform, some students might never be required to show their skills. If carried to extremes, this situation could lead to the development of graduates who range from extremely effective to completely incompetent. Obviously, modules cannot solve all the problems associated with vocational and technical instruction but they may be able to improve the quality control process, particularly as students move toward completion of the curriculum. Although some students may proceed more rapidly than others and complete a number of learning experiences, there should always be a minimum level of competence associated with successful completion of a curriculum. By using the standards specified in each module, the instructor is given a unique opportunity to specify these standards and provide them to students. Thus each student knows exactly what standards are expected and can work toward their achievement.

Relevance within the curriculum.   A final advantage of module use is improved relevance. But just how is relevance increased within a curriculum, particularly from the student's vantage point? Since each module is designed to assist students in the mastery of specified objectives, the effects of this approach on students are fairly simple to judge. The students should easily see that objectives are actually spelled out and detailed guidance with regard to meeting these objectives is provided. Thus each student should be able to note the relationship between instruction and outcomes.

Limitations of instructional modules

By virtue of their characteristics, modules have certain limitations in the instructional environment. However, it may be best to call them potential limitations, since, in many cases, problems may be reduced or even eliminated if a concerted effort is made in this direction. What, then, are some of the major limitations associated with the use of modules? These generally include difficulties in module development, scheduling and grading processes, and instructional support.

Module development.   Logically, a module is only as good as the person or persons who develop it. And at this juncture, the success or failure of modular instruction is often decided. A finished module may contain meaningful objectives and assessments, but if the various learning experiences are tedious or poorly written, the package will most likely be rejected by students. Furthermore, a module with major shortcomings is worse than no module at all, since the effect is students being turned against modular instruction. It is imperative that all modules used in a curriculum be of high quality in terms of *both* instruction and subject matter content. Problems in these areas will surely cause students to react in an adverse manner. The limitation that presents itself in this regard is one's ability to write. If the instructor can communicate well in writing and is creative and precise, the development of high quality modules should present no problem. However, if he or she cannot develop and arrange content so that it flows smoothly and logically and stimulates students to master objectives, the finished product will not be accepted by learners. A second limitation associated with the development process is time. All too often, the vocational and technical instructor has numerous responsibilities besides writing instructional packages; and writing a module becomes a lower priority when one is "asked" to develop next year's budget or participate in preparations for an accreditation visit. Time, the ingredient needed so much when modules are being developed, is often absent. This absence can certainly affect module quality, since many hours must be devoted to development if the finished product is to be acceptable and usable.

Scheduling and grading processes. Some of the processes associated with traditional instruction can severely limit the use of modules. Even though an instructor wants to develop a program that is individualized and competency-based, scheduling requirements may dictate otherwise. Rigid rules such as no provision for incompletes or nonacceptance of module completion as evidence of progress toward program completion make it difficult for any instructor to implement instruction that really meets students' individual needs. Grading can also present a significant problem. Since each module is designed to help students attain mastery of its objectives, the basic "grade" would be either a pass or a no-pass instead of a letter grade (e.g., A, B, C, D, F). The instructor who decides to use modules should, therefore, be sure that module mastery is compatible with some sort of grading scheme if the school requires that grades be given. Perhaps different levels of mastery can be stated that are, in turn, associated with different grades; or, it may be possible to note achievement in accordance with the number of modules a student completes. In any event, as long as grading is being used in a school, provision must be made for compatibility with modular instruction. Otherwise, there will be severe limitations imposed on the use of modules in the vocational and technical program.

Instructional support. The individualization of instruction is often enhanced by single-concept films, slide-tape presentations, and other types of media; and it is this very enhancement that may become a problem for the instructor. Media are often quite expensive and may necessitate the use of expensive equipment that neither the instructor nor the school is able to afford, even though the item in question can make a significant contribution to the learning process. For example, a film might be available for purchase that assists students in understanding problems associated with job interviews. Although this film may make the best addition to a module, its use is dependent upon purchase and availability, two factors that are often problems as far as films are concerned. Instructional support, then, can become a major problem when one decides to establish individualized, competency-based instruction. This is in terms of both financial and logistical support. If a resource is needed to assist students in achieving certain objectives, it should be acquired and made available to them. Otherwise, some students may not be able to achieve the objectives and will suffer from this lack of achievement.

Module components

Modules developed by different persons and groups often assume a variety of shapes and sizes. The variety is only limited by a developer's expertise and experience in creating an instructional package. It should be noted, however, that modules typically contain certain basic components; otherwise, they are not classified as modules. These components are an introduction, objectives, learning experiences, resource materials, and assessments.

Formatting

Numerous individuals and groups have devised module formats that appear useful for particular instructional needs. Russell (1974) and Johnson and Johnson (1973) describe the development of modules that can be used in a variety of settings including science, history, and drafting. An International Labor Office booklet (ILO, 1973) presents a vocational training system that utilizes modules of employable skill. The approach used by ILO emphasizes that modules should be *directly* related to employment needs. The modules of employable skill concept looks at a person and asks what that person will do and what training he or she will need. The UNIPAC approach to instruction enables a broad range of instruction to be packaged in module form. UNIPACs have been developed for a number of curriculum areas such as science, social studies, humanities, business education, and physical education (Projects 81 Center). Extensive use has been made of the Learning Activity Package (LAP) in vocational and technical education, particularly in the area of distributive education. Numerous LAPs have been developed under the auspices of the Interstate Distributive Education Curriculum Consortium that focus on a broad range of distributive education skills (Ditzenberger, 1977).

Obviously, locating modules that have already been developed and using them would be the easiest approach. Unfortunately, modules have not been developed for all vocational and technical areas, nor does it appear likely that they will be for some time. Realistically, the vocational and technical instructor should plan to become involved in some module development if he or she intends to have an individualized curriculum.

Since formatting is based upon both teacher and learner considerations, no attempt will be made to show all of the various formats one might use. Instead, a general format and specific examples are presented as a useful guide for module development. Figure 10–2 shows a typical module formatting arrange-

---

FIGURE 10-2. Typical module format

Introduction. In this section, the student is told how the module may serve as a means of developing certain skills, knowledges, and attitudes. Specific prerequisites (if any) are detailed and directions for proceeding with the module are provided. Also included are a cover page and table of contents.

Objectives. Provided here are specific statements of performance the student should be able to demonstrate while progressing through the module and when completing it. Terminal and enabling objectives specify the activities to be performed, the conditions under which they are to be performed, and the levels of acceptable performance.

Preassessment. This section is useful in determining student entry performance and provides a means of "testing out" of the module if he or she can demonstrate mastery. Student instructions and an assessment form with explicit criteria are placed here to ensure that there is no question about what constitutes module mastery.

Learning Experiences. Learning experiences are detailed that correspond with each of the enabling objectives. They are designed to provide each student with the best means of mastering module objectives. Each learning experience consists of one or more activities followed by assessment and feedback to the student. Learning experiences may include resource materials such as information sheets, references, audiotapes, etc., that serve to enhance the learning process and help individualize instruction.

Resource Materials. This section serves to reference all resource materials used in the various learning experiences so that both teacher and student may locate them rapidly. The resource materials listing aids the teacher in "setting up" for students and ensuring that all materials are available when they are needed.

Postassessment. This section is quite similar to the preassessment and, in many cases, may be exactly the same. The postassessment focuses on the terminal objective and an assessment form is used to determine whether or not it has been met.

---

ment. It should be noted that provision is made to ensure meeting the individual needs of students. Included are the following:

1. Each student is afforded the opportunity to "test out" of the total module or any of the learning experiences.

2. The student receives feedback as to his/her performance on each learning experience and the entire module.

3. No specific time limit for module completion is imposed on the student. Instruction is self-paced.

4. There is no question as to what the student should do to demonstrate module mastery.

In some instances, certain portions of the module are included in a teacher's section or guide. If it is felt that assessment keys should not be used by students, the keys may be included in the teacher's guide. Likewise, if a performance examination is to be used, details for its administration would be provided there. Special procedures might need to be included such as organizing for a role-playing situation or planning a field trip. Since details of this nature are only relevant to the instructor, it is best to omit them from the student's material. Formatting is a personal matter, so the module developer may want to experiment with different approaches until one (or more) is found suitable to both instructor and student. Above all, it should be remembered that the format serves as a means to an end—module mastery. If it does not help in this regard, modification is in order.

Basic components

Each module contains basic components that work in concert to assist students in achieving mastery of the package. Even though Figure 10–2 provides a brief glimpse at these components and what they consist of, a developer needs to have more details about the module introduction, objectives, preassessment, learning experiences, resource materials, and postassessment prior to the time this task is begun. One must be aware that even though they may appear to be quite simple and straightforward, components may be deceptive, since they are closely articulated with each other to ensure that the individualization process is successful.

Module introduction.   The module introduction sets the stage for learning by providing each student with an understanding of how this module relates to other modules or experiences he or she may have had. It bridges the gap between known and unknown and aids in stimulating the learner to complete the module learning experiences. As is the case with other module components, the introductory statement is written clearly and concisely and at the appropriate reading level for students. The total statement does not usually exceed two pages in length and focuses on relevance of the module to the student. Also included as part of the introduction component are specific prerequisites (if any), directions for proceeding with the module, and a table of contents. Prerequisites can consist of other modules, out-of-school experiences, or demonstrated achievement of certain basic skills such as reading or mathematics. Basically, prerequisites should specify what the student should be able to do *before* he or she is allowed to proceed with the module. Module directions can be short or lengthy depending upon the comprehensiveness of the particular module. In either case, provisions for "testing-out" of the module should be detailed and information about general procedures the student will follow must be provided. Typically, the student is given three alternatives. He or she can decide to either 1) take the preassessment and, if successful, proceed to another module; 2) take the preassessment and, if unsuccessful, proceed with the present module; or 3) not take the preassessment and proceed with the present module. These three alternatives seem to provide a great deal of flexibility, since the student is not forced to take a test if he or she does not feel ready to do so. Figure 10–3 contains an example of a module introduction including the introductory statement, prerequisites, and table of contents.

Objectives.　Module objectives are provided so the student will always know what is expected of him or her. They are stated in the performance terms that were detailed in Chapter 7, which include the activity, conditions under which the activity is to be performed, and level of acceptable performance. Thus no question should exist as to whether or not the student has mastered a particular objective. There are two types of objectives found in each module. These are the *terminal* objective and the *enabling* objectives. In order for a module to be classified as competency-based, the terminal objective should align closely with that which is expected of a person in the worker role. For example, if a competency-based module were to be developed that culminates in a student being able to compute using a calculator, the author should 1) be sure this was, in fact, a competency associated with the occupation being taught; and 2) develop a terminal objective that specifies standards acceptable to at least entry level employment. The terminal objective, then, may be defined as *the specification of student performance [activity, conditions, and level] that is most closely aligned with competence expected in the worker role.*

　　　Much as the term implies, the enabling objective serves as a means to an end. It is an education-related objective that, together with other enabling objectives, contributes to the student's mastery of a terminal objective. The enabling objective can focus on a student's verbal comprehension (e.g., write down the sequence in which a task is performed), physical action (e.g., perform a complex manipulative skill), or attitude (e.g., state the consequences of an action). Aside from being stated in performance terms, the only requirement is that the enabling objective contribute to mastery of a terminal objective. An example of terminal and enabling objectives for a module is presented in Figure 10–4. Note that the terminal objective specifies performance in an actual work setting, whereas each of the enabling objectives contributes to this terminal behavior.

Preassessment.　The preassessment provides a means for each student to "test out" of the module if he or she is capable of doing so. This, of course, means the preassessment should be closely correlated with the activity, conditions, and level of performance specified in the terminal objective. Usually the preassessment is developed in conjunction with the terminal objective so that each aligns closely with the other. This alignment is important, since one can seldom state a terminal objective that does not refer to some sort of supporting test or checklist. A frequent shortcoming of the preassessment is its being written to measure student knowledge while the terminal objective reflects applied performance. If this sort of practice is followed in a module, students will be able to "test out" even though they may not be able to demonstrate application.

　　　Many proponents of individualized instruction state that the preassessment should be diagnostic in nature, and thus enable the teacher to determine

---
FIGURE 10–3.   Example of a module introduction*

Module Title: Administering Insulin

Introductory Statement: As a part of your experience as a student nurse, you will be caring for patients with Diabetes Mellitus. When dealing with patients who have diabetes, it is important to have a working knowledge of health care areas such as diet, exercise, personal hygiene, urine testing, and the administration of insulin and oral hypoglycemic agents. In order to help patients understand this illness and deal with it effectively, you must have a thorough understanding of the disease and its treatment. This module is designed to provide you with a basic knowledge of insulin and its administration.

Prerequisites: Before beginning this module, you should have 90% of the items correct on a basic mathematics test (P.S–6) and a knowledge test dealing with techniques for administering parenteral medications (P. 7–9).

Directions: Check to be sure that you have completed the prerequisites. Then review the introductory statement and objectives. If you think you can demonstrate mastery of the terminal objective and successfully complete the preassessment, start on another module. If you think that you can demonstrate mastery of the terminal objective and do not successfully complete the preassessment, or if you decide not to take the preassessment, start the first learning experience of this module.

Table of Contents:

---

*Adapted from a module developed by Patsy Rinehart.

FIGURE 10–4. Examples of terminal and enabling objectives*

Module Title: Stockkeeping in Distributive Business

Terminal Objective: In an actual work setting, demonstrate your skill at stockkeeping. Your competency will be evaluated by your job sponsor using a stockkeeping checklist. Specific standards of performance are provided on the checklist.

Enabling Objectives:
1.   Give three advantages of good stockkeeping to the salesperson and the customer. Explain how these advantages lead to increased sales profit (Learning Experience I).
2.   Name twelve specific duties you can perform in your work station as a part of stockkeeping, and briefly describe what is involved in completing each of these duties (Learning Experience II).
3.   Using a sample inventory sheet and related information provided, complete a simulated physical inventory (Learning Experience III).

---

*Adapted from a module developed by Harry C. Lunsford III.

which portions of the module a student should and should not take. Although this concept is fine in theory, the development of a measure that diagnoses student shortcomings accurately and consistently is very difficult. Also, since each learning experience contains an assessment of its own, progress can be ascertained as the student proceeds through a module and corresponding instruction provided to meet individual needs and capabilities. It might be best to reemphasize the necessity of stating meaningful prerequisites for each module. If this is done, the prerequisites can serve a diagnostic function as far as student capabilities and limitations are concerned. Thus, between the stated prerequisites and individual learning experience assessments, an instructor should be able to diagnose student needs in a meaningful manner.

The preassessment consists of instructions and the assessment form. Instructions must be concise and to the point with no ambiguity. The student should be told exactly how to proceed and what is to be performed. If a particular task is complex, it may be necessary to list procedures to be followed or limitations imposed on the assessment process. The assessment form itself consists of problems, items, or standards associated with mastery of the terminal objective. Just as the terminal objective may vary, so will the assessment form. Preparation of a technical report would have certain unique standards or criteria, whereas preparation of meat or fowl for consumption would reflect others. Assessment of applied performance usually takes the form of a checklist or set of explicit standards (e.g., $\pm.0010$ inch on all machined surfaces). The basic approach depends somewhat upon how accurate one can be in assessing a student's performance. The examples in Figure 10–5 serve to illustrate two different types of preassessment. The first deals with an area that can be assessed more objectively and includes mechanically measurable standards. The

---

FIGURE 10–5.   Examples of module pre/postassessments

Module Title: Planning Adjustments*

Directions: A worksheet with a trial balance and the necessary data for merchandise inventory, supplies, and prepaid insurance is provided on the following pages. You are to record necessary adjusting entries on the worksheet in general journal form. On the blue worksheet, record the adjust entries for merchandise inventory supplies and prepaid insurance. Total the adjustments, prove, and rule. The level of acceptable performance is 100% of the entries correct.

The following is information you need in order to complete the worksheet.

1.   The amount of merchandise inventory at the end of the fiscal period is $42,000.

*Adapted from a module developed by Judith A. Allen.

Module Title: Oxyacetylene Cutting†

Directions: Your proficiency at oxyacetylene cutting will be evaluated by your instructor using the items provided below. Each item should be at a level of "good" or "excellent." If any item is below "good," you should continue to practice until you have reached this standard.

Item	*Proficiency Level* [*circle one*]			
1. Cut is square horizontally	Excellent	Good	Fair	Poor
2. Cut is square vertically	Excellent	Good	Fair	Poor
3. Little slag is present	Excellent	Good	Fair	Poor

†Adapted from a module developed by Eugene M. McIlwee, Jr.

---

second example reflects assessment in a more subjective area. In this case, criteria are of a more relative nature, since absolutes are not readily available.

Learning experiences.   Each learning experience serves as a vehicle to assist the student in mastering enabling and terminal objectives; and, since learning experiences are used by individual students, they *must* communicate on their own. They should be designed so that they provide each student the *best* means of meeting specified objectives. This reflects the necessity of having alternatives available for students that align with their particular learning styles. As a rule of thumb, there should be at least one learning experience for each enabling objective. This will ensure the students of having formal assistance in mastering every objective in the module.

Every learning experience consists of one or more activities followed by assessment and feedback. An *activity* is a specific way that the student becomes involved in moving toward learning experience (and module) mastery. It specifies participation on the part of the student such as listening, viewing, reading, analyzing, constructing, and so forth. There are variants to the basic activity. These include the alternate and the optional activity. The *alternate activity* is one that provides a different but equally good route to achieving mastery of the learning experience. An alternate activity is used so that each student may have a choice of several activities from which one may be selected that is most compatible with his or her learning style. An *optional activity* is designed to give the student enrichment beyond basic mastery of the learning experience. It may contribute to learning experience mastery, but because the optional activity is not required, there is no way of ensuring that a particular student will select the activity. Therefore it must be considered as being supplemental to the basic instruction. This sort of activity is best suited for students who want to go beyond the basic activity and gain a broader base of instruction or who seek further information about an area of special interest. By developing alternate and optional activities and letting students know they exist, the instructor is providing an individualized learning environment that is difficult to improve upon.

The *assessment* accompanying a learning experience is designed to let each student know whether he or she has mastered its corresponding enabling objective. Although usually not as formalized as the pre- and postassessments, it should still accurately measure the student's progress and let him or her know whether or not a particular learning experience has been mastered. Provision may be made for self- and peer assessment as well as assessment by the instructor. The decision as to which should be used is somewhat arbitrary, depending most upon whether or not the objective can be assessed meaningfully by a student or peers. Typically, when the objective deals with a critical task that requires professional judgement, the instructor is the designated evaluator. Of utmost importance is the provision made for giving a student immediate feedback about his or her performance. This consideration must be incorporated into every module learning experience, since the student knows where he or she stands relative to module completion and what deficiencies have to be corrected or changes made. The module learning experience example provided in Figure 10-6 includes a restatement of the enabling objective followed by various activities. The assessment that would be provided on a subsequent page is of a self-examination nature. In this case, the student would have access to a key so that answers might be checked for accuracy.

Resource materials.   The developer is only limited by his or her imagination in the selection and development of resource materials for modules. Besides the more basic resources such as textbooks and manuals, use can be made of information sheets, audiotapes, slide/tapes, single-concept films, videotapes, programmed instruction, 16-millimeter films, laboratory equipment, and others. In fact, the range of resources goes beyond use with individual students. Directions

---

FIGURE 10–6.   Example of a module learning experience*

Module Title: Measurement of Body Temperature, Counting Pulse, and Respirations

Learning Experience I

Objective: Measure the oral temperature of a seated classmate with 100% accuracy, applying the basic principles of patient comfort, therapeutic efficiency, economy, and safety.

Alternative #1:

Read the information sheets provided on pages 6 to 12 of this module.

Practice the procedures outlined in these information sheets by taking the oral temperature of a classmate.

Feedback may be obtained by taking the self-test on page 14. If you answer the questions with 90% accuracy, take the temperature of a seated classmate using the checklist and standards on page 16 to evaluate your performance.

Alternative #2:

Read pages 26 to 29 and 99 to 112 in the programmed unit of instruction *AIDS TO DIAGNOSIS.*

Feedback is continuous in programmed instruction. After completing the reading, take the self-test on page 14 and check your answers on page 15.

Practice the procedures listed on pages 27 to 29, *RIVERSIDE HOSPITAL PROCEDURE MANUAL*, by taking the temperature of a seated classmate.

Feedback may be obtained by using the checklist on page 15 to evaluate your performance.

---

*Adapted from a module developed by Leona C. Eastwood.

for role playing and other forms of simulation may be included; brainstorming and buzz group sessions may be utilized. The main constraint regarding use of resources is their availability and practicality. If an item is not readily available or the cost is prohibitive, it will probably not fit into a module very well. Likewise, if the resource is cumbersome to use or requires special technical assistance, the instructor is not likely to make use of it. Even though the above considerations rate much concern, they are overshadowed by a basic consideration in the selection of any resource material. Does the resource actually contribute to mastery of the enabling and terminal objectives? If the developer says no, then there is no real reason to use the resource. Combining this consideration with cost, it might be best to *select the least costly resource that will assist students in mastering the particular objective* (Butler, 1974). If this basic rule is followed, resource materials should certainly be used more realistically and, at the same time, more stringently.

Postassessment.   As each student completes the final learning experience or feels ready to demonstrate mastery of a module terminal objective, he or she is given the postassessment. As with the preassessment, focus is on the terminal objective and the extent to which it has or has not been met. In fact, certain modules may have a postassessment that is identical to the preassessment. This is particularly true when a terminal objective specifies applied performance that does not allow a student to become "test-wise." For example, a module whose terminal objective deals with welding a joint or typing a letter uses a tangible product as evidence of performance. In either of these cases, both a pre- and postassessment would not be needed. If, however, the terminal objective indicated that a student should score at a certain minimum level on a multiple choice examination, it might be best to have a separate pre- and postassessment. This situation would require that two assessments be constructed that are different and yet measure mastery of the same terminal objective. Development of postassessments would follow the previously mentioned guidelines established for preassessments. Since they both relate directly to the terminal objective, there is no reason for construction methods to vary.

Developing modules

Basically, developing a quality module is not unlike the preparation for any good instruction. Content must relate to objectives in a meaningful manner and be arranged in such a way that learning is maximized. However, since the module is used for individualized learning and is usually self-contained, the developer should recognize that any errors may spell disaster for students. Even a deficiency as small as faulty page numbering can seriously disrupt student learning, since the package does not "stand alone." The module must be both accurate and precise, since an instructor's time is better spent assisting students than correcting development errors or the results of these errors. In the development of modules, a basic set of steps may be followed, starting with planning for module development. This is followed by determining objectives and prerequisites, developing assessments, developing learning experiences, developing resources, and trying out the module. To better aid the development process, a Module Development Checklist is provided (Figure 10–7). This should be referred to as a module is being developed, since it focuses on key areas that might affect quality of the finished product.

Planning for module development

Module planning involves the determination of how the developmental process will actually take place and what competency or set of competencies (if any) will

FIGURE 10–7.   Module development checklist

I. *Introduction*

    A. The introduction is clear and concise.   Yes ? No
    B. The introductory statement shows how this module relates to other
        modules or experiences.   Yes ? No
    C. Prerequisites specify what the student should be able to do before
        proceeding with the module.   Yes ? No
    D. Directions to the student include an explanation of how to "test
        out."   Yes ? No
    E. An easy to follow table of contents is included.   Yes ? No

II. *Objectives*

    A. Terminal and enabling objectives are provided.   Yes ? No
    B. Each objective specifies the activity to be performed, conditions,
        and level of acceptable performance.   Yes ? No
    C. The terminal objective focuses directly on application.   Yes ? No
    D. Enabling objectives contribute to student mastery of the terminal
        objective.   Yes ? No
    E. Objectives reflect a logical flow from basic awareness and under-
        standing to applied performance.   Yes ? No

III. *Pre- and Postassessments*

    A. Pre- and postassessments align closely with the terminal objective.   Yes ? No
    B. Instructions for completing the assessment are provided for the
        student.   Yes ? No
    C. The assessment procedure used is the most objective one for the
        particular situation.   Yes ? No
    D. Pre- and postassessments are identical when the student cannot
        become "test-wise."   Yes ? No

IV. *Learning Experiences*

    A. Each learning experience is correlated with an enabling objective.   Yes ? No
    B. Every learning experience provides students with the best means of
        achieving specified objectives.   Yes ? No
    C. Learning experience activities provide specific ways that the student
        may participate in the learning process.   Yes ? No
    D. Alternate activities are used as necessary to provide different (but
        equally good) routes to module mastery.   Yes ? No
    E. Optional activities are used as necessary to supplement and enrich
        basic instruction.   Yes ? No
    F. Learning experience assessments provide the student with feedback
        about his or her progress.   Yes ? No

FIGURE 10–7. [continued]

V. *Resource Materials*

    A. All resource materials used in the module are listed in sufficient detail so that they can be readily identified and located.   Yes ? No

    B. Each listed resource actually assists students in mastering module objectives.   Yes ? No

    C. Each resource is the least costly with regard to assisting students in achieving mastery of a particular objective.   Yes ? No

VI. *General*

    A. All written material is at a reading level that is suitable for the intended audience.   Yes ? No

    B. Continuity exists between the various segments of the module.   Yes ? No

    C. Technical content is accurate and up-to-date.   Yes ? No

    D. There is no sex or racial bias in the module.   Yes ? No

VII. *Tryout*

    A. Teachers perceive the module as being an effective teaching-learning device.   Yes ? No

    B. Students perceive the module as being an effective teaching-learning device.   Yes ? No

    C. Students master module learning experiences in an efficient manner.   Yes ? No

---

serve as a base for the package. Since a module may be used by one teacher or a number of teachers, the employment of a developmental process that aligns with this eventual use is important. Likewise, the students who will be involved with a particular module largely determine the various teaching strategies to be used. Let us say that only one teacher will use a module. If this were the case, he or she would probably be best suited to develop the module and involvement from others would not be necessary. However, if a number of teachers plan to use a particular module, their active participation in the developmental process is essential. A basic concern here is with generalizability. When it is desired to have a module that can be used by a number of teachers, the package must be accepted by each one and have content applicable to diverse instructional settings. In sum, any development process should take into account the teachers and students who will use the module, for they are the ones who eventually pass judgement.

    If the module is to be truly competency-based, the particular competency or set of competencies to serve as its foundation needs to be identified. This entails examining available lists of competencies and selecting one or more that can be packaged in a meaningful, challenging manner. The arrangement is largely dependent upon an individual's professional judgement or consensus of several persons who are experienced in curriculum development and knowledgeable about the occupational area. This first conceptualization is somewhat arbitrary and a module may be reconceptualized if feedback obtained from users (teachers and students) suggests that a revision be done.

Determining objectives and prerequisites

Once module competencies have been established, it is relatively easy to develop a terminal objective or objectives that deal with student performance. First, the activity to be performed is specified. This is followed by the delineation of criteria used to determine whether or not the student has been successful and, finally, the conditions under which performance is to be demonstrated and assessed (e.g., in the worker role). Criteria and conditions may be gleaned from sources such as technical manuals, interviews with workers and supervisors in the occupational area, and process or product specifications. It is extremely important that each criterion and condition be clearly stated and not be open to misinterpretation, since the information will be made available to both student and teacher. This process is followed by the development of enabling objectives. These objectives have the same three components; however, their focus is more specifically in the direction of interim outcomes. Further details about the development of objectives are presented in Chapter 7.

The specification of prerequisites flows logically from stated objectives and should ask this question: What does the student need to complete the module that will *not* be provided for in any of the learning experiences? Those knowledges, skills, and so forth that are not taught in the module become its prerequisites and serve as a quality control point for the instructor. Although almost any number of prerequisites may be indicated, it is a good idea to keep them at an absolute minimum. Excessive numbers of prerequisites affect both the instructor and the student because there may be an undue burden placed on each in terms of testing time. Additionally, since many traditional prerequisites are artificial, it appears best to justify each one placed in a module and to document the justification. This will ensure students being treated fairly.

Developing pre- and postassessments

As soon as objectives and prerequisites have been specified, the development of pre- and postassessments is possible. If these assessments are one and the same, it is a relatively simple task but still one that should not be taken lightly. Since a well stated objective forms an excellent base for assessment, a close look should be taken at how the terminal objective is put together. If the activity, criteria, and conditions are clearly delineated, there should be little problem in moving from objective to assessment. On the other hand, lack of clarity will surely require the developer to go back eventually and revise his or her objectives. One key to meaningful assessment is the preciseness with which criteria are stated. Another key is the extent to which criteria actually sample the activity being measured. It becomes clear that, to be of value, each assessment should focus directly on the area to be measured and do this in an exacting manner. While this is difficult to accomplish, it adds immeasurably to module quality.

Developing learning experiences

Since learning experiences are typically associated with enabling objectives, it is reasonable to expect that they each contribute to student mastery of these objectives. As each learning experience is being developed, thought should be given to the ways that students can be assisted in meeting module objectives. With a commitment to individualized instruction goes the obligation to ensure that *each* student's needs are met; and the learning experiences with vaious alternate and optional activities have the potential to meet these needs. This is an area where developers can be maximally creative in the approaches used to reach students. Reading and nonreading alternatives may be used. Extensive enrichment can be provided via optional activities. Students can be required to become actively involved in their own learning instead of maintaining a passive role. In other words, the developer is only limited by his or her imagination and budget.

Learning experiences seem to follow some of the basic rules of instruction. From the initial to the final learning experience, instruction typically flows from simple to complex and from the known to the unknown. Most important to competency-based education, however, is the flow from basic awareness to applied competence. This flow relates to student progression through various learning experiences in a module. The initial learning experience may deal with developing the student's knowledge or awareness of a particular competency. This might be followed by other learning experiences focusing first on specific skills, knowledge, or attitudes, and then combinations of these. Finally, the student is required to demonstrate competence in an applied setting.

Developing resources

Since many instructors are not media specialist, it is best to focus on those resources which can be developed and used with a minimum amount of skill. The business of instructional resource development actually begins when learning experiences are being developed, for it is there that decisions are made regarding the strategies best suited to various objectives. Once a decision has been made to use resources in a module, the most pressing concern is resource selection and development, an area that may cause great frustration. Although many resources are available to the teacher, few go beyond awareness and knowledge. This means, of course, that the teacher may have to develop resource materials dealing with application.

Trying out and revising the module

The ultimate test of any module is how well it performs. Even though a great amount of time and effort may have been put into a module, this is no guarantee of success. Trying out modules and examining their effectiveness is an integral part of the development process, and here at least two questions can be answered. Did students perceive the module as an effective teaching-learning device? Did the students master module learning experiences in an efficient manner? There are other questions that could be asked but these serve as a minimum set of concerns for the developer. Only through actual use can the teacher really tell whether or not a module does the job it was intended to do. In the revision process, it is best to focus on making changes to correct deficiencies rather than making wholesale modification. This will save time, and in the long run, may aid the developer in identifying specific problem areas common to several modules.

SUMMARY

Competency-based education represents a meaningful alternative to conventional forms of education. Its direct focus on the development of tasks, skills, attitudes, values, and appreciations critical to successful employment makes competency-based education most relevant to vocational and technical education. CBE is often enhanced through the use of individualization, instructional technology, and systemization. While by no means mandatory parts of CBE, these elements greatly improve the operation of such a program.

The instructional module is often found to be an integral part of CBE. Modules or self-contained packages are typically individualized to assist in meeting students' learning needs. The utility of modules may be seen through focusing instruction on the individual student, aiding with the quality control process, and adding relevance to the curriculum. There are, however, certain limitations associated with modules. These include the time available to develop them as well as instructional support, and scheduling and grading processes.

The typical module format is set up in such a way that learning will be enhanced. Various components of a module include the introduction, objectives, preassessment, learning experiences, resource materials, and postassessment. While the individualized, competency-based module does represent a break from conventional instruction, it is a most important approach for the contemporary curriculum developer to consider, particularly in light of the potential it has to better meet individual students' needs.

REFERENCES

Banathy, Bela H. *Instructional Systems*. Palo Alto, Calif.: Fearon Publishers, 1968.

Butler, F. Coit. *Instructional Systems Development for Vocational and Technical Training*. Englewood Cliffs, N. J.: Educational Technology Publications, 1972.

Clark, Francis E. "Now You Can Teach Classes of One," *Industrial Education Magazine* 62, No. 12 (December, 1973), pp. 28–29.

Ditzenberger, Roger. "Perceived Barriers to Implementing a Distributive Education Learning System," *Journal of Vocational Education Research* 2, No. 1 (Winter, 1977), pp. 49–59.

Elam, Stanley. *Performance-Based Teacher Education, What Is the State of the Art?* Washington, D.C.: AACTE, December, 1971.

Finch, Curtis R. "Individualizing Instruction: What Can You Learn from Research?" *American Vocational Journal* 49, No. 6 (September, 1974), pp. 28–29.

Finch, Curtis R., and Hamilton, James B. "Performance-Based Teacher Education Curricula: Implications for Programs," *The Changing Educational Scene*. Columbus: The Center for Vocational Education, Ohio State University, 1974.

Goldschmidt, Barbara, and Goldschmidt, Marcell. "Modular Instruction: Principles and Applications in Higher Education," *Learning in Higher Education* 3, No. 8 (April, 1972).

Impellitteri, Joseph T., and Finch, Curtis R. *Review and Synthesis of Research on Individualizing Instruction in Vocational and Technical Education*. Columbus: The Center for Vocational Education, Ohio State University, 1971.

International Labor Office. *Introduction of a Vocational Training System Using Modules of Employable Skill*. Geneva, Switzerland: ILO, 1973.

Johnson, Rita B., and Johnson, Stuart R. *Assuring Learning with Self-Instructional Packages*. Boston: Addison-Wesley, 1973.

Projects 81 Center. *UNIPAC Format*. Spokane, Wash.: Projects 81 Center, West 25 Fifth Avenue, undated.

Russell, James D. *Modular Instruction*. Minneapolis: Burgess Publishing Company, 1974.

11

Evaluating
the Curriculum

Introduction

There can be no doubt that the way a curriculum is planned and established has great impact on its quality. However, the process used to define and determine that quality is of at least equal importance. The role of evaluation in curriculum development cannot be overemphasized. When utilized properly, evaluation can help ensure that the curriculum is of a high quality and that deficiencies are identified before they cause major problems to arise.

What, then, constitutes evaluation? Within the context of curriculum development, evaluation may be defined as *the determination of the worth of a curriculum [or portion of that curriculum]. It includes gathering information for use in judging the worth of the curriculum, program, or curriculum materials* (Worthen and Sanders, 1973). Obviously, the task of evaluating an entire curriculum is quite complex and time-consuming. Thus evaluations often tend to focus on *programs* and *materials* (sometimes called educational products). While programs and materials are indeed closely related, the evaluation of each takes on a somewhat different air. This may be easily seen in the evaluation literature, where a clear distinction is made between the evaluation of educational programs and materials. Programs are often viewed as being synonymous with curricula; however, they more logically focus on formal aspects of education and typically on a specific course or instructional area (e.g., production agriculture, reprographics, child care). Materials, on the other hand, are typically instructional items such as guides, modules, texts, or multimedia packages that the developer feels have utility beyond a single teacher.

While it is recognized that an entire text could be devoted to curriculum evaluation, the information presented in this chapter should provide the curriculum developer with a foundation for conducting meaningful evaluation activities. Initial emphasis is given to the presentation of an evaluation framework that aligns with curriculum development. Next, various aspects of planning for evaluation are discussed including evaluation objectives and the development of an evaluation plan. The conduct of a program evaluation is then described. This is followed by a description of curriculum materials evaluation. Finally, thought is given to the ways evaluation results may be used to effect curriculum improvement.

A framework for evaluation

Curriculum evaluation in vocational and technical education is often dreaded and avoided. While many give lip service to evaluation by making comments such as, "Every time I meet with a student I am evaluating" or, "We evaluate whenever it is appropriate," the fact remains that few curricula are actually subjected to rigorous, systematic evaluations. The reason for this is quite simple. Educators often feel they have neither the time, the expertise, nor the inclination to carry out the type of comprehensive evaluation actually needed. Unfortunately, few realize that an evaluation does not have to take up much extra *time*. In fact, much of the curriculum development work that is already taking place can easily be part of an evaluation effort if meaningful standards and measures are used. In terms of *expertise*, there should be at least one person in a school district, community college, or area vocational school who is knowledgeable about evaluation and can bring his or her expertise to bear on this area. Likewise, professionals at the state level as well as college and university faculty may be in a position to provide needed assistance with evaluation plans. With regard to *inclination*, attitudes must change if evaluation is expected to have more than minimal impact on the curriculum. Administrators, deans, division chairpersons, supervisors, department heads, and teachers must all recognize the value of evaluation and integrate evaluation efforts into ongoing curriculum development and refinement activities.

One way this integration may take place is through the acceptance and use of a comprehensive evaluation framework. Just as curriculum development activities must be systematic, curriculum evaluation must, likewise, follow some sort of meaningful structure. Since the contemporary curriculum is quite comprehensive, evaluation must also be comprehensive, taking into account the various aspects of curriculum initiation, structuring, and operation. The diagram presented in Figure 11–1 serves to illustrate various aspects of evaluation that relate to curriculum initiation, structuring, and operation (Finch and Bjorkquist, 1977). It portrays an evaluation scheme that is both comprehensive and systematic. The four elements of evaluation include:

> *Context evaluation*, which deals with whether or not to offer a curriculum and, if so, what its parameters will be including focus, goals, and objectives.
>
> *Input evaluation*, which relates to deciding what resources and strategies will be used to achieve curriculum goals and objectives.

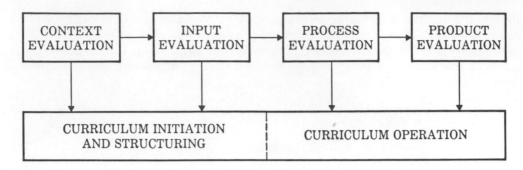

FIGURE 11–1.   A framework for curriculum evaluation

Process evaluation, which focuses on determining what effect the curriculum has on students in school.

Product evaluation, which deals with examining the curriculum's effects on former students.

Context, input, process, and product (CIPP) have been espoused by Stufflebeam (1969) as the key elements of a comprehensive evaluation, particularly when information is gathered and used for decision making. As emphasized in previous chapters, proper decision making is a key to the development of quality curricula. Thus it is most appropriate to use these four elements as a foundation for meaningful curriculum evaluation. Context and input evaluation are employed as the curriculum is being initiated and structured. These two elements focus on gathering information and making decisions relative to curriculum planning (e.g., whether or not to offer a curriculum), curriculum development (e.g., what content should be included in a curriculum), and curriculum materials development (e.g., whether or not materials are of a sufficient quality). Process and product evaluation relate to curriculum operation. Process evaluation focuses on decisions associated with curriculum effects on students (e.g., whether or not content is learned by students), whereas product evaluation is more closely aligned with decisions about curriculum effects related to former students (e.g., whether or not the curriculum affects graduates' employability).

Context evaluation

Context evaluation is basic to the curriculum development process, since it is closely associated with decisions about whether or not the curriculum should be offered and what goals and objectives should be used. Realistically, a comprehensive planning effort may include the essential elements of context evaluation. Specifically, context evaluation may define and describe the environment in which the curriculum will be offered, identify needs that have been used, and pinpoint constraints that keep them from being met. The aggregate data and information gathered serve as a basis for curriculum decisions and the subsequent development of objectives (Stufflebeam, 1971).

While there are numerous curriculum questions one might seek answers to in relation to context evaluation, the following are representative:

Should the curriculum be offered?

What student population will the curriculum serve?

What business or industrial population will the curriculum serve?

What content will be included in the curriculum?

What goals should the curriculum have?

What objectives will be used in the curriculum?

A variety of strategies and measures are associated with context evaluation. Among those discussed in previous chapters include the needs assessment, task analysis, and introspection, as well as others. By its very nature, context evaluation is quite speculative, particularly when a new curriculum is being initiated. Decisions are mostly subjective, since "hard" data may not always be available. Likewise, the rapidly changing nature of social needs, as well as the state of our economy and rapid advances in technology, present a rather amorphous state of conditions within which the evaluator must operate. The result is that context evaluation serves as a precursor to other more objective evaluation elements (Finch and Bjorkquist, 1977).

Input evaluation

Input evaluation, with its focus on resource and strategy decision making, has important implications for the curriculum developer. As the curriculum is being structured, every effort should be made to ensure that the best resources are chosen and that provision is made for their proper use. Decisions made in this regard are all too often based upon conjecture rather than data. Input evaluation serves to aid the developer in making more objective decisions about the ways content might be provided to students. This is accomplished by systematically identifying and assessing relevant capabilities of the educational agency, resources for achieving curriculum objectives, and alternate plans for their implementation (Stufflebeam, 1971). Resources can range from teaching, media, modules, and learning environments to teaching strategies and learning experiments. Information based on this identification and assessment is used to select specific resources and strategies to meet stated curriculum objectives.

The use of input evaluation is somewhat restricted, with a basic prerequisite being that a decision has been made to offer a vocational or technical curriculum. Since input evaluation is used to determine how resources might be best utilized to achieve curriculum objectives, the evaluator should be aware that data-based decisions are somewhat more arbitrary than their counterparts in process and product evaluation. The logic for this is simple: input evaluation focuses on *intended* rather than actual outcomes. Thus the extent to which input evaluation is meaningful depends on its true relationship to curriculum process and product (Finch and Bjorkquist, 1977). For example, a decision might be made to utilize team teaching in a curriculum because there is some feeling it will enable students to meet a greater number of objectives. This decision obviously is classed as tentative until such time as data show team teaching to be a significant contributor to student achievement.

Curriculum questions related to input evaluation include (but are by no means limited to):

What curriculum materials might be most useful in a particular educational setting?

Which materials are most acceptable to teachers and students?

How might individualized instruction be best implemented?

What are the relative effects of different materials on student achievement?

Data gathering for input evaluation can range from relatively simple to complex with instruments representing varying degrees of objectivity. Techniques utilized in the data-gathering process may include group consensus, expert judgement, literature and curriculum examination, management by objectives, and pilot experimental and quasi-experimental efforts (Finch and Bjorkquist, 1977).

Process evaluation

Process evaluation is most closely aligned with instruction. While all evaluation ultimately needs to focus on how the curriculum actually helps students, process evaluation appears most appropriate when the immediate effects of instruction are being examined. Since process evaluation deals directly with operation of the curriculum, the information associated with this element is most meaningful for the instructional staff. In the traditional sense, process evaluation is what many think of as being evaluation. However, it is but one part of a total evaluation framework. While the student's success in school is very important, it is meaningful only to the extent that inferences may be drawn to out-of-school success. Thus, while conclusions drawn from process evaluation are useful for curriculum improvement, they may not align very closely with employment-related outcomes.

Process evaluation can be used to examine a variety of areas. For example, it might be appropriate to determine the extent to which students have achieved certain curriculum objectives or whether a certain innovative program is operating properly. Examples of curriculum questions that could be associated with process evaluation include:

> How well are learners performing?
>
> What is the quality of instructional and support personnel?
>
> What are the costs associated with operating the curriculum?
>
> To what extent are students satisfied with their instruction?
>
> Which (if any) of the curriculum components are deficient?

The ways that process evaluation data may be gathered are numerous. These include the use of teacher behavior measures, teacher rating measures, standardized achievement measures, expert referenced measures, and teacher constructed knowledge and performance instruments (Finch and Bjorkquist, 1970).

Product evaluation

Evaluation must accomplish more than just focusing on the student in school. Major consideration must be given to ways the curriculum has aided former students. Product evaluation uses the former student as a focal point in determining this aspect of curriculum quality. The end product of any curriculum is the graduate, and this product (as well as his or her counterpart who did not graduate) needs to be studied if realistic statements are to be made about the worth of the curriculum.

Product evaluation typically takes place "in the field," with information being gathered from sources such as employers, supervisors, and incumbent workers (former students). These sources of information are extremely important, since process evaluation only deals with short-range in-school effects (Wentling and Lawson, 1975). In terms of curriculum questions associated with product evaluation, the following are illustrative:

> What is the mobility of former students?
>
> How satisfied are former students with their positions?
>
> How do employers view the performance of former students?
>
> How adequate is the curriculum preparing individuals for job entry?

Measures associated with product evaluation must be selected with care to ensure that an accurate assessment is made of curriculum effectiveness. Among those measures most frequently utilized in product evaluation are the skills survey, job satisfaction, job satisfactoriness, and value of the curriculum. Information that may be gathered via questionnaire items includes worker mobility, salary, unemployment, and additional training taken by the worker (Bjorkquist and Finch, 1969).

Planning for evaluation

While some may feel that evaluation just happens, this is far from the truth. The quality of any evaluation is closely related to the amount and type of planning that go into it. Planning to conduct a meaningful curriculum evaluation usually involves a great deal of time as well as systematic effort. The planning process is composed of several key elements. These include the establishment of sound evaluation objectives and the development of a comprehensive evaluation plan.

Evaluation objectives

Most curricula being developed today include performance objectives that specify the activity to be accomplished, the conditions under which the activity is to be performed, and the level of acceptable performance. These types of objectives have been detailed in Chapter 7. Although performance objectives are excellent from an instructional standpoint, they do not relate directly to the curriculum evaluation process.

It appears most efficient to focus initially on evaluation objectives as they relate to curriculum quality. Assume that a curriculum developer is interested in evaluating some materials such as modules that are hopefully of a "high quality." Translating this rather vague statement into more explicit standards related to quality, the curriculum developer might first ask the following broad questions:

1. Do students master the modules?

2. Is each module accepted?

3. Can the materials be used in the regular school setting?

The next logical step would be to develop more detailed questions related to each of these areas. Some of the questions that might be included under these broad areas are as follows:

Do students taking each module achieve mastery of learning experience objectives?

Do students have positive attitudes toward modularized instruction?

Do teachers perceive the modules as making a meaningful contribution to the teaching-learning process?

Will use of the modules require special facilities?

Will use of the modules require special equipment?

Will use of the modules require other resources?

Next, taking the first question and combining it with performance objectives, we can develop an evaluation objective such as:

> 70 percent of the students taking each module must complete each learning experience attempted and must master the objective in a given learning experience on the first trial.

This level of specificity is important when curriculum materials are being assessed, since it provides a clearly defined quality control level and cutoff point for recycling purposes. That is, if the objective was not met, the module would need to undergo revision and then be assessed again. The 70 percent is somewhat arbitrary, being based primarily on the type of subject matter involved, characteristics of the students, and the expected error associated with the testing process. Johnson and Johnson (1970) recommend 70/70 as a basic standard for the first draft of individualized instructional materials. That is, 70 percent of the students who are taught from the materials master at least 70 percent of the objectives. Wallbesser and Carter (1968) pose a more stringent standard of 90/90.

The next two questions might be translated into the following assessment objectives:

> 80 percent of the students completing each module must score 160 or higher on the Instruction Attitude Inventory.

> Teachers administering the modular instruction must react favorably to at least 80 percent of the items on the Teacher Reaction Form.

Each of these evaluation objectives is combined with an instrument to ensure that accurate assessments can be made. The attitude objective utilizes a summated rating instrument, with individual items on the inventory being combined to form a composite attitude score. The perception objective utilizes a form with items that are individually scored. In this case, items are not summed, they are examined individually with the 80-percent minimum for each teacher serving as a standard.

The three final questions might possibly be answered by merely reading the modules and speculating that special equipment would or would not be needed. However, since the real test of quality takes place when materials are being used, the following assessment objectives might be developed:

> None of the teachers using the modules indicate that materials required the use of special facilities.

> None of the teachers using the modules indicate that materials required the use of special equipment.

> None of the teachers using the modules indicate that additional resources were required.

Information associated with these objectives might be gathered via personal interviews with teachers or by way of items inserted on the Teacher Reaction Form. No matter how this information is gathered, it is important that instructors are given an opportunity to provide their personal views about the curriculum materials.

Similar types of evaluation objectives may be developed when a program evaluation is being planned. Let us say that it is desired to examine the effects of a cosmetology program on its graduates (product evaluation). While recognizing that the determination of actual program effects may be quite difficult, it is possible to pinpoint some indicators in this regard via the following broad questions:

1. Are program graduates employed as cosmetologists?

2. Are program graduates' supervisors satisfied with their work performance?

3. Are program graduates satisfied with their work?

Then, translating the first question into a meaningful evaluation objective, we might come up with the following:

> 80 percent of the 1978–1979 graduates who are available for employment
> as cosmetologists have positions in this occupational area.

Note that the objective specifies a certain employment percentage. This is important to spell out so that quality is clearly defined. Additionally, the group is clearly identified (1978–1979 graduates available for employment) to ensure that there is no question about the data source. If it were merely stated as "1978–1979 graduates," persons might be included in the group who were currently in the military service or who were physically incapacitated. The figure of 80 percent is merely illustrative, since the actual percentage would be determined through group consensus or some similar process.

The second question could be developed into the following evaluation objective:

> 90 percent of the 1978–1979 graduates employed as cosmetologists are
> rated at or above the mean by their supervisors on the Job Satisfactoriness Scale.

In this case, supervisors play an important role in determining quality, since they would be asked to complete Job Satisfactoriness Scales for 1978–1979 graduates. By specifying a standard (90 percent at or above the mean), there is no room for ex-post-facto standards to be established. In the absence of explicit standards, persons have occasionally been known to let the results form the standard. Thus, by providing a clear, measurable standard *before* data have been gathered, there is much greater assurance that an expected level of quality is not modified at a later date.

An evaluation objective based upon the third question might consist of:

> 75 percent of the 1978–1979 graduates employed as cosmetologists rate
> their work at or above 42 on the Job Satisfaction Index.

This objective allows the graduates to serve as a data source. Each graduate
employed as a cosmetologist is afforded an opportunity to indicate his or her job
satisfaction by completing a standardized instrument. The actual level of quality
(in this case, 42 or above) would most likely be determined through group consensus (e.g., the cosmetology advisory committee). As with the other objectives, standards are established before data are gathered so the evaluator will
be sure of what constitutes a measure of program quality.

While there are a host of additional evaluation objectives that could be
presented, the ones provided serve to illustrate the range of possibilities a curriculum evaluator might use. Whether the task is to evaluate curriculum materials, a specific program, or an entire curriculum, it is extremely important that
evaluation planning include meaningful, measurable evaluation objectives. Otherwise, there is not much point in conducting any evaluation at all.

Developing the evaluation plan

After evaluation objectives have been developed, a framework for gathering and
examining data may then be established. This framework, which is called the
evaluation plan, details the evaluation procedures to be followed and helps assure that a thorough, accurate evaluation will be conducted.

Need for the evaluation plan.   There are several reasons for using an evaluation plan. The first relates to the general value of planning. If an evaluation
were conducted without any prior planning, the result might be a faulty design
for data gathering, missing data, or invalid results. From a practical standpoint,
time spent in the planning process pays large dividends in helping to determine
curriculum quality accurately. Planning can assist the curriculum developer in
overcoming a number of potential problem areas such as scheduling, data gathering, and data analysis.

A second need for the evaluation plan may be associated with documentation. As an example, although many curriculum materials are "tried out," the
user seldom sees the detailed results of this tryout. What the evaluation plan
does in this regard is to help the curriculum developer document procedures
that were followed and results that were drawn for the data analysis. This documented evidence, together with the ways that the evidence was gathered, may
be used by others who want to know just how well the curriculum materials are
suited to their needs.

Evaluation plan components.   The plan for evaluation typically consists of five
components. Each component serves a useful purpose in the clarification of eval-

uation by detailing what is actually going to be evaluated, why it will be evaluated, and how it will be evaluated. While recognizing that some curriculum evaluation may be conducted without first developing a detailed plan, it is nonetheless important to keep the plan's content in mind when preparing to evaluate. The five components that make up an evaluation plan are: the rationale; objectives of the study; curriculum, program, or materials description; evaluation design; and description of the evaluation report (Worthen and Sanders, 1973). An example of a table of contents from an evaluation plan is provided in Figure 11–2.

FIGURE 11–2.   Table of contents from an evaluation plan

   I. Rationale   1

       A. Need for Evaluation
       B. Evaluation Approach
       C. Benefit Derived from the Evaluation

  II. Objectives of the Evaluation Study   3

 III. Curriculum Description   4

       A. Curriculum Objectives
       B. Philosophy and Content
       C. Curriculum Procedures
       D. Student Population
       E. Curriculum Setting

  IV. Evaluation Design   12

       A. Constraints
       B. Evaluation Model
       C. Appropriateness of Evaluation Design
       D. Determination of Achievement of Objectives
       E. Sources of Information
       F. Information Collection Methods
       G. Analysis Techniques
       H. Schedule of Events
       I. Proposed Budget

   V. Description of the Evaluation Report   18

Appendix A: Evaluation Instruments   19

Rationale. In this section of the evaluation plan, a need for the evaluation is specified. It is imperative that the need be clearly established so others will know exactly why the particular curriculum should be evaluated. Since an evaluation plan may be used to help sell people on the idea or convince them to allocate resources in this direction, the rationale section can serve as an introduction to the evaluation process and encourage the reader to read further. In addition to a specific statement of need, the general evaluation approach should be stated. This helps the reader obtain a feel for the evaluation's overall scope. A final item in this section consists of detailing the benefits derived from conducting the evaluation. These benefits should focus on the groups served (e.g., teachers and students) and how the evaluation will actually help them.

Objectives. This section includes the evaluation objectives. Precise evaluation objectives are provided so that there is no question about standards the curriculum should meet. In some cases, the objectives may not yet have been developed. If this situation exists, the plan should detail procedures that will be used to generate these objectives.

Description. At this point in the plan, it is important to describe thoroughly the curriculum, program, or materials being evaluated. The instructional objectives are provided and content is described. Any unique aspects of the content are explicated. Items such as media and personnel that must be available to support the curriculum need to be described; and, finally, details are given about the types of students who will use the curriculum and the settings in which it will be used.

Evaluation design. The evaluation design is the heart of the plan. It builds upon the rationale, objectives, and description in such a way that relevant data can be gathered and valid results generated. In this section, a general organizational design for the evaluation is provided. This design should take into consideration the specific curriculum being evaluated as well as evaluation constraints. If, for example, there are certain factors such as time, dollars, or legal barriers that might limit the scope of the evaluation, these should be detailed so the reader may see exactly why the evaluation is being conducted in a particular manner. Information needed to determine whether or not objectives have been met is detailed. This would include information sources and collection methods as well as a collection schedule. Whether the evaluation involves a simple survey of users or a complex experimental design, the exact process used to collect information must be specified. Techniques for analyzing the collected information are also provided. While the actual data analysis process might be somewhat dependent upon its specific nature, it is most meaningful to have in mind the various ways data may be dealt with. Also included in the design section is a proposed budget for the evaluation. This budget should detail expenditures that are directly associated with the evaluation process. Items that might conceivably be related to evaluation efforts include printing, travel, data processing, typing, and personnel costs. Instruments that will be used to gather information about curriculum quality are generally included in an appendix so that the reader may see exactly what will be used in this regard. This might include standardized measuring instruments and/or initial drafts of instruments that will undergo validation before the evaluation is conducted.

Evaluation report.   This section is useful as a means of planning for the eventual development and distribution of a formal evaluation report. The report should be such that the quality and the process used to determine this quality are clearly indicated. In many instances, the evaluation plan can serve as a basis for the report. With minor modification, the first four sections of the evaluation plan can make up the first part of a comprehensive evaluation report. This, together with sections dealing with evaluation results, conclusions, and recommendations, constitutes a report that should be most acceptable to administrators and/or sponsors. An outline of the evaluation report to be eventually produced is provided in this section so that the reader will know what to expect with regard to documentation of the evaluation effort. Also of value would be an indication of those who are tentatively scheduled to receive copies of the report. This information need not be of a specific nature (i.e., actual names) but should include classes of persons who might find the report to be of value (e.g., teachers in specific schools, administrators at certain levels, and other curriculum developers).

Conducting the program evaluation

The actual conduct of a program evaluation varies in relation to a number of operational constraints. While it would be most profitable to examine the program context, input, process, and product, this is not always feasible. Say, for example, it is desired to evaluate a program that is already in operation. In this particular situation, it could be quite difficult to conduct a context and input evaluation. However, if a program is being initiated or revised, these two evaluation areas might be quite easily examined as a part of the total evaluation effort.

Once the scope of the evaluation has been determined, it is necessary to examine what evaluation roles will be assumed by various staff members. While basic consideration is given to this in the evaluation plan, it is imperative that activities be initiated to ensure that staff members are supportive and will do their part. Consideration might be given to faculty and administrator orientation, staff input sessions, and the provision of incentives for involvement. Even though there will be those few who do not accept evaluation, every effort should be made to bring these persons "into the fold."

As the program evaluation is being conducted, staff members should be kept informed of progress that is being made and have an opportunity to participate in the evaluation to the extent that their schedules permit. For example, it might be most appropriate for a power sewing machine operator instructor to visit local industries and conduct a personal follow-up of former students. A distributive education coordinator might feel that it is best to combine evaluation of former students with visits to students who are involved in cooperative work experience activities. In the case of input evaluation, staff most definitely should play an active role in the establishment of program goals and objectives. Process evaluation, with its close relationship to school-related success of students, cannot be conducted unless teachers are involved in the assessment of student performance. Thus it is evident that staff members should know what the evaluation entails and be given every opportunity to become partners in the assessment process.

Once data have been gathered and compared with established evaluation objectives, results should be immediately conveyed to all staff members. Delays in this regard could give rise to thoughts of suppressed information and might otherwise adversely affect staff morale.

While each program evaluation is closely aligned with its particular evaluation plan, there are a number of concerns that cannot be easily committed to paper. These have to do primarily with interpersonal activities. Above all, it should be recognized that evaluation is not a mechanical procedure one follows to get from point A to point B. The most meaningful evaluation effort is one founded upon sound objectives, that has a clear framework within which it is to be conducted, and that gives major consideration to staff input and involvement.

Evaluating curriculum materials

Traditionally, the curriculum materials writing process has served as a setting for establishing curriculum materials quality, with the writer or writers serving as the sole means of quality control. After a decision is made to develop a particular item, an individual or group writes it and then the material is reproduced and distributed to appropriate teachers and students for their use. While it must be acknowledged that the writer is a key figure in the development process, he or she may not always be capable of determining exactly how teachers or students might react to use of the materials. Obviously, the writing environment is different than the teaching environment, and because of this difference, each situation serves a useful role in the determination of curriculum materials quality.

Chapters 8 and 9 have dealt extensively with the processes of determining which materials to select and developing materials in a systematic manner. Each of these areas is of considerable value to the individual who is selecting or preparing curriculum materials for vocational and technical education. Chapter 10 has provided detailed information about developing a special type of curriculum material—the individualized, competency-based package or module. This type of material places further emphasis on the need for precision in the curriculum materials development process. It must be noted, however, that systematic development is only the initial step in the establishment of curriculum materials quality. The contemporary curriculum developer goes beyond materials selection and preparation to actual testing in realistic educational settings.

Need for curriculum materials evaluation

In recent years, educators have placed greater and greater emphasis on the area of curriculum materials evaluation. Whether this emphasis has evolved from administrative pressure, public displeasure, a shrinking funding base, or professional concern is dependent upon the particular educational environment; however, the fact remains that educators are increasingly aware of the need to gather information about the worth of materials they use. Two most useful resources have been developed that relate directly to program evaluation; namely, *Educational Evaluation: Theory and Practice* (Worthen and Sanders, 1973) and *Evaluating Occupational Education and Training Programs* (Wentling and Lawson, 1975). The Worthen and Sanders book deals with evaluation from a more general frame of reference and provides information about the various models one might apply to an evaluation effort. Wentling and Lawson focus directly on evaluation as it relates to vocational and technical education and detail the ways that occupational education programs may be systematically evaluated. This book would be of value to anyone who desires to evaluate a vocational program. However, much less may be found in the literature that relates directly to systematic evaluation of curriculum materials for vocational education.

When giving consideration to the evaluation of curriculum materials, it is important to distinguish between two levels of evaluation: formative and summative. *Formative evaluation* is used to improve materials while they are being formulated and developed. This sort of evaluation is typically conducted by someone such as a curriculum developer who is familiar with the materials and/or has worked closely with them. *Summative evaluation*, on the other hand, involves the examination of a completed item to determine its impact on the potential consumer. An unbiased person or persons from outside the organization are brought in to conduct the summative evaluation (Scriven, 1967). Although much of the remainder of this chapter applies equally well to formative and summative evaluation, the focus will be on the formative type, since this level of evaluation is seen as a major role of the curriculum developer.

Why, then, is there a need to determine curriculum materials quality? The need appears to parallel determination of any curriculum's worth. This includes the contribution materials make to student growth, curriculum materials credibility, and practical considerations associated with their use.

Contribution to student growth. While development and review by experts serve as useful means of gathering information about the worth of curriculum materials, these experts do not deal directly with the concern about how students are actually helped. No matter how much writers or reviewers praise a particular item, their praises may be in vain if it is not of value to the students for whom it has been designed. This factor represents the single, most important aspect of curriculum materials quality; for if an item is not able to effect some positive change in students, it is certainly of little value as a component part of the vocational education curriculum.

Credibility.   A second need for determining curriculum materials quality lies in the area of credibility. Not only should the materials be tangible contributors to student growth; they must also be readily accepted by both teachers and students. No matter how useful curriculum materials are in effecting student learning, they may be considered worthless if teachers and their students will not accept them as being meaningful ways to learn. One must recognize, however, that credibility does not substitute for a contribution to student growth. This is merely one of several dimensions that must be closely scrutinized if quality materials are to be developed.

Practical considerations.   Any curriculum materials that may be easily introduced to the classroom and laboratory setting and can be utilized by teachers and students with a minimum of effort will most likely be used again and again. Conversely, materials must fit well in the educational setting to be of genuine value. Even though teachers and students may accept the materials as being worthwhile and as helping students to learn, they must have practical utility as well.

Establishing evaluation standards

When one is faced with the task of evaluating curriculum materials quality, initial consideration must be given to the development of meaningful evaluation standards. While quality may have numerous interpretations, the curriculum developer's job is to spell out exactly what quality is in relation to his or her particular materials. Quality then is operationally defined for each of the materials that undergoes development, with standards for some being different than standards for others. The variation in standards from item to item is typically a function of time and associated resources available to the developer; however, each standard must be one that professional educators can live with. Otherwise, the evaluation results will not be accepted by them. In many cases, standards may be established before development begins. If this were always the case, there would be no need to deal with setting up standards at this juncture. However, since some materials have their standards established on a post-hoc basis, information about the process is presented here rather than in Chapter 9.

　　The establishment of evaluation standards typically follows a three-step process. Initially, a definition of quality is developed for the particular curriculum materials. Next, evaluation objectives are prepared, each of which aligns with the definition of materials quality. Finally, instruments are identified that focus on the various evaluation objectives. Two of these steps are detailed in the sections that follow. The third step, preparing evaluation objectives, was presented earlier in this chapter as part of the overall planning process.

Defining curriculum materials quality

The quality of curriculum materials can be viewed as multidimensional. Any materials used by teachers and students must meet a number of practical standards, each of which represents a unique dimension of their overall quality. The specification of materials quality can only be limited by one's creativity. As long as the curriculum developer can assure that objectives are specified and instruments identified, there is virtually no limit to the set of specifications one may associate with quality. There is, however, a practical problem of time and resources available to assess the various aspects of materials quality. One solution to this problem involves selection and evaluation of those dimensions which appear to be the major contributors to materials quality. For example, a curriculum developer might identify twenty areas of quality that relate to a particular set of materials but may have sufficient resources to assess only three of these areas. He or she would then select the three areas felt to be most critical to quality and evaluate the materials on these dimensions. In the selection process, consideration should be given to use of a professional team consisting of vocational teachers and curriculum developers who are charged with the responsibility of ranking the various quality areas and selecting those which are most important to evaluate.

Evaluators have given much thought to the various aspects of curriculum materials quality. Tyler and Klein (1974), Alkin and Fink (1974), and Wright and Hess (1974) focus on several areas of quality that might be considered by the curriculum developer. Although a discussion of all these areas is beyond the scope of this volume, it may be of value to deal with several that should be considered when materials are being evaluated. These dimensions are materials effectiveness, efficiency, acceptability, practicality, and generalizability.

Effectiveness.   This area of quality deals directly with assessing the effects of materials used. Questions that might be raised about materials effectiveness include: Does use of the materials change student behavior? What changes occur with what types of students? Do the materials effect a greater change than other materials?

Efficiency.   Efficiency is concerned with materials effectiveness as it relates to time and cost. Materials may be deemed effective but at an increased cost or with a greater time allocation. If this is the case, vocational educators might find it more beneficial to remain with the original instructional arrangement. Efficiency may be represented by either greater effectiveness than materials now in use with no increase in time and/or cost, or equal effectiveness to other materials with a decrease in time and/or cost. Questions that can be raised about materials efficiency include: Do the materials effect a greater student success rate than alternate modes of instruction while not being greater in time or cost? Does it cost less to achieve a specified student success rate with the materials than with other materials? Does it take less time to achieve a specified student success rate with the materials than with other materials?

Acceptability. The area of acceptability deals with students and teachers who use the materials. Concern here is with the users' acceptance of materials as a useful contributor to the teaching-learning process. Questions one might elicit about materials acceptability include: Do students perceive the materials as making a meaningful contribution to the teaching-learning process? Do students have positive attitudes toward instruction received via the materials? Do teachers perceive the materials as making a meaningful contribution to the teaching-learning process? Do teachers have positive attitudes toward instruction via the materials?

Practicality. This area of quality is associated with materials use in the school environment. It is concerned with potential constraints that might restrict materials use even though they show up well in other quality areas. Questions related to materials practicality might include: Will use of the materials require special facilities or equipment (e.g., laboratories, audiovisual aids, references)? Is the cost-per-unit price of the materials prohibitive? Will in-service teacher education be required before the materials may be used? If so, how extensive will the in-service program be?

Generalizability. The generalizability area focuses on curriculum materials potential to be used by students in other schools, school districts, community colleges, or subject matter areas. Since a number of materials go through an extensive and costly development process, it is important to know if an item can be used by students other than those for whom it was initially designed. A parallel concern is the gathering of evidence about possible new applications for the materials (Wright and Hess, 1974). Questions one might raise with regard to generalizability include: To what extent may the materials be used with students in other educational settings? To what extent may the materials be used by students with different characteristics than those for whom they were originally intended? To what uses might the materials be put that have not heretofore been identified?

Instruments for curriculum materials evaluation

A most important aspect of curriculum materials evaluation involves identifying instruments that can be used to determine whether or not the specified standards have been met. It becomes obvious that some evaluation objectives cannot be developed unless immediate consideration is given to instruments that will be used in the evaluation process. Thus the curriculum developer must sometimes consider the kind of instruments he or she will use concurrently with the development of evaluation objectives.

Instrument selection can be a rather personal matter, since the curriculum developer needs to be sure that an accurate evaluation is being made of his or her materials. The actual selection is based upon an instrument's alignment with a particular quality question and evaluation objective. This alignment often presents problems, since the numerous standardized instruments listed in documents such as Burros's *Mental Measurement Yearbook* do not align well with many of the evaluation objectives developed for curriculum materials. If, for example, one desires to determine the effectiveness of a particular learning package that focuses on development of skills in using the metric system, a standardized general mathematics test might be inappropriate, since it may not be sensitive enough to any change produced by the package. In this case, the curriculum developer might utilize tests that focus directly on the package's objectives. These tests could already be a part of the package; otherwise, they would need to be developed locally for use in the evaluation process.

The types of instruments used to evaluate materials quality are numerous, and with so many possibilities to choose from, the curriculum developer may find it quite difficult to select an instrument that is appropriate. In order that the developer may be provided with a better picture of how instruments align with areas of materials quality, the following discussion focuses on instrumentation as it relates to assessing various aspects of quality.

Knowledge instruments. If the objective is to produce a change in the cognitive area, a knowledge examination might need to be developed for use in evaluating materials effectiveness. As was mentioned earlier, a curriculum developer is often faced with the task of developing instruments, since there appear to be few commercially-produced instruments that closely align with materials outcomes.

Numerous books are available that describe the procedures used in developing knowledge instruments (e.g., Erickson and Wentling, 1976). The curriculum developer would do well to locate a good applied measurement book and use this as a guide in the development process. Of course, central to instrument development is the concept of relevance. Any instrument that is developed must focus directly on the curriculum materials outcomes. If this is not done, the materials probably will not fare very well when being evaluated. Equally important concerns in the development of knowledge instruments are the establishment of *validity* (the extent to which an instrument measures what it is supposed to measure), and *reliability* (the extent to which it measures something consistently). These elements can, likewise, affect the success of an evaluation and should, therefore, be an important aspect of the instrument development process. Figure 11–3 provides an example of a knowledge instrument together with its source of validity and reliability. Whether a knowledge instrument is selected or developed, it is extremely important to have validity and reliability information available so that no questions will be raised about the instrument's value.

Attitude and opinion instruments. Attitude and opinion instruments focus directly on the affective aspects of curriculum materials quality. These instruments align most closely with materials acceptability; however, they can also be used to gather information about materials practicality. The attitude instrument is especially difficult to develop, since attitudes are generally measured by in-

FIGURE 11–3.   Example of a knowledge instrument

INSTRUMENT SUMMARY

TITLE: Automobile Engine Knowledge Examination

NUMBER OF ITEMS: 46

VALIDITY AND RELIABILITY INFORMATION SOURCE: *Troubleshooting Instruction in Vocational-Technical Education Via Dynamic Simulation*
(ERIC ED 055 204)

AUTOMOBILE ENGINE KNOWLEDGE

Name _____ School _____

Date _____Instructor's Name _____

Directions: For each of the following questions, select the correct answer from the four possible answers listed. Circle the letter of your choice in each question.

1. A condenser is charged by the collapsing field of the circuit known as
   A. secondary.
   B. ignition.
   C. generator.
   D. primary.

2. The secondary current begins to flow in the ignition coil when the

   A. condenser discharges.
   B. primary current flows.
   C. points open.
   D. points close.

3. The compressed mixture between the spark plug electrodes causes a high degree of

   A. tension.
   B. resistance.
   C. conductance.
   D. combustibility.

FIGURE 11–3.   [continued]

4. An ignition coil increases battery voltage by principles of

    A. constant-potential.
    B. nonconduction.
    C. polarization.
    D. electromagnetism.

5. The ignition condenser discharges into the

    A. secondary circuit.
    B. primary circuit.
    C. ground circuit.
    D. radio circuit.

direct rather than direct means. This necessitates the use of more subjective procedures than would be associated with the knowledge instrument. In the development of an attitude instrument, one does not simply write down items, give them to students, and then come up with a composite score for each individual. The attitude instrument must be a valid and reliable measure that meets basic educational measurement standards. An example of an attitude instrument, together with information about the supporting data source, is provided in Figure 11–4. Note that the instrument is of the Likert-type with item scores being summed to produce a composite score. Other types of item arrangements such as the Thurstone and Semantic Differential approaches might work equally well for a variety of curriculum materials assessment situations.

FIGURE 11–4.   **Example of an attitude instrument**

INSTRUMENT SUMMARY

INSTRUMENT TITLE: Instruction Attitude Inventory

NUMBER OF ITEMS: 47

VALIDITY AND RELIABILITY INFORMATION SOURCE: "An Instrument to Assess Attitude Toward Instruction," *Journal of Educational Measurement* **6**, No. 4 (Winter, 1969), pp. 257–258.

FIGURE 11–4.   [continued]

Instruction Attitude Inventory [IAI]

LAST NAME   FIRST   INITIAL   DATE

COURSE   INSTRUCTOR

DIRECTIONS: Below are several statements about the period of instruction which you have just completed. Read each statement carefully and indicate how much you agree or disagree with it according to the following scale:

SD = STRONGLY DISAGREE   D = DISAGREE   N = NEUTRAL   A = AGREE   SA = STRONGLY AGREE

USE A # 2 PENCIL FOR MARKING. DO NOT USE BALL POINT PEN OR RED PENCIL. ERASE ALL UNINTENDED MARKS.

1. I would like more instruction presented in this way....

2. I learned more because equipment was available for me to use ....

3. This instruction was very boring ....

4. The material presented was of much value to me ......

5. The instruction was too specific ....

6. I was glad just to get through the material ....

7. The material presented will help me to solve problems

8. While taking this instruction I almost felt as if someone was talking with me....................

9. I can apply very little of the material which I learned to a practical situation ....

10. The material made me feel at ease....................

11. In view of the time allowed for learning, I felt that too much material was presented ....

12. I could pass an examination over the material which was presented ....

13. I was more involved with using equipment than with understanding the material ....

14. I became easily discouraged with this type of instruction

15. I enjoy this type of instruction because I get to use my hands....................

16. I was not sure how much I learned while taking this instruction ....

17. There are too many distractions with this method of instruction ....

18. The material which I learned will help me when I take more instruction in this area ....

19. This instructional method did not seem to be any more valuable than regular classroom instruction ....

20. I felt that I wanted to do my best work while taking this instruction ....

21. This method of instruction makes learning too mechanical....................

22. The instruction has increased my ability to think .....

23. I had difficulty reading the written material that was used ....

24. I felt frustrated by the instructional situation ....

25. This is a poor way for me to learn skills...............

26. This method of instruction does not seem to be any better than other methods of instruction....................

27. I am interested in trying to find out more about the subject matter....................

28. It was hard for me to follow the order of this instruction

29. While taking this instruction I felt isolated and alone....

30. I felt uncertain as to my performance in the instruction ..

31. There was enough time to learn the material that was presented ....

32. I don't like this instruction any better than other kinds I have had ....

33. The material presented was difficult to understand ......

34. This was a very good way to learn the material ....

35. I felt very uneasy while taking this instruction ....

36. The material presented seemed to fit in well with my previous knowledge of the subject ....

37. This method of instruction was a poor use of my time ...

38. While taking this instruction I felt challenged to do my best work ....

39. I disliked the way that I was instructed ....

40. The instruction gave me facts and not just talk.........

41. I guessed at most of the answers to problems...........

42. Answers were given to the questions that I had about the material....................

43. I seemed to learn very slowly with this type of instruction

44. This type of instruction makes me want to work harder...

45. I did not understand the material that was presented ....

46. I felt as if I had my own teacher while taking this instruction....................

47. I felt that no one really cared whether I worked or not ...

The opinion type instrument or opinionnaire serves as a useful means of gathering information about specific user concerns. The opinionnaire may include a variety of items, each of which focuses on a different aspect of product quality. Each item then becomes somewhat of a separate entity; items are not summed to produce a composite opinion score. The value of using an opinionnaire rests in its ability to gather information that might otherwise "fall between the cracks." While an attitude instrument may be extremely useful in determining whether or not materials are basically acceptable to students, it does not usually tell where certain specific deficiencies may exist. The opinionnaire enables a curriculum developer to obtain feedback from users about specific aspects of the materials. For example, items might be included that ask students how clear the objectives were or ask teachers how relevant the learning experiences were. An additional advantage of the opinionnaire is that it has the capability of soliciting the degree of user commitment to materials. If instructors were asked, "Would you use these materials again with another class?", their collective answers to responses such as "Yes," "Yes with revision," and "No" would give the developer a good idea of how the materials would fare with regard to continued use. Additionally, opinionnaires allow the user to provide free response information about how well the materials are accepted. Even though this information is very difficult to code, it may provide useful ideas about the materials' specific strengths and weaknessess. These particular ideas may then be discussed with users to help determine exactly where revisions should be made.

The opinionnaire works equally well with students and teachers. Realistically, it is important to obtain opinionnaire type information from both of these groups, since they may each see the materials in a different light. The student may view a particular set of materials in relation to his or her learning a certain aspect of the vocational education curriculum; whereas the instructor might see the same materials as one of several ways students can be assisted in mastering certain specified objectives. Examples of opinionnaires that are useful for gathering information from students and teachers are provided in Figures 11–5 and 11–6. The student opinionnaire deals with reactions to use of a learning activity package, while the teacher opinionnaire focuses on feelings about the use of a teaching machine. These two examples represent the range of information that might be gathered about curriculum materials. Depending upon the type of information desired, it may be possible to develop some items that reflect common concerns of both teachers and students. Then, after data have been collected and summarized, an examination may be made of similarities or differences that exist between these groups.

Performance instruments. The performance instrument may be used when materials have been designed to develop student capability to perform certain tasks or activities in applied settings. The procedures used to develop this type of instrument are detailed by several authors (e.g., Finch and Impellitteri, 1971; Finch and O'Reilly, 1974; Erickson and Wentling, 1976). Development procedures provided in these sources should aid greatly in constructing an instrument

---

FIGURE 11–5.   Example of a student opinionnaire

LEARNING ACTIVITY PACKAGE OPINIONNAIRE

I.   SPECIFIC REACTIONS

INSTRUCTIONS: Please read each of the following statements. Circle the term on the right of each statement that most nearly represents your opinion of this learning activity package. The terms on the right are defined as follows:

SA	A	D	SD
Strongly Agree	Agree	Disagree	Strongly Disagree

Your carefully considered responses will definitely be used in our revision of this package!

1. I easily understood each of the learning activity package objectives before I began working with the learning experiences.................... SA   A   D   SD
2. Each learning experience assisted me in achieving its related objectives... SA   A   D   SD
3. I was well aware of my progress (or lack of progress) as I worked through this learning activity package... SA   A   D   SD
4. The evaluations (self-tests, rating sheets, checklists) measured my achievement of the objectives.. SA   A   D   SD
5. The learning experiences made the best use of my time in achieving objectives.. SA   A   D   SD
6. I felt that the instructional materials helped me achieve the learning activity package objectives... SA   A   D   SD
7. I feel that the performance objectives included in this learning activity package are important to my success in this program................. SA   A   D   SD

II.   GENERAL REACTIONS

INSTRUCTIONS: In this section we want your reactions to *any* aspects of the learning activity package that you like or dislike.

1. What did you like *best* about this learning activity package?
    A.
    B.
    C.

2. What did you like *least* about this learning activity package?

    A.
    B.
    C.

3. Any additional comments?

that is both meaningful and practical. A key aspect of performance instrument development is its content validity. That is, does the instrument's content accurately portray the performance required in applied settings? If this standard is not met, the instrument will not give a true picture of student performance. An additional aspect of instrument development involves determining how easily the instrument may be administered to students. Even the most valid performance instrument will cause a curriculum developer problems if it cannot be administered to students with relative ease.

Performance instruments may already be a part of curriculum materials. If this is the case, instrumentation problems are solved, since the evaluation of performance can take place as students complete their required instruction. If a product does not include a performance instrument, performance may have to be evaluated during a special testing session. Either situation requires that the

---

FIGURE 11–6.   Example of a teacher opinionnaire

TEACHING MACHINE OPINIONNAIRE

Name:_____School:_____

DIRECTIONS: Below are several statements about the teaching machine that you have been using with your classes. Read each statement carefully and indicate the extent to which you agree or disagree with it according to the following scale:

SD—Strongly Disagree; I strongly disagree with the statement.
D—Disagree; I disagree with the statement, but not strongly so.
A—Agree; I agree with the statement, but not strongly so.
SA—Strongly Agree; I strongly agree with the statement.

CIRCLE YOUR RESPONSE

1. The teaching machine requires a great deal of maintenance.......... SD   D   A   SA
2. The teaching machine provides my students with a good way to learn skills.. SD   D   A   SA
3. The teaching machine should be used in conjunction with instructional materials such as booklets and instruction sheets.............. SD   D   A   SA
4. The teaching machine should be located in the classroom............ SD   D   A   SA
5. The teaching machine should be used instead of classroom instruction... SD   D   A   SA
6. Teaching machine breakdowns did not occur very frequently........ SD   D   A   SA
7. The teaching machine should be located in the school laboratory area.. SD   D   A   SA
8. Instructors should be provided with time to develop instructional materials that can be used with the teaching machine.................. SD   D   A   SA
9. Students should work on the teaching machine in groups............. SD   D   A   SA

examiner ensure control over the testing environment so each student is given an equal opportunity to do his or her best work. The performance instrument example provided in Figure 11-7 is but one of the many applied activities that can be evaluated. Other areas that performance tests may be developed for include (but are not limited to) marketing, treating, diagnosing, adjusting, building, displaying, selecting, calculating, planning, drawing, administering, preparing, repairing, developing, and compiling.

FIGURE 11-7.   Example of directions for a performance instrument

---

NAME_____ DATE _____

STUDENT INSTRUCTIONS FOR THE TROUBLESHOOTING
PERFORMANCE EVALUATION

This evaluation is designed to find out how well you can troubleshoot a receiver. You will try to find two troubles that have been placed in a receiver, one at a time. It will be your job to find each trouble using the procedure and checks that were learned in your electronics instruction. No charts or books may be used to help you; however, you may use the tools provided by the instructor. After the exam has started, you may not talk unless the instructor asks you a question. The indication for each trouble is, "The receiver will not operate."

In order to get the highest possible score in this evaluation, you should observe the following suggestions:

1. Use the procedure and sequence that were taught in your electronics instruction.

2. Find each trouble as quickly as possible; you will be timed.

3. Try to make only those checks that will help you to find the trouble.

4. Try to make each check in its proper sequence.

5. Touch only those parts of the receiver which you feel will help you to find the trouble.

When you think you have found each trouble, write the trouble in the space provided below:

The first trouble is _____

The second trouble is _____

After you are sure that you understand these instructions, tell the instructor that you are ready and he or she will have you start.

Questionnaires. The questionnaire serves a useful purpose in gathering information about curriculum materials users and the educational setting. Questionnaires may be used to identify what the teachers' and students' personal characteristics are such as age, occupational experience, teaching experience, and education. This kind of information is important when the curriculum developer wants to determine how different groups of teachers might react to the materials or how different types of students might perform after having received the instruction. Other kinds of information that can be gathered via questionnaires include student grade level, location of the evaluation, and time required to complete the materials.

While questionnaires can be developed and administered separately from other instruments, they are often combined with opinionnaires, with each taking up one or more parts of a composite instrument. This procedure makes the evaluation process go more smoothly by reducing paperwork and allowing the user to feel that he or she is not burdened with so many pages of material to complete. Items representative of those used in questionnaires are presented in Figure 11–8. While each of the items may be applicable to a certain evaluation situation, it would be quite easy to modify them for use in another setting. Spaces to the right of each item are used for coding purposes so that data may be easily keypunched and processed by computer.

Conducting the curriculum materials evaluation

Once sufficient planning has been done, including the establishment of meaningful evaluation objectives and instruments, the curriculum developer is ready to carry out the evaluation. This is a relatively simple task if proper steps have been detailed in the evaluation plan and one that is most rewarding, since the developer now has an opportunity to find out just how well materials fare in realistic educational settings.

The extent to which one can actually evaluate curriculum materials is dependent upon available resources. Dollars or time available to evaluate materials destined for use at the local level may be considerably less than for evaluating materials to be used by state and national audiences. Thus the developer may be faced with decisions about how extensive an evaluation can be accomplished for a given set of materials. Ideally, the evaluation is a two-phase process consisting of pilot testing and field testing. Realistically, this might be limited to pilot testing if time and/or dollars are unavailable, with the recognition that both pilot and field testing are necessary in order to make a most meaningful check of materials quality.

Pilot testing

The pilot-testing activity consists of trying out materials in the "setting of use," generally in one site (Contract Research Corporation, 1975). By "setting of use"

FIGURE 11–8.   Example of a questionnaire

STUDENT INFORMATION SHEET

	D	S	S
	1	2	3
	0	1	
	4	5	
	6	7	8
	9	10	

1. Name: _____ 2. Date: _____

11   12   13

3. Mailing Address: _____

14   15

4. City: _____ State: _____ Zip: _____

16   17   18

5. Area Vocational-Technical School: _____

19

6. Course Area (Major): _____

20

7. Teacher's Name: _____

21   22

8. Birth Date: Day: _____ Month: _____ Year: _____

23   24   25

9. Sex (circle one):   Male   Female

26

10. Year in School (circle one):   10   11   12   Adult

27   28

11. Have you ever had any sales experience in school?
    (circle one)   Yes   No

29

12. Have you ever had any sales experience outside of school?
    (circle one)   Yes   No

30

13. List the part-time and full-time jobs you have held:

_____

31   32   33

_____

34

14. List your hobbies: _____

35

_____

36   37   38

15. How would you classify the area where you live?
    (circle one)   Farm   Town   City

39

16. How would you classify the area where you live? (circle one)
    everyone has jobs   some don't have jobs   many don't have jobs

40

17. What is (or was) your father's occupation? _____

41

18. How would you classify your father's occupation? (circle one)

42

           Unskilled   Semiskilled   Skilled
           Technical   Professional

43   44   45

is meant that testing will be conducted in school environments and with students who are similar to those who will eventually use the materials. Since the pilot test represents an initial tryout effort, testing is limited to one location.

Pilot testing focuses on the acceptability and practicality aspects of curriculum materials quality. While it is recognized that materials effectiveness, efficiency, and generalizability are of equal if not greater importance, the pilot test serves as an initial trial that does not usually allow the evaluator sufficient time to deal directly with these key areas. The pilot test might be said to serve as a prerequisite to field testing. Since any product must be deemed functionally sound before additional tryouts are conducted, the pilot test is an important means of obtaining this sort of information.

A pilot test typically involves one or more regular classes of vocational students who can benefit from the materials. The evaluator must first identify a site where the test may be conducted and then coordinate the efforts with appropriate school administrators, teachers, and students. Groups should know exactly what their respective roles will be and procedures to be followed during the test. Even though information gathered is of a more descriptive nature, it is important for all teachers to recognize that accuracy of information is paramount. If it is not possible for teachers to gather data, the evaluator may choose to gather his or her own data. This course of action must meet with teachers' and administrators' prior approval.

Field testing

Field testing involves the trial of materials in the intended "setting of use," generally utilizing multiple sites (Contract Research Corporation, 1975). The field-testing process builds upon pilot testing and typically focuses on all five aspects of curriculum materials quality: effectiveness, efficiency, acceptability, practicality, and generalizability. While acceptability and practicality have already been examined during the pilot testing, field testing provides an additional opportunity to gather data about these areas and see how the materials fare with other students and teachers.

The field test is characterized as being more rigorous than the pilot test and may include one or several rather sophisticated designs. Most of the basic approaches one can use to conduct field tests are drawn directly from research and evaluation in the behavioral sciences; and with so many possibilities available, it sometimes becomes difficult to decide which design or combination of designs will be best for a particular situation. When designing the field-test process, it is best to give initial consideration to internal and external validity. This, in effect, means a close look should be taken at the field-testing process to ensure that test results will be interpretable and that they can be generalized to appropriate populations, settings, etc. (Campbell and Stanley, 1963). Obviously, a true experimental design would be the best means of obtaining internal and external validity. Its use enables the curriculum developer to control for sources of invalidity in an efficient manner. The developer should recognize, however, that experiments cannot always be conducted when evaluations are done. As Walbesser and Carter (1968) point out,

> In general, the present school environment can be characterized as one in which the opportunities for manipulation of experimental variables do not exist for all practical purposes.

Other factors such as available time and dollars work against the use of experiments in field testing. Because of these restrictions, developers often turn to quasi-experimental and nonexperimental or (as Campbell and Stanley call them) preexperimental designs. Although these designs are acknowledged as lacking in terms of internal and external validity, they are typically used by evaluators. Since field testing is often a compromise situation, these designs seem at least to align with the basic evaluation constraints of a vocational and technical education setting. It should be emphasized that if the preexperimental design is used, serious consideration must be given to conducting a number of field tests. Satisfactory performance over repeated testing with different students should indicate that the materials are of a high quality in terms of both effectiveness and generalizability.

When considering the sample size to use in a field test, it is best to keep in mind that a random sampling of students just cannot be accomplished. It is impossible to take a completely random sample from all present and future populations to which the field-test results are to be inferred (American Educational Research Association, 1970). The logical alternative is to conduct the field test with students whose personal characteristics are representative of those who will eventually use them. This helps to ensure that, when the materials are implemented on a large scale, they will be as effective as when they were field tested.

The question is often raised as to what size a sample of students should actually be. A rather vague answer to this question would be to use as large a sample as can be afforded. In experimental research, a minimum of ten to fifteen subjects is usually assigned to each group (Bruning and Kintz, 1968). This minimum number is perhaps a good one to use. However, before numbers are actually firmed up, the curriculum specialist should ask an important question about sample size: "How much difference will one student's performance make to the composite evaluation results?" If one student represents 10 percent of the field-test sample, success or failure by that individual will have much greater impact on results than would a student who is part of a forty-student sample.

Site selection and coordination of the testing effort are equally as important in field testing as they are in pilot testing. In fact, since field testing includes the use of multiple test locations, it is imperative that detailed arrangements for testing be worked out as the evaluation plan is being developed. When multiple-location testing is being conducted, it is too late to back up and make major revisions to the process. This is why testing arrangements should be thought out and committed to paper far in advance of the time testing begins.

Utilizing evaluation results for curriculum improvement

Curriculum evaluation is only useful to the extent that results have a positive impact on the curriculum, program, or materials. While it may be necessary on occasion to conduct an evaluation to comply with some external mandate, the real strength of evaluation lies in its potential to effect educational improvement. Whether concern is with a total curriculum, a vocational program, or curriculum materials used in that program, it is essential that evaluation results serve as a basis for determining if and when appropriate educational changes should be made.

Program improvement

The vocational program, which represents a substantial portion of the curriculum, can certainly benefit from sound evaluation. Benefit is, of course, relative and tends to parallel the comprehensiveness of evaluation. Logically, an evaluation that only focuses on the educational process is not going to produce as much meaningful data as one that deals directly with context, input, process, and product.

Context evaluation data may be used to help improve the educational environment and refine the program's goals and objectives. Input evaluation data can assist the curriculum developer in determining which resources and strategies have the greatest potential as well as how content might be arranged. Process evaluation data may be utilized to focus on improving both teaching and learning, while product evaluation can aid in determining which programs are more successful in producing work force members.

With regard to the aforementioned areas, it is important to ask the following questions:

> Have the specified evaluation objectives been met?
>
> If the objectives have not been met, what program changes can be made to ensure that they are met in the future?
>
> If the objectives have been met, is it worthwhile to raise the specified quality standards?

These questions are based on the assumption that realistic, measurable evaluation objectives have been established. Obviously, anything less than this will not enable questions to be answered. Vocational program improvement, then, is most dependent upon the objectives used in the evaluation effort. If objectives are vague, it may never be known whether they have been met, much less what action should be taken to effect program improvement.

Program improvement is typically incremental. Certain changes are made based upon evaluation results and then future evaluations focus on the results of these changes. Since it is usually not feasible to make wholesale changes in a program, only those changes are made that will benefit students the most. Program evaluation has the potential to assist vocational educators in making meaningful improvements. However, the extent to which these improvements may actually be made depends upon the quality and comprehensiveness of the evaluation effort.

Curriculum materials improvement

Once an evaluation of curriculum materials has been conducted, how can a curriculum developer best utilize the results? While this question appears easy to answer, the testing process does not always provide the clear results that one might like to have. The findings of pilot and field tests "do not always offer clearcut and positive direction for revision and dissemination activities. The developer must responsibly confront ambiguous or negative findings and exercise the necessary judgment to act on the evidence available" (Contract Research Corporation, 1975). This situation might well occur even if explicit evaluation objectives have been prepared. For example, upon testing a particular instructional package, the data might indicate that the material is effective and acceptable but not efficient or practical. In this situation, the burden of responsibility rests with the curriculum developer to decide whether materials should be either discarded, revised and retested, or allowed to be released with deficiencies clearly documented. The decision made in this situation might depend upon how serious the deficiencies are or how much revision time is available. In either case, the developer is faced with making a decision; and, hopefully, this decision will be based upon data gathered during pilot and field testing.

If deficiencies do exist, it is important to identify exactly where they are so that appropriate revisions may be made. One fruitful approach is to examine individual opinionnaire items and determine if the specific problem areas may be pinpointed. An item indicating that a high number of students felt their time was wasted might lead to revision of content such as eliminating nonrelevant material. Students' negative reactions to reading assignments might lead the developer to provide nonreading alternatives. Whatever the deficiency may be, it is important to identify exactly where the problem is and make necessary revisions.

In some cases, it may be obvious that materials have major deficiencies which cannot be resolved. If this situation occurs, the developer could be faced with terminating a development effort and admitting that work has been unsuccessful. This is certainly a difficult task but a necessary one if the need should ever arise. All too often, curriculum materials are made available to the public that do not meet standards of the profession. The curriculum developer's role is clearly one of controlling materials quality and, if necessary, he or she should be ready to point up identified shortcomings. Evaluation is more than simply confirming materials quality; it involves determining their worth and reporting that worth to the public. The curriculum developer should be prepared to report what this worth is, regardless of the evaluation findings.

SUMMARY

This chapter has focused directly on curriculum evaluation in realistic educational settings. A clear distinction has been made between educational programs and materials, the latter of which is somewhat synonymous with curriculum products. The evaluation process is initiated with the establishment of evaluation standards. This includes actually defining what quality is as well as developing evaluation objectives.

A key to the success of any evaluation effort is the development of a practical evaluation plan. This plan serves as a framework for gathering and examining evaluation data. Included in the plan should be a rationale for the evaluation as well as a description of the curriculum and the evaluation design that will be utilized. After the evaluation has been carried out, provision must be made to use the results for curriculum improvement. It is only in this way that the evaluation effort will have fulfilled its purpose.

REFERENCES

Alkin, Marvin C., and Fink, Arlene. "Evaluation Within the Context of Product Development: A User Orientation," in G. Borich, ed., *Evaluating Educational Programs and Products*. Englewood Cliffs, N. J.: Educational Technology Publications, 1974, pp. 98–119.

American Educational Research Association. "Socrates Instructs Crito on Sampling," *Educational Researcher* (April, 1970), p. 21.

Bjorkquist, David C., and Finch, Curtis R. "Use and Critique of Product Measures in Evaluation," *Journal of Industrial Teacher Education* 6, No. 3 (Spring, 1969), pp. 66–73.

Bruning, J., and Kintz, B. *Computational Handbook of Statistics*. Glenview, Ill.: Scott, Foresman and Company, 1968.

Campbell, D., and Stanley, J. *Experimental and Quasi-Experimental Designs for Research*. Chicago: Rand McNally, 1963.

Contract Research Corporation. *Guidelines on Pilot and Field Testing of Curriculum Products*. Belmont, Mass.: Contract Research Corporation, 1975.

Erickson, Richard C., and Wentling, Tim L. *Measuring Student Growth: Techniques and Procedures for Occupational Education*. Boston: Allyn and Bacon, Inc., 1976.

Finch, Curtis R., and Bjorkquist, David C. "Review and Critique of Context and Input Measures in Evaluation," *Journal of Industrial Teacher Education* **14**, No. 2 (Winter, 1977), pp. 7–18.

––––––. "Review and Critique of Process Measures in Occupational Education Evaluation," *Journal of Industrial Teacher Education* **7**, No. 1 (Summer, 1970), pp. 37–42.

Finch, Curtis R., and Impellitteri, Joseph T. "Development of Valid Work Performance Measures," *Journal of Industrial Teacher Education* **9**, No. 1 (Fall, 1971), pp. 36–49.

Finch, Curtis R., and O'Reilly, Patrick A. "Assessing Troubleshooting Proficiency: Application of a General Strategy for Work Performance Measurement," *Journal of Industrial Teacher Education* **11**, No. 4 (Summer, 1974), pp. 32–39.

Johnson, S., and Johnson, R. *Developing Individualized Instructional Material*. Palo Alto, Calif.: Westinghouse Learning Press, 1970.

Scriven, Michael. "The Methodology of Evaluation," in B. Worthen and J. Sanders, *Educational Evaluation: Theory and Practice*. Worthington, Ohio: Charles A. Jones, 1973, pp. 60–104.

Stufflebeam, Daniel Z. "Evaluation as Enlightenment for Decision Making," *Improving Educational Assessment*. Washington, D.C.: Association for Supervision and Curriculum Development, National Education Association, 1969.

Stufflebeam, Daniel Z., et al. *Educational Evaluation and Decision-Making*. Itasca, Ill.: F. E. Peacock Publishers, Inc., 1971.

Tyler, Louise L., and Klein, M. Frances. "Evaluation Within the Context of Curriculum Development and Instructional Materials," in G. Borich, ed., *Evaluating Educational Programs and Products*. Englewood Cliffs, N. J.: Educational Technology Publications, 1974, pp. 120–139.

Walbesser, H., and Carter, H. "Some Methodological Considerations of Curriculum Evaluation Research," *Educational Leadership* **26**, No. 1 (October, 1968), pp. 53–64.

Wentling, Tim L., and Lawson, Tom E. *Evaluating Occupational Education and Training Programs*. Boston: Allyn and Bacon, Inc., 1975.

Worthen, B., and Sanders, J. *Educational Evaluation: Theory and Practice*. Worthington, Ohio: Charles A. Jones, 1973.

Wright, William J., and Hess, Robert J. "A Criteria Acquisition Model for Educational Product Evaluation," in G. Borich, ed., *Evaluating Educational Programs and Products*. Englewood Cliffs, N. J.: Educational Technology Publications, 1974, pp. 153–185.

Appendix A

AGRICULTURAL STUDENT INTEREST SURVEY

Date _____

1. Name _____ Age _____ Sex _____

2. Father's name _____ Occupation _____

3. Mother's name _____ Occupation _____

4. Grade in school _____ Do you plan to continue formal education beyond high school?

   Yes _____ No _____

5. Where do you live?   Town _____ Rural Community _____ Farm _____

6. What type of curriculum are you enrolled in now? _____

   College Preparatory _____ Vocational _____ General _____

7. In what occupation do you prefer to receive training? _____

   1st Choice _____ 2nd Choice _____ Undecided _____

8. What type of work do you like? _____

   _____

9. What are your hobbies? _____

10. Will you be available for part-time work experience?   Yes _____ No _____

    If yes, after school _____ Weekends _____ Summer _____

AGRICULTURAL STUDENT INTEREST SURVEY   (continued)

11. Do you think you might be interested in any of the following occupations after gradua-
     tion from high school? Check (✓) all that might interest you. Place an (X) on the line if
     you would like more information about that occupation.

_____ Farm advisory to bank and   _____ Buying agricultural products
         other lending agencies
                                             _____ Servicing machinery and
_____ Hatcheryman   equipment

_____ Florist   _____ Artificial breeding technician

_____ Field representative for buying   _____ Crop-dusting or spraying (aerial
         and selling activities in farm   and otherwise)
         organizations
                                             _____ Conservation service employee
_____ Selling feed, seed, fertilizer,
         machinery, and spray materials   _____ Forestry technician

_____ Landscape consultant   _____ Agricultural missionary

_____ Tree surgeon   _____ Poultry specialist

_____ Land appraiser   _____ Veterinarian

_____ Seed, feed, milk, and meat   _____ Herdsman
         inspector
                                             _____ Beekeeper
_____ Agronomist (crops and soils)
                                             _____ Vegetable grower
_____ Agricultural journalist for radio,
         television, newspaper, or   _____ Farm manager
         magazines
                                             _____ Veterinary-hospital attendant
_____ Dairy farmer
                                             _____ Tree pruner
_____ Agricultural conservationist
                                             _____ Tractor driver
_____ Agriculture teacher in high
         school or college   _____ Landscape gardener

_____ Agricultural economics   _____ Fire warden

_____ County agricultural extension   _____ Campground caretaker
         agent
                                             _____ Cruiser
_____ Forester

AGRICULTURAL STUDENT INTEREST SURVEY (continued)

———————— Farm management specialist   ———————— Animal keeper

———————— Food technician   ———————— Other (please list)

———————— Horticulturist

——————————————————————

———————— Landscape architect

——————————————————————

———————— Agricultural engineer

Appendix B

QUESTIONNAIRE TO PARENTS OF VOCATIONAL EDUCATION STUDENTS

Please provide the following information. All information received will be kept confidential and no individual responses will be identified. If possible, we would prefer a joint effort of the parents to complete this questionnaire.

1. Name of parents _____

2. Occupation (please specify)

   Father_____Mother _____

3. What is the highest level of formal education completed?

   Father   Mother

   _____   _____   1. Less than 8th grade

   _____   _____   2. Less than high school

   _____   _____   3. Graduated from high school

   _____   _____   4. Two-year college or school

   _____   _____   5. Four-year college

   _____   _____   6. Other (specify) _____

QUESTIONNAIRE TO PARENTS OF VOCATIONAL EDUCATION STUDENTS   (continued)

---

4. Who completed this form?

    1. Father only _____

    2. Mother only _____

    3. Both parents _____

Section I. *Concerns and Expectations of Vocational Education in a Local School*

General Directions

There is no time limit in completing this questionnaire. We urge you to read each statement carefully and give us your personal reaction.

PART I

Specific Directions

1. The statements on the following pages are possible concerns and expectations of vocational education programs. If the statement expresses a concern that you have with the present vocational program, place a check ($\vee$) under the column, "Yes." If the statement is not a concern, place a check ($\vee$) under the column, "No."

    We have defined a *concern* as "an interest or feeling characterized by uneasiness about the present vocational education program."

    All responses will be kept confidential.

Reminder: 1. If the statement is a concern, check ($\vee$) "Yes."
2. If it is not a concern, check ($\vee$) "No."
3. Review the following examples.

Check One ($\vee$)
Yes   No

Example A.   The safety of your son or daughter during school hours.   ✓ _____

Example B.   Procedure for securing supplies for the teachers.   _____ ✓

QUESTIONNAIRE TO PARENTS OF VOCATIONAL EDUCATION STUDENTS   (continued)

	Check One (✓)
Possible Concerns	Yes No

The amount of time or class periods required in vocational education programs. ____ ____

Provision of liability insurance coverage of students while attending the area vocational center or the home school. ____ ____

Provision of accident insurance coverage of students while attending the area vocational center or the home school. ____ ____

The image in the community of the vocational education program. ____ ____

Not enough emphasis placed on vocational education programs. ____ ____

The entrance requirements of a vocational course. ____ ____

Type of training experiences being offered. ____ ____

Whether a student will be prepared to enter a job at an entry level upon completion of the program. ____ ____

Availability of work experience programs. ____ ____

The lack of a vocational program designed for out-of-school youth and adults. ____ ____

The lack of a vocational program designed for students with special needs. ____ ____

Adequacy of guidance counseling for prospective vocational education students. ____ ____

Adequacy of information available on vocational opportunities for any students. ____ ____

Opportunities for job placement after program completion. ____ ____

Vocational competency of the guidance coordinator. ____ ____

Cost of required special clothing. ____ ____

Cost of required tools or equipment. ____ ____

Conflict between student and parents about the selection of a vocational goal. ____ ____

Vocational education students being subjected to adverse or harmful remarks upon selection of the vocational education course. ____ ____

The effectiveness of the present vocational education program for out-of-school youth and adults. ____ ____

QUESTIONNAIRE TO PARENTS OF VOCATIONAL EDUCATION STUDENTS   (continued)

Possible Concerns [*continued*]

Check One (✓)
Yes   No

The effectiveness of the present vocational education program for students with special needs.

_____ _____

That the selection of a vocational course may hinder the opportunity of continuing further education and/or training.

_____ _____

Please list any other concerns that you may have which were not on this list.

PART II

Specific Directions

1. The statements on the following pages are possible expectations of a vocational education program. If the statement expresses an expectation that you have with the present vocational program, place a check (✓) under the column, "Yes." If the statement is not an expectation, place a check (✓) under the column, "No."

   We have defined an *expectation* as "an anticipation or hope of what a vocational education program should provide to the student."

2. If you answered "Yes" to a particular statement, express the degree to which your expectation is being fulfilled. Select either "Completely Fulfilled," "Partially Fulfilled," or "None."

Possible Expectations

Check One (✓)
Yes   No

If "Yes," Check One (✓)
Completely Partially None

That an advisory board composed of community leaders be used to establish, plan, and assist in the operation of a vocational program.

_____ _____   _____ _____ _____

That students have the opportunity to obtain instruction in several different vocational areas, if needed for employment.

_____ _____   _____ _____ _____

That students receive training for a specific occupation.

_____ _____   _____ _____ _____

QUESTIONNAIRE TO PARENTS OF VOCATIONAL EDUCATION STUDENTS (continued)

Possible Expectations [*continued*]	Check One (✓) Yes No	If "Yes," Check One (✓) Completely Partially None

That students be prepared for an appropriate entry level position upon completion of the program.

That directed work experience be provided for students in vocational education.

That vocational education be provided only at the eleventh- and twelfth-year level.

That a student organization be established for each vocational area.

That vocational programs meet the employment needs of the students.

That vocational programs meet the needs of employers for entry level workers.

That employment be available immediately to qualified students upon completion of a vocational program.

That students may alter or change their occupational goals during the first year of their vocational programs.

That selection of the vocational curriculum does not prohibit the opportunity to continue further education and/or training.

That students can enter a vocational program even if their vocational goals are not definite.

That students in the twelfth grade in high school can enter a two-year vocational program.

Please list any other expectations that you may have which were not on this list and specify the degree to which those expectations are being fulfilled.

QUESTIONNAIRE TO PARENTS OF VOCATIONAL EDUCATION STUDENTS   (continued)

Section II. *Concerns and Expectations of Vocational Education Offered in an Area Vocational Center*

PART III

Check One (✓)

Possible Concerns   *Yes*   *No*

	Yes	No
The distance to travel between the area vocational center and the home school.	____	____
The amount of time required to travel between the area vocational center and the home school.	____	____
The effect of the area vocational education program on the extracurricular activities of the home school.	____	____
The effect of the extracurricular activities of the home school on the area vocational education program.	____	____
Fair representation of home schools on the administrative board of the area school.	____	____
Losing local control with an increase in size of the area school district.	____	____
That a budget of the area school dictates the number of students allowed to enroll in the area vocational education program.	____	____
Whether the area vocational center will help graduates find jobs.	____	____
Adequacy of information available on the area vocational center's program for prospective vocational students.	____	____
The degree of teacher-parent contact in an area vocational school program.	____	____
Adequacy of tools and equipment in the area vocational education program.	____	____

Please list any other concerns that you may have which were not on this list.

QUESTIONNAIRE TO PARENTS OF VOCATIONAL EDUCATION STUDENTS   (continued)

PART IV

	Check One (✓)		If "Yes," Check One (✓)		
Possible Expectations	Yes	No	*Completely*	*Partially*	*None*

That local schools are active participants in the area vocational education program.

That coordination of scheduling of the area vocational program allows students to participate in home school extracurricular activities.

That all local schools have a representative on the area school board.

That area vocational education programs will serve the needs of out-of-school youth as well as in-school youth.

That vocational education programs be available in the area center for the re-training of adults.

That area vocational education programs be designed to meet the needs of special groups; i.e., disadvantaged and others.

That area program staff should help the vocational education students locate positions upon graduation.

That opportunity to transfer within the area vocational education center be provided.

That the area vocational center has available modern, adequate facilities and equipment.

That all tools or equipment needed by students be provided by the area vocational center.

Please list any other expectations that you may have which were not on this list and specify the degree to which those expectations are being fulfilled.

Appendix C

CURRICULUM MATERIALS ASSESSMENT FORM*

| SECTION I | GENERAL DESCRIPTION

TITLE _____

AUTHOR_____PUBLISHER/SUPPLIER_____

YEAR PUBLISHED_____PLACE_____COST_____

PACKAGING (check one)

_____ 1. Single piece (item)   _____ 3. Set of ____ items, available separately

_____ 2. Set of ____ items, packaged   _____ 4. Other _____
            together   (specify)

TYPE OF MATERIAL (check all appropriate items)

1. *Printed Matter*   2. *Audiovisual Materials*   3. *Manipulative Aids*
   (pages   )

____ A. Manuals   ____ A. Graphics   ____ A. Puzzles
____ B. Workbooks   ____ B. Pictures   ____ B. Games
____ C. Pamphlets   ____ C. Posters   ____ C. Models
____ D. Study guides   ____ D. Audiotapes   ____ D. Specimens
____ E. Reference books   ____ E. Transparencies   ____ E. Puppets/figures
____ F. Textbooks   ____ F. Filmstrips   ____ F. Learning kits
____ G. Magazines   ____ G. Slide series   ____ G. Experiments
____ H. Newspapers   ____ H. Records   ____ H. Other_____
____ I. Other_____   ____ I. Films
                             ____ J. Film loops
                             ____ K. Videotapes
                             ____ L. Other_____

VOCATIONAL AREA

____ 1. Agricultural Education   ____ 6. Home Economics Education
____ 2. Business Education   ____ 7. Trade & Industrial Education
____ 3. Career Education   (specify subject area_____)
____ 4. Distributive Education   ____ 8. Other_____
____ 5. Health Education

TARGET POPULATION

____ 1. Grades K–1   ____ 4. Grades 7–8   ____ 7. Special Needs
____ 2. Grades 2–3   ____ 5. Grades 9–12   _____
____ 3. Grades 4–6   ____ 6. Postsecondary/Adult _____

BRIEF DESCRIPTION OF MATERIAL _____

_____

_____

_____

*Adapted from Instructional Materials Assessment Form in *Instructional Materials for Occupational Education*, Martha C. Muncrief and James G. Bennett, authors. (Project funded by Grants Administration Unit, New York State Education Department, under the Education Professions Development Act, Section 554.)

CURRICULUM MATERIALS ASSESSMENT FORM   (continued)

| SECTION II | READABILITY GRADE LEVEL

_____ 1. Not Applicable _____2. Readability Check Performed_____ Grade Level Is

Readability Formula Used _____

COMMENTS _____

_____

_____

| SECTION III | BIAS

Materials that stereotype sex roles, show bias toward age, race, ethnic or religious groups, and/or impose artificial hierarchies of social values on occupational categories (job denigration) should be avoided. Bias may also be evident in advertising that detracts from the educational value of the material.

1. Is bias present in the material? (check all appropriate bias and indicate Evaluation Coefficient Analysis—ECO)

	ECO			*ECO*
_____ Job denigration	_____	_____ Ethnic bias		_____
_____ Sex-role stereotyping	_____	_____ Religious bias		_____
_____ Age discrimination	_____	_____ Other (explain)_____		_____
_____ Racial bias	_____	_____ Objectionable advertising		_____

2. Is the material sufficiently free of bias to justify its use? (check one)

_____Yes   _____No

COMMENTS _____

_____

_____

_____

CURRICULUM MATERIALS ASSESSMENT FORM   (continued)

SECTION IV   ACCURACY

Materials that provide inaccurate or misleading information have little utility in the total teaching-learning process.

1. To what extent is the content accurate?

_____1   _____2   _____3   _____4   _____5

Unrealistic or incorrect   Realistic and correct

2. To what extent is the content timely and up-to-date?

_____1   _____2   _____3   _____4   _____5

Outdated in information, ideas, and/or   Current in information, ideas,
illustrations   and/or illustrations

3. To what extent is the content clear and complete?

_____1   _____2   _____3   _____4   _____5

Vague and inconclusive   Sufficiently detailed to prevent
                                                                         misinterpretation

_____ TOTAL SCORE FOR SECTION IV
              (add numerical values checked)

COMMENTS _____

_____

_____

_____

CURRICULUM MATERIALS ASSESSMENT FORM   (continued)

SECTION V   APPROPRIATENESS

Appropriateness of materials should be judged in relation to the target population and the total subject matter area.

1. To what extent are the language and/or visuals appropriate to the target population?

    _____1   _____2   _____3   _____4   _____5

    Stilted; antiquated language used; trite or   Fluent and easy to understand;
    too complex   appropriate to maturity level of
                                                         learner

2. To what extent is the content appropriate to the target population?

    _____1   _____2   _____3   _____4   _____5

    Lacking in challenge or too difficult to   Challenging but not beyond the
    comprehend   ability of the learner

3. To what extent is the content relevant to the total subject matter area?

    _____1   _____2   _____3   _____4   _____5

    Unnecessary; emphasizes an unimportant   Important and necessary to
    aspect of the subject   the subject matter area

                                   _____ TOTAL SCORE FOR SECTION V
                                             (add numerical values checked)

COMMENTS _____

_____

_____

_____

CURRICULUM MATERIALS ASSESSMENT FORM   (continued)

SECTION VI   VERBAL AND VISUAL FLUENCY

Instructional materials should make learning easier by presenting the subject matter in a simple and attractive way.

1. To what extent is the material appealing to the learner?

   _____1   _____2   _____3   _____4   _____5

   Unattractive; cluttered; poor in design   Attractive; simple; effective in
                                                     design

2. To what extent is the organization of the material easy to follow?

   _____1   _____2   _____3   _____4   _____5

   Too many ideas treated inadequately;   Ideas developed adequately in a
   distracting or extraneous parts   logical manner; clear general
                                                 theme

3. To what extent is the material interesting and stimulating?

   _____1   _____2   _____3   _____4   _____5

   Treats too few ideas in a redundant   Contributes to the development
   manner; dull and boring   of critical thought and creativity

   _____ TOTAL SCORE FOR SECTION VI
   (add numerical values checked)

COMMENTS_____

_____

_____

_____

CURRICULUM MATERIALS ASSESSMENT FORM   (continued)

| SECTION VII | USEFULNESS AND VERSATILITY

Instructional materials should be useful in a variety of situations and adaptable to varied needs of students.

1. To what extent can the material be used with learners having varying needs?

_____1   _____2   _____3   _____4   _____5

Suitable for a limited group of learners

Appropriate to target group with varying level of maturity, economic backgrounds, and learning styles

2. To what extent can the material be used in a variety of learning environments?

_____1   _____2   _____3   _____4   _____5

No provisions for adaptability; useful in only one type of situation

High level of adaptability; suitable for varying learning environments

3. To what extent are cost and packaging of the material consistent with the degree of usability?

_____1   _____2   _____3   _____4   _____5

Poorly constructed or packaged; more costly than is justified by probable use

Durably packaged; easy to handle and store; available at a cost commensurate with value

_____ TOTAL SCORE FOR SECTION VII
(add numerical values checked)

COMMENTS _____

_____

_____

CURRICULUM MATERIALS ASSESSMENT FORM   (continued)

| SECTION VIII | SUMMARY PROFILE

SECTIONS	MAXIMUM POINTS POSSIBLE	SCORE OF TASK
IV	15	————
V	15	————
VI	15	————
VII	15	————
TOTAL	60	

1. Overall assessment of material (check one)

2. Does the rating above accurately reflect your general assessment of the material?

_____Unacceptable; below 36 points
_____Useful; 36 to 48 points
_____Excellent; 49 to 60 points

_____Yes   _____No (explain)

COMMENTS _____

CURRICULUM MATERIALS ASSESSMENT FORM   (continued)

SECTION IX | LEARNING ENVIRONMENT USE

1. Have you used this material in your classroom?

    _____Yes   _____ No

2. Have you used this material in your laboratory?

    _____Yes   _____ No

3. Does this material require in-service training for effective use?

    _____Yes   _____ No

4. Are consultant services available to provide in-service training for use?

    _____Yes (explain)   _____No

Where?_____

_____

_____

5. Do you know of any type of validation that has been done on this material; i.e., learner verification, pre/posttests, ratings, etc.?

    _____ Yes (explain)   _____ No

_____

_____

_____

6. Are there other discipline areas or target populations for whom this material might be appropriate? (list)

_____

_____

_____

Sign-off by Material Assessor

Name_____

Date_____

SECTION X   OVERALL SUMMARY OF RATINGS

SECTION II —READABILITY GRADE LEVEL   Score_____

SECTION III—BIAS   ECO Subject: _____ _____ _____

                                    ECO Scores: _____ _____ _____

SECTION IV—ACCURACY (score of ____)

SECTION V—APPROPRIATENESS (score of ____)

SECTION VI—VERBAL AND VISUAL FLUENCY (score of ____)

SECTION VII—USEFULNESS AND VERSATILITY (score of ____)

SECTION VIII—OVERALL RATING (score of ____)

SECTION IX—LEARNING ENVIRONMENT USE

Name of Task Force Chairperson Or Materials Assessor

Index